Edmund O'Donovan

Merv

A Story of Adventure and Captivity

Edmund O'Donovan
Merv
A Story of Adventure and Captivity
ISBN/EAN: 9783337178185

Printed in Europe, USA, Canada, Australia, Japan

Cover: Foto ©ninafisch / pixelio.de

More available books at **www.hansebooks.com**

M.ERV

A STORY OF ADVENTURES AND CAPTIVITY

EPITOMISED FROM 'THE MERV OASIS'

BY

EDMOND O'DONOVAN

SPECIAL CORRESPONDENT OF 'THE DAILY NEWS'

WITH A PORTRAIT

LONDON
SMITH, ELDER, & CO., 15 WATERLOO PLACE
1883

[All rights reserved]

ADVERTISEMENT.

The account of Mr. O'Donovan's Travels East of the Caspian, with his five months' residence among the Tekkés of Merv, having been published in two large volumes, which of necessity places it beyond the reach of many readers, it has been thought desirable to give an epitome of the work, which, leaving out political matters, presents the marvellous story of his adventures and captivity in a concise and popular form.

CONTENTS.

CHAPTER I.
PAGE

Across the Steppe—Delays in landing—The Troïka—The Steppes—Russian stations—A sporting country—Thievish Tartars—The Grand Hotel—General Lazareff—A dreary ride—Reaching Baku . 1

CHAPTER II.

A petroleum city—Petroleum—Fire worship—A strange rite—The Turcomans—Chatte—Flies and mosquitoes—A reconnaissance—In gorgeous array—Caucasian horsemen—The *handjar* . . . 12

CHAPTER III.

Searching for sulphur mines—A desert post—Bitter waters—The Black Gulf—Sulphur Mountain—Turcoman steeds—A night alarm—The attack—A race for life—Worn out 22

CHAPTER IV.

Waiting to advance—Water snakes—Quaint humanity—Caucasian cavalry—Uniforms—Ideas and fashion—Punishment of the knout—An angler's paradise 32

CHAPTER V.

Sickness—The death of an old friend—Funeral at sea—General Tergukasoff—Notice to quit—A start for Persia—A slimy waste—A home for reptiles—Robber Turcomans—The faithful dog—A Jack-of-all-trades—Night alarms—An unpleasant welcome—Asterabad 39

CHAPTER VI.

A Persian town—Wild boars—Sanitary features—The bazaar—Manufactures—Felt-making—A finished carpet—Persian costume—A story-teller—Persian pottery—A lost art 52

CHAPTER VII.

Rumours of activity—A fresh venture—Another dismissal—A snowstorm—Severe losses—Fresh plans—General Skobeleff . . 63

CHAPTER VIII.

Persian boatmen—A Persian river—Sturgeon and silkworms—The ice torture—Venomous serpents—A ghastly burden—The 'Bite the Stranger'—Effects of a bite—The kanots—The Shah's capital—His Majesty's servants—Court splendour—Flower-scatterers . 70

CHAPTER IX.

Important telegrams—Visit to a magnate—The Towers of Silence—Fortifications—Dwellers in the tombs—A false alarm—Beauty of villages—Bitten—A human churn 83

CHAPTER X.

Female pilgrims—Dervishes—A strange escort—Joining the hadjis—A night march—A council of hadjis—A skirmish—A threatened massacre—Results of the fight—An awkward position—A weird procession—A dangerous ravine—A fresh halt 92

CHAPTER XI.

The caravanserai—Flies and scorpions—A Persian residence—Offer of an escort—An act of lunacy—Insect pests—Fond of the sword—An awkward look-out—The Emir's palace—An Eastern dinnertable—The Emir of Kuchan—A banquet—The following of a feast—Critical illness—After the fever—Abundance of fruit—Beauty of Meshed—Bazaar inmates—Persian officials—Ancient coins—My bedroom—Meshed water 105

CHAPTER XII.

Persian obstruction — Opening communications — Turcoman heads — Persian ruins — Tarantulas and snakes — A strange drink — Kurdish castles — Beauty of mountains — A border chieftain — The Khan's kiosk — A Turcoman raid — Held to ransom — Brigandage . . 128

CHAPTER XIII.

A Persian passion play — The theatre — The drama — An apology for grief — A stage combat — A stirring scene — Sanguinary performance — A religious dance — Convenient pigtails — Doing penance — Displays of grief — The drama murdered, ... 141

CHAPTER XIV.

Fresh obstacles — Taken in ambush — Fall of Geok Tepé — The Russian advance — The Tejend swamp — Objects on the march — Skobeleff's contribution — Invited to Merv — The Russian agent . . . 153

CHAPTER XV.

Onward to Merv — Atmospheric deceptions — The Merv Tekkés — Taken for a spy — Insect torments — A meeting in the desert — Turcoman wigwams — A prisoner — The Tejend river — Boars and lynxes — A wet night 162

CHAPTER XVI.

The 'Queen of the World' — My personal appearance — Reception by the Mervli — An awkward position — A sanguinary threat — First impressions of Merv — My residence — Under inspection — An eager audience — The Merv chiefs — Showy costumes — A Merv Israelite — The Ichthyar — Petty persecutions — A mischief-making servant — A formidable examiner — Result of the council — Held a prisoner . 173

CHAPTER XVII.

My new home — A hut interior — The Turcoman costume — Merv fortifications — Captured cannon — Quaint ideas on artillery — The great earthwork — A weak defence — A tour of inspection — A naïve proposal — My purpose at Merv — My servant's departure . . . 191

CHAPTER XVIII.

The waterworks—Holding the stirrup—The guest-chamber—How to show gratitude—Delights of a siesta—A generous host—The Benti dam—The sluice—An awkward crossing—A dainty dish—Porsa Kala—Snakes in the desert—Hunting a runaway—Glimpse of the old cities—Homeward bound 203

CHAPTER XIX.

Makdum Kuli Khan—Promised gifts—A doubtful ruler—Another present—Small jealousies—Signs of the times—A Russian prisoner 218

CHAPTER XX.

A fresh council—Political questions—I become a Khan—An expedition—A visit to Baba Khan—Merv vegetables—Peculiarities of teeth—The ride to the ruins—An ancient city—Traces of the past—Crumbling palaces—Old tombs—Giaour Kala—Rampart and citadel—A caravanserai—Brazen vessels—Manners of prayer—Religious customs—Traditions of Alexander—Treasure-seekers—Tomb of Sultan Sanjar—Melon-growing—Strange offerings—The voiceless wilderness 225

CHAPTER XXI.

Mad racing—Imitation raiders—Ready for combat—Heat of the desert—Hospitable customs—A Turcoman belle—Danger of whistling—An antique lamp—Troubles of the night—A cure for wounds—Value of stones—Snake-killing 249

CHAPTER XXII.

The revolution—Coming of the Khans—A singular spectacle—Overthrow of Kadjar—The triumvirate—A theatrical spectacle—Dress—Differences of clan—Making presents—Festivities—My surprise—Playing the host 261

CHAPTER XXIII.

A dilemma—Branding horses—A Georgian prisoner—Other captives—Prisoners in chains—The black present—A camel's bite—Dread of poison—Turcoman pipers—A morning scene—My pets—An oil mill—Offers of hospitality—The Khan's vineyards—Tea-drinking—Tea etiquette—The Guinea worm—The Russian prisoner—Torture of Kidaieff—Offers of ransom—A cure for fever . . . 272

CHAPTER XXIV.

Bazaar day—An accident—The market-place—Food supplies—Punishments—Turcoman steeds—The town crier—Sheep-tail fat—Abundance of game—Breakfast difficulties—Starving out enemies—My *sumsa* stealer—Beg Murad's present—Turcoman life—Customs—Cleverness of women—Carpets 292

CHAPTER XXV.

Religious proposals—Generous offers—A request to Teheran—Russia leather—Raiding—The Old Man of the Sword—Mourning customs—Effects of a storm—Shampooing 309

CHAPTER XXVI.

Diseases—Thirst for remedies—An unsatisfied patient—Plans for the future—A fast for liberty—The Khan's proposal—A change of front—Squeezing a Jew—Unwelcome visitors—Traits of the people—The Moullah's watch—Ink *v.* blacking—Marriage—Settlement of divorce 318

CHAPTER XXVII.

Breach of etiquette—Important document—My ultimatum—Sale of a horse—The last arrow!—Largess—Summoned—An imposing spectacle—A Turcoman joke—My advocate 332

CHAPTER XXVIII.

Fresh delays—Turcoman inertia—Final presents—Sun-burning—The Tandara Pass—Down with fever—Back to civilisation . . . 342

…
THE STORY OF MERV.

CHAPTER I.

Across the Steppe—Delays in landing—The Troïka—The Steppes—Russian stations—A sporting country—Thievish Tartars—The Grand Hotel—General Lazareff—A dreary ride—Reaching Baku.

I LEFT Trebizond at sunset on Wednesday, February 5, 1879, *en route* for Central Asia. It was my intention to travel to Central Thibet, but subsequent circumstances obliged me to alter my resolution, and directed my steps to a locality perhaps not less interesting. I started by the English steamer 'Principe di Carignano,' reaching Batoum early on the morning of the 6th. I found that place wonderfully increased in size, even during the short time which had elapsed since the Russian occupation. The number of houses had almost trebled, and, after the fashion of Russia generally, the majority of these consisted of rum and *vodka* shops. At least one barrel-organ was to be heard grinding in the streets, and, for the first time in the history of the town, public vehicles—the Russian *phäeton*, or gig—plied for hire. The same afternoon, the 'Principe di Carignano' continued her voyage, arriving at the mouth of the Rion river in two and a half hours. Here one became fully impressed with the necessity felt by Russia for a

B

better naval station than Poti on the Southern Black Sea littoral. The extreme shallowness of the water obliged us to anchor at least a mile and a half from the low pebbly beach, and, owing to the violent off-shore wind which prevailed, which would neither allow us to send boats ashore, nor the usual tug steamer, employed for disembarking passengers, to come off, two days and a half elapsed before the slightest chance of landing occurred. At length some of the fishing luggers ventured to put out from the river's mouth, and brought us and our baggage ashore.

Arrived within the mouth of the river, we were taken in tow by a small steamer, which tugged us a distance of two miles, finally landing us at the town of Poti itself. The river banks on either side presented a dismal aspect. Everything seemed but lately to have been inundated. Rotting 'snags' stuck out from the slimy surface of the semi-stagnant water; the lower portion of those trees which stood along the margin looked black and rotting, and a general odour of decomposing vegetable matter permeated the air. Poti is notorious for its unhealthy, feverish climate, and, considering its immediate surroundings, I am not surprised at this. As a naval station there can be no comparison between it and Batoum. Leaving Poti late in the afternoon, after plenty of trouble and delays connected with passports and baggage examinations, one arrives by rail at Tiflis, the capital of the Trans-Caucasus, early on the following morning. The first thing that strikes the eye is the semi-Asiatic, semi-European aspect of the place—the old town, with its narrow streets, its old-fashioned booths, and artisans plying their trades in full view of the public, together with Tartar head-dresses and fur-lined coats, contrasting violently with the palatial houses, wide *prospects*, and great open gardens, thronged with persons of both sexes, wearing Western European fashionable attire. I was unfortunate enough to miss seeing Prince Mirski, the governor of the town, he being absent in the interior; so, after a couple of days' delay at the Hotel Cavcass, I prepared for my journey across the steppes.

On the strength of the Russian official order, which after a good deal of trouble I obtained, the people of the hotel undertook to find me the orthodox postal vehicle with the due number of horses and the official conductor. At the moment of which I speak I had never seen a *troïka*, but I had a kind of preconceived idea about four fiery steeds and a fur-lined carriage, in which the traveller is whirled in luxury to his destination. Judge of my surprise when, on a raw winter's morning, I saw a nameless kind of thing drawn up before the door of the hotel. Though I had just been summoned from bed to take my place, I had not the slightest suspicion that the four-wheeled horror before me was even intended for my luggage. The hall porter and some chilly-looking waiters were standing around, impatiently awaiting a 'gratification,' and I was beginning to get stiff with cold. At length I asked, 'Where is this coach?' 'Your Excellency,' said the porter, 'it is there before you.' When I shall have described a *troïka*, no one will wonder at the exclamation of amazement and terror which burst from my lips at the bare idea that I had to travel four hundred miles in such a thing. Imagine a pig-trough of the roughest possible construction, four feet and a half long, two and a half wide at the top, and one at the bottom, filled with coarse hay, more than half thistles, and set upon four poles, which in turn rest upon the axles of two pairs of wheels. Besides these poles, springs, even of the most rudimentary kind, there are none.

The driver, clad in a rough sheepskin tunic, fitting closely at the waist, the woolly side turned inwards, and wearing a prodigious conical cap of the same material, sits upon the forward edge of the vehicle. With a combination of patched leather straps and knotted ropes by way of reins, he conducts the three horses. The centre animal is between the two shafts, which are joined by a high wooden arch of a parabolic form. From the summit of this arch a leather strap, passing under the animal's chin, keeps his head high, while two pretty large bells, hung just where he ought to keep his ears, force him to carry the latter in a painfully constrained position, while during the whole of the stage he must be almost deafened by the clang. The horses on either side are very loosely harnessed; so much so, that while the central one is, with the vehicle, running along a deep narrow cutting, the flankers are on the top of high banks on either side, or *vice versâ*. Once for all, I give a description of a *troïka* as the species of carriage in which I made my journey to the Caspian. As the stations at which relays are usually found are but twenty-seven or twenty-eight miles apart, they are gone over, almost the whole time, at full gallop. In such guise, mingled with heterogeneous portions of luggage, and wallowing in thorny hay, I was whirled out of Tiflis, and across the long rolling sandy expanses that form the steppes—past Mohammedan tombs, amidst whose walls nomadic shepherds cowered over their fires, with their flocks of sheep and goats hard by—past strings of groaning camels laden with petroleum from Baku. Flocks of pigeons start from the dusty track. They fly on a hundred yards, and then, with a curious obstinacy, settle again and again before us, to be driven on again. Away to the left the giant range of the Caucasus trembles in ghastly whiteness athwart the cloudless sky, and at its base stretches widely a blue mirage that mocks the Kur, alongside of which we go. To the right, farther off still, fainter and more visionary than the Caucasus, are the Persian mountains. Between, a vast dun expanse, fifty or sixty miles across, the horizon ahead, clear and uninterrupted as that of mid-ocean. At length, after a weary ride, the postal station is reached; generally a collection of a few small buildings, under the management of a station-master, who, with his military uniform and flat regulation cap, is the only sign of officialism about the place. As a rule, I found these station-masters exceedingly obliging, and ready to afford the traveller every assistance. At each station-house is a 'guest-chamber,' as the Mohammedans style the apartment in their houses which is appropriated to the reception of strangers. It is generally a small room containing two wooden camp-beds, a table, a fireplace, and sometimes a couple of chairs. No bedding is provided, the traveller being supposed to bring this with him, as well as his food, tea, sugar, &c. A petroleum lamp burns all night within the chamber, and another is attached to the blue and white striped post at the door, which indicates the station, with its distance from the last centre of Government, in versts. Usually it is difficult to procure food, unless some of the women of the establishment can supply a few eggs and some sheets of the peculiar leathery bread, rivalling in size and consistency a cobbler's apron, which seems to pervade the entire East. The only thing the traveller can be certain of finding is the redoubtable *samovar*. This instrument is to be found in the humblest Tartar hovel, for tea—morning, noon, and night—seems an absolutely indispensable necessity of Russian populations. Weak tea swallowed, the traveller again mounts his chariot, which at once dashes away in the most reckless fashion, utterly regardless of the nature or state of the road. The drivers make all kinds of short cuts, very much as a rider would after the hounds. In fact, at times I can only compare our progress to a headlong steeplechase over a violently accidented ploughed field, with continually occurring mad dances across steep-sided torrent-beds filled with large boulders, the banks on either side having a slope of thirty or forty degrees, sometimes more.

At the third station from Tiflis the traveller may be said to bid adieu for the time to civilisation, and encounters swampy riverside, primeval forest-patch, and endless temptations for the sportsman, for one is amidst the homes of the wild boar, the lynx, the wolf, and the wild cat. These latter are really formidable creatures —little less in size than a leopard, of a lion-tawny coloured stiff fur, with flat heads and noses, half-way between those of an otter and a bull-dog. One had just been shot by a peasant close to the station. The habitations of the Tartar families are even more troglodytic than those of Central Armenia. In the latter place there is, at least, something like a slightly raised tumulus to suggest to the experienced eye that a dwelling exists, or did so formerly. Here advantage is taken of some scarped bank, into which a broad deep trench is cut. This is covered over with hurdles and branches, and the earth which covers all is scarcely, if at all, above the level of the surrounding surface. Here and there a wooden cask-like construction acts as chimney; but in most instances this last is simply a hole in the ground, with stone coping, and a small wooden fence erected round it to prevent human beings or cattle from falling through. Buffaloes and goats wander at will over these singular house-tops. A stranger is often startled,' while strolling over what he considers solid ground, to come upon an oblong opening, through which he can hear human voices, while huge wolf-like dogs are prowling about, making him pass them by with a sidelong edging movement by way of precaution. These places are very unhealthy. At one time I feared that I had caught the much-dreaded Astrakan plague, but I recovered after a couple of days and a good deal of quinine. A still worse mishap, however, occurred at one station. I had a small leather writing-case, closed by a lock, and containing all my maps, notes, and writing material. There are always prowling round a large station a number of thievish Tartars, and while seeing to the transfer of my baggage to the place where I was to pass the night, one of these itinerant gentlemen, evidently mistaking the article for a money-box, made off with it. On missing it I at once called on the officer at the station to despatch men to pursue the thief. Everything possible was done, but in vain, and in the interim my sword-belt disappeared.

Endless objects of interest meet the eye to relieve the toilsome journey. Camels trailing loads of osiers, and looking like gigantic porcupines; trains of huge waggons from Persia drawn by four or five horses abreast; a Tartar cavalcade with indigenous ladies on horseback clad in staring red garments, and closely veiled; and at last, all white in the glaring sun, you reach the half-Asiatic, half-European town of Elizabethpol, a sort of halfway house between the last traces of Europe and the Caspian shore. There are Tartar shops in the bazaar, there are

Tartar minarets on the mosques, there are kalpaked Tartars in the streets; the latter contrasting with the patrols of from thirty to forty soldiers, with long grey coats and fixed bayonets, marching slowly along the public ways. There are Turkish *cafés*—holes in the wall, as we should probably call them—mere niches, within which the proprietor crouches, nursing his charcoal fire wherewith to light water-pipes for his customers.

My battered conveyance drew up at the door of what I should be tempted to call a caravanserai, but it was the Grand Hotel of Elizabethpol, and here I was at last shown into a bedroom without bed, and where I could not wash because *the* basin was in use. There was a *table-d'hôte*, but the bill of fare was an illusion, for the only things procurable were ham and caviare. The latter is said to be a delicacy. A spoonful I once by accident tasted at Constantinople reminded me of cod-liver oil.

Here, according to Russian etiquette, I donned the best suit my saddle-bags afforded, and called at the palace of the Government, where I paid my respects to the local governor, Prince Chavchavaza. I was received in a chamber hung with ancient tapestry, the walls of which were garnished with arms of different periods, captured during the protracted struggle in which Schamyl led the Caucasians. The Prince was most courteous, but he did not understand French, and our conversation was carried on by means of his secretary. Here I learned news that entirely changed my plans. For after a short conversation on political matters, suddenly turning to me, the Prince fixed his dark eyes upon my face with a piercing glance, and said, 'Do you know that we expect an army corps shortly, bound for the shores of the Caspian?' 'My prince,' I replied, 'I was unaware of the fact. Where are they going to?' 'There is an expedition against the Turcomans,' he said, 'commanded by General Lazareff.' This was news for me, and I resolved, instead of proceeding on my original mission, to follow the operations of the Russian columns. Having thus determined, nothing was left but to await the arrival of the Commander-in-Chief, General Lazareff, and to ask his permission to accompany his expedition. I waited several days, amid the usual spendthrift extravagance of Russian border towns, and at length the colossal old general made his appearance. General Lazareff was no ordinary individual. He was over six feet in stature, and broadly made in proportion. A mass of jaw was surmounted by a more than Cæsarian nose, and the large grey eye, half hidden by the heavy eyelid, denoted the amount of observation which as a specialty belongs to his race— the Armenian. Up to the age of twenty years he worked as a journeyman tailor. Then joining the Russian army he soon became sergeant. He was the capturer of Schamyl in his stronghold in the Caucasus; and, later on, it was owing to his intrepidity and intrigues that Kars became a Russian citadel, instead of remaining under Turkish rule.

After two days I once more set off to encounter the same undulating plains, the same dust, the same groaning camels; with an occasional change in the shape of mountain, river, and Armenian villages, with vineyards stretching around. Sometimes I was glad to walk over the rough ground to avoid the risk of broken bones, and pick my way through the rocks or miry loam. Here and there we came upon a solitary camel abandoned by some passing caravan, his depleted hump hanging over on one side like an empty sack, and indicating an absolute state of exhaustion.

At last the road began to rise, and we crossed an

elevated mountain chain, the route leading us into the
region of cloud, and cold, and mountain torrent. On one
occasion we were five hours in traversing the most dreadful mountain tracks, often along the top of some great
landslip which the torrent at its base had sapped from
the mountain side. The country seemed alive with field
mice, rats, and ferrets. Leaving the mountain with its
snow and fog behind, it was an inexpressible relief to
reach once more the dry, warm plain that stretched to
Shumakha, where I spent my night upon the rude benches
of the guest-chamber. I started again early on the
morning of Wednesday, the 27th, passing another exceedingly disagreeable and difficult series of mountains
deeply covered with snow, and at last, after endless
troubles at various stations, where horses were wanting,
with an obstinate driver who objected to leave the place
on account of a wedding, and on my insisting upon proceeding upsetting the *troïka* and breaking the harness, it
was at seven o'clock in the morning when, after a weary
night drive, we came in sight of Baku, lying some ten
versts off; the Caspian, glittering beyond, being seen at
intervals between the low hills that flanked its border.
The country at this point is inexpressibly dreary and
volcanic-looking; the salt incrustations lying thick upon
the earth. Here and there were straggling Tartar villages,
with their flat houses and preposterously large conical
chimneys, looking like gigantic mushrooms. From time
to time we passed along the road the peculiar-looking
carts characteristic of the country. The wheels were
not less than eight feet in diameter, and very close to
each other, the body of the cart being but two feet
wide, a structure like a pulpit rising in front, gaudily
painted, and probably intended for the use of the conductor. Entering Baku itself, the driver descended for

a moment from his seat to tie up the bells hanging from the wooden arch above the central horse, the municipal regulations forbidding the entry of postal vehicles accompanied by their usual jangling uproar, lest the horses of the town *phäetons* should take fright.

CHAPTER II.

A petroleum city—Petroleum—Fire worship—A strange rite—The Turcomans—Chatte—Flies and mosquitoes—A reconnaissance—In gorgeous array—Caucasian horsemen—The *handjar*.

WHILE I was staying in Baku I was a good deal interested in the peculiar nature of the soil. During the storms that are very frequent, dense clouds of dim yellow dust arise, and this contains so much bitumen that the least glow of sunshine fixes it indelibly upon one's clothes. The streets are moistened with the coarse black residual naphtha that remains after distillation of the raw petroleum, and this effectually lays the dust for about a fortnight. Petroleum abounds in the neighbourhood, and its mineral springs are busily worked by means of well-borings which are sometimes sunk to a depth of 150 yards. At times the naphtha rises to the surface, and even flows over abundantly, occasionally springing fountain-like into the air to a height of eight or ten feet for hours together, as in the case of the artesian well. In such cases the ground around the boring is often flooded to a depth of six inches with the mineral oil, which, to avoid the danger of a conflagration, has to be let off by channels constructed so as to lead it seaward. Under ordinary circumstances, it has to be drawn up from a considerable depth. The boring is generally ten, or at most eighteen, inches in diameter. A long bucket, or rather a tube stopped at the bottom, and fifteen feet in length, is lowered into the well, and drawn up full of crude petroleum—fifty gallons at a time. This, which is a blue-pink transparent liquid, is poured into a rudely constructed, plank-lined trough at the door of the well-house, whence it flows by an equally rude channel to the distillery.

Apart from the local use of petroleum for lighting, and its exportation for a similar purpose, is its application to steam navigation. With the old-fashioned boilers in use, which have a central opening running longitudinally, no modification is necessary for the application of the new fuel. A reservoir, containing some hundred pounds' weight of the refuse (*astatki*), is furnished with a small tube, bearing another at its extremity, a few inches long, and at right angles with the conduit. From this latter it trickles slowly. Close by is the mouth of another tube, connected with the boiler. A pan containing tow or wood saturated with *astatki* is first introduced to heat the water, and, once the slightest steam pressure is produced, a jet of vapour is thrown upon the dropping bituminous fluid, which is thus converted into spray. A light is applied, and then a roaring deluge of fire inundates the central opening of the boiler. It is a kind of self-acting blowpipe. This volume of fire can be controlled by one man, by means of the two stop-cocks, as easily as the flame in an ordinary gas jet.

Baku was one of the last strongholds of the fire-worshippers, not at all a surprising fact when I state that in some places I have seen fifty or sixty furnaces for burning lime, the flame used being simply the carburetted hydrogen that issued from fissures in the earth.

In the midst of the busy petroleum works, where the chimneys of the distilleries no doubt far surpass in height the fire towers of old, is a real specimen of the religious architecture and practices of ante-Mussulman days. After stumbling through the black naphtha mud, and over uneven foundations, a hole roughly broken in a modern wall gives entry to a small chamber, twenty feet by fifteen, adjoining which is a smaller one to the right. In the opposite wall and to the left is another low door opening on a semi-circular yard, fifteen feet wide at its greater diameter. It is the remaining half of the once celebrated fire temple, or rather of the small monastery connected with it. The exterior wall, eleven or twelve feet high, on which is a parapeted walk, is composed of rough stone. From the courtyard one can enter thirty-five roomy cells, accessible by as many doors. These cells, formerly occupied by the monks or pilgrims, are now rented at a moderate price to some of the workmen who belong to the factories immediately surrounding, by the priest, the last of his race, who still lingers beside his unfrequented altars. The priest is called for. He dons a long white robe, taken from a rude cupboard in the whitewashed wall, and, drawing near a kind of wide altar tomb at the south-western corner of the chamber, railed off from the outer portion of the apartment by a low wooden balustrade, applies a lighted match, which he has previously sought for in a most prosaic manner in his breeches pocket, to a small iron tube. A jet of pale blue lambent flame is produced, rising to the height of eight inches or a foot. Seizing the rope of a bell hung over his head, he rings half a dozen strokes upon it, then takes in his hand a small bell, and, ringing it continually, proceeds to bow and genuflect before the altar. The light wanes gradually, and goes out. And then, advancing towards the curious spectator, the priest proffers on a small brass dish a few grains of barley or rice, or, as I once saw, three or four pieces of candied sugar, which the envelope indicated had been manufactured in Paris! A person in the East always gives a present with the view of receiving at least fifty times its value in return; so we present the last of his race with a couple of roubles, and retire.

On the afternoon of Tuesday, April 2, 1879, having received permission from General Lazareff to accompany the expedition against the Akkal Tekké Turcomans, a permission endorsed by H.I.H. the Grand Duke commanding at Tiflis, I went on board the Russian war steamer 'Nasr Eddin Shah,' and three days later we anchored two and a half miles off the low sandy shore of Tchikislar, having to land in boats at a rude pier that ran out some hundred and fifty yards. The General was received by a party of Yamud elders, who, drawn up at the extremity of the pier, offered him, as he landed, a cake of bread, a plate of salt, and a large fish newly caught; meantime, the guns in the small redoubt adjoining the camp thundered out their salute. The Turcomans of the entire surrounding neighbourhood had assembled to do honour to the General, and were drawn up on either side of the pier along which he passed to the shore. At its landward extremity, a number of these people held prostrate on the ground half a dozen black-haired sheep, and, as he passed, a knife was drawn across the throat of each animal, the blood streaming, hot and reeking, across his path, and flooding the ground to such an extent that our shoes were all ensanguined as we walked in procession across it. It was the first time I had had a good opportunity of seeing genuine Turcomans. Each wore the enormous sheepskin shako affected by the inhabitants of Central Asia, and a long tunic of some bright colour, tightly girt at the waist by a broad white sash, knotted in front, a long dirk thrust through it. Over this was an exterior garment of some sombre tint, with long sleeves, which the wearers were continually pulling backwards in order to leave their hands free. Each, together with his poniard, wore a curved, leather-sheathed sabre, with cross guard. One might have imagined them a battalion of the Foot Guards, robed for the nonce in dressing gowns. Some, also, wore the enormous pelisse of sheepskin so common among the dwellers in Central Asia.

The General then gave audiences to the chiefs of these Yamud Turcomans, and finding they had fifteen or sixteen prisoners of their enemies, the Akkal Tekkés, with a view of propitiating their companions of the distant oasis, the General ordered the immediate release of these prisoners, and sent them away to their homes, giving to each some trifling present in money or articles of European manufacture. To them, as well as to the Yamud chiefs and elders, he gave silver watches, silver-mounted *handjars*, pieces of bright-coloured cloth, and such like articles as he thought might be pleasing to them. On the following morning, April 6, a little before daybreak, we started for the advanced post of Chatte, at the junction of the Atterek and Sumbar rivers, the former being the nominal division between Persia and the Russian and Turcoman possessions. We were strongly escorted by Cossacks, and the early part of our journey was most unpleasant, for our wheels sank deeply in the sand of the low region, over which during a westerly wind the waters of the Caspian are often driven for the distance of a league. Two miles inland I saw the bleaching skins of the Caspian carp; and multitudes of sea anemones lay around. Far from the shore, too, we met with Turcoman *täimuls*, or dug-out canoes, lying about over the plains in the places where they had been left stranded by the retiring waters. The heat was intense, and the eyes were pained by the constant glare from the white plains, unrelieved by anything more than an occasional tamarisk bush or clump of camel thorn, the marl around seeming as if it had been calcined in some mighty furnace. Fresh water was extremely scarce, the expeditionary force spending much time in digging wells, while travellers upon these plains are often tortured by the mirage—that oft-repeated atmospheric delusion which has frequently beguiled me into a bootless ride of many a league in search of the wished-for water.

Chatte is one of the dreariest places imaginable. At the time of my visit the garrison consisted of two battalions. The heat was intense; and the cemetery, not far off, and ominously large for so small a garrison, spoke in eloquent terms of the unhealthy nature of the locality. Fully eighty feet below, in the midst of their tremendous ravines, ran the canal-like streams of the Atterek and Sumbar, at this time shrunk to comparative threads of water, all white with suspended marl, and almost undrinkable from the quantity of saline matter held in solution. Myriads of flies rendered life unbearable by day, as did gnats and mosquitoes by night; and the intense heat, aggravated by the simoom-like winds sweeping across the burning plain, made Chatte anything but a desirable abiding-place. 'I would ten times rather be sent to Siberia than left here any longer,' I one day heard an officer of infantry exclaim to a newly-arrived comrade. After a short experience I felt quite in the same mind as this officer, for between heat and flies by day, and mosquitoes by night, I never passed such a miserable time in all my existence. In view of the domed edifices and extensive foundations, spreading far and wide, there can be no doubt that a populous community once flourished there. Now, owing to the fact that the river has cut its bed low down in the marly soil, and that irrigation is impossible, civilisation has perished from the spot. Very possibly, too, Zenghis Khan and his hordes had something to do with laying waste what are now trackless solitudes.

General Lazareff having made his reconnaissance, and satisfied himself, returned at once to the Caspian, to take the necessary steps before finally committing himself to a forward movement into the heart of the enemy's territory. In the middle of one of the stages on our backward way, the horses of the General's carriage, broken down by the rapid pace at which we were proceeding, had foundered, and we had to leave them behind us, gasping on the dusty plain. To replace them, Cossacks of the escort were ordered up. Each horseman, taking one of the ropes which served as traces, placed it under his left thigh, held the extremity in his hand, and then galloped forward with the surviving horses of the team, over the plain already dotted with the bones of camels and mules, which, bleaching in the sun, strewed every foot of the way—ghastly evidences of the dangers awaiting the traveller across these silent tracts. Save ourselves, not a living being of any description was in sight. Not even a prowling Turcoman was to be seen.

The advanced guard, now that all danger was over for the moment, amused themselves with chasing the wild asses and antelopes which constantly came in sight as we topped some undulation of the ground, the horses seeming to enter into the sport quite as thoroughly as their riders, though we never had a chance of coming within shot. One of my last reminiscences of this journey was having supper with General Lazareff and his second in command, General Lomakin. We sat upon the edges of three drums, and bayonets stuck point downwards in the ground served us as candlesticks. In our company was the Caravan Bashi, a Khivan, whose dress merits description. He wore a silk tunic, of the brightest possible emerald green, with lavish gold embroidery; sky-blue trousers, of semi-European make; a purple mantle profusely laced; and, contrary to all Mussulman precedent, his fingers were covered with massive rings of gold. A gold-embroidered skull-cap was stuck upon the back of his head, and, perched forward, the brim almost upon the bridge of his nose, was a cylindrical cap of black Astrakan fur, which allowed almost the whole of the elaborately decorated skull-cap to be seen behind.

We arrived in Tchikislar about six o'clock in the evening, and I hoped to obtain a good night's rest, so far as such was consistent with the presence of great redbodied, long-legged mosquitoes, but to my dismay an aide-de-camp announced to me that I must be ready to go on board the steamer at nine o'clock to proceed to the northward.

Krasnavodsk, which we reached at eight o'clock next morning, is simply a Russian military colony. It would be impossible to conceive anything more bleak or desolate-looking than the scarped, scraggy cliffs of rose-coloured alabaster which face the town. Did it lie in the bottom of a volcano crater, the barrenness and dryness could not be greater. The natural water of the site, very limited in quantity, is absolutely unfit for human use, and the needs of the place are supplied by the distillation of sea water, the wood fuel being brought at an immense cost from Lenkoran on the opposite

Caspian shore. Here there has been made an attempt at a public garden; but only a few very scrubby-looking tamarisk bushes have been able to hold their own in the midst of the sandy soil and the scorching sun-glare. The greatest care is necessary in order to foster even these few bushes, which would look faded and miserable beside the most withered furze bush that ever graced a highland mountain-top. One evening during our stay at Krasnavodsk, I had an opportunity of seeing the peculiar method of fighting of the Caucasian and Daghestani horsemen, who happened to be on the station. They are natives of the north-eastern portion of the Caucasus, and are esteemed among the best cavalry in the Russian service. Their uniform is almost precisely similar to that of the Circassians, save that the Daghestani have their long tight-waisted tunics of white flannel instead of the usual sober colours affected by the Circassian horsemen. Hanging between the shoulders, and knotted around the neck, is the *bashlik*, or hood, worn during bad weather, this hood being of a crimson colour. On either side of the breast are one or more rows of metal cartridge-tubes, now worn simply for ornament, for I need scarcely say that these horsemen are armed with modern breech-loading carbines, and carry their cartridges in the orthodox regulation pouches, instead of after the fashion of their forefathers. Their sabres are of the usual guardless Circassian pattern, almost the entire hilt entering into the scabbard. Hanging from the front of the waist-belt is a *handjar*, or broad-bladed, leaf-shaped sword, very similar to the ancient Spanish weapon adopted by the Roman soldiery, or resembling perhaps still more those bronze weapons found upon the old battle-fields of Greece and within early Celtic barrows. These weapons they are accustomed to use as projectiles, much as the North American Indians use their long-bladed knives.

On the evening in question, a squadron of these Daghestani horsemen were paraded, in order that we might witness their skill in throwing the *handjars*. A large wooden target was erected, in front of which was suspended an ordinary black bottle. Then, one by one, the horsemen dashed up at full speed, hurling their *handjars*, as they did so, at the mark. It was intended to plant the point of the knife in the target, so close to the bottle that the flat of the blade should almost touch it. One after another the knives of the whole squadron were thrown, until they stuck like a sheaf of arrows round the mark, and so good was the aim that in no one case would there have been the slightest possibility of missing so large a mark as a man's body.

After this exhibition of skill, the Lesghi, as the Daghestani are occasionally called, performed some of their national dances, to the music of the pipe and tabor. Two dancers at a time stepped into the circle formed around them by their comrades. Each placed the back of his right hand across his mouth, holding the elbow elevated in the air; the left arm was held at its fullest extent, sloping slightly downwards, the palm turned to the rear. In this somewhat singular attitude they commenced sliding round the ring with a peculiar waltzing step; then, suddenly confronting each other, they broke into a furious jig, going faster and faster as the music increased in pace, and when, all breathless, they retired into the ranks, their places were immediately taken by another pair. Occasionally one of the more skilful would arm himself with two *handjars*, and, placing the points on either side of his neck, go through the most violent calisthenic movements, with the view of showing the perfect control he had over his muscles.

CHAPTER III.

Searching for sulphur mines—A desert post—Bitter waters—The Black Gulf—Sulphur Mountain—Turcoman steeds—A night alarm—The attack—A race for life—Worn out.

DURING my stay at Krasnavodsk, I made the acquaintance of an Armenian gentleman who had come there with the intention of scientifically exploring the neighbourhood, and discovering what its mineral resources might be. He was especially in search of certain sulphur mines reported to exist upon the shores of the Kara Boghaz, the great expanse of shallow water lying to the north of Krasnavodsk. He had succeeded in obtaining from General Lomakin a guard of fifteen Yamud Turcomans, acting as Russian auxiliary irregular horse, and, gathering from some conversation with me that I was interested in geological researches, asked me to accompany him on his expedition. We started early in the morning, and, mounted upon hardy little Khirgese ponies, climbed the horrid-looking, burnt-up ravines that lead through the amphitheatre of hills which guard Krasnavodsk, to the plain beyond. These rocks, as I have said, are of rose-coloured gypsum, though sometimes a blue and yellow variety is to be met with. Once outside the rocky, girding scarp, the Turcoman *sahra*, here affording an unusually luxuriant supply of coarse bent-grass, reaches away in one unbroken tract to the banks of the Sea of Aral. The Yamud shepherds, perched upon every slight elevation around, kept watch and ward lest a party of Tekké Turcomans should sweep down upon them and bear both themselves and their charges into captivity. At the time of which I am writing some four or five thousand camels, destined for the transport service of the Akhal Tekké expedition, were concentrated in the neighbourhood of the town, the greater portion of them having been most unwisely sent to pasture at a distance of some twenty miles from the garrison.

Though it was early in the year, the heat of the sun was overwhelming; and as in the midst of our wild-looking escort we rode across these naked, burnt-up plains, I could well appreciate how welcome was the 'shadow of a great rock in a weary land.' Far, far off, on either hand, loomed, faintly violet, some minor hills, which, my companion assured me, were replete with mineral treasures, especially with a very pure kind of natural paraffin, or mineral wax (*osocheryte*), as it is commonly called. Apart from the stray camels and flocks, the only living things to be seen were huge spotted lizards, who stared eagerly at us as we went by, and tortoises, crawling about over the marly surface.

It was two o'clock in the afternoon as we reached a Russian military post, some sixteen miles distant from Krasnavodsk. It consisted of a small rectangular redoubt, garrisoned by two companies of infantry and about twenty-five Turcoman horse. The captain shared with us his not very luxurious meal of dried Caspian carp and almost equally dry sausage, washed down by the never-failing glass of *vodka*, and then we again started on our forward journey. We varied the monotony of the journey by racing, and dangerous work it was, for the ground was everywhere burrowed into by great chameleon-like lizards—sometimes two feet long—and every now and then a horseman came to grief, owing to his steed involuntarily thrusting a leg into one of these pitfalls. At ten o'clock in the evening we reached a kind of basin, situated in the midst of low hills, if I may call elevations of fifty feet or so by that name. This basin might have been a mile and a half across. Near its centre were half-a-dozen wells, which gave the place the name of Ghoui-Sulmen. Each well was surrounded by a low parapet of yellowish-grey nummulitic limestone, and close by the mouth stood a couple of rude troughs of the same material. Their workmanship was of the very rudest description, and I have no doubt that these traces of man's handiwork must be of great antiquity. The water lay at least forty feet below the level of the well-mouth, and could only be procured by being fished up in the nose-bags of our horses, let down by the united tethering-ropes of several of the party. This water was execrable in the extreme. I understand that it contains a large percentage of sulphate of soda and common salt; but whatever be the matter which gives it its peculiar taste and flavour, it is very nauseous, especially when it has become heated from being carried in the leather bags in which water is stored during long journeys in these parts of the world. It then becomes emetic, as well as strongly purgative. Coming from the great depths at which it lies beneath the soil, it is icy-cold when brought to the surface, but even then it is intolerable to anyone who has been accustomed to different water elsewhere. Not being able to drink, I tried to assuage my thirst by bathing my face and hands, but I soon discovered what a mistake I had made, for when the moisture had evaporated I found the surface of my skin covered with an extremely irritant saline matter, the eyes and nose especially suffering. Our escort prepared their tea with this water, and seemed to enjoy it, though after the first mouthful I was obliged to cease drinking.

The Turcomans rarely smoke anything but a water-pipe, or *kalioun*, but as this is too cumbrous to be carried about on horseback, a simpler expedient is resorted to. An oblong steep-sided hole is dug in the ground, some five inches wide, and a foot deep. Some red-hot charcoal is taken from the camp fire, and placed in the bottom of the cavity. A handful of *tumbaki*, a coarse kind of tobacco used in these regions, is thrown in, and the smoker, kneeling beside the hole, places his expanded palms on either side of his mouth, stoops over the orifice, and inhales the fumes of the tobacco, mingled with air. Three or four whiffs from this singular smoking apparatus seem quite sufficient for the most determined smoker among them, and I am not surprised at it. I nearly choked myself at my first attempt.

We broke camp about half-past one, and continued our journey towards the shores of the Kara-Boghaz (Black Gulf), on the borders of which lay the sulphur mines which it was the mission of my friend to explore. The stars gave but feeble light, and as the edges of projecting strata now began to make their appearance the road became so dangerous that after two miles we were obliged to halt again and wait for dawn. As the sun was rising we found ourselves on the margin of a vast creek reaching inland from the Kara-Boghaz. The waters lay still and death-like, and the entire surroundings were more lifeless and ghastly than any I had hitherto witnessed. Not even a bird of any description was to be seen, far or near. To reach the level yellow shore at the water marge it was necessary that we should scramble down the almost vertical face of the cliff, some sixty or seventy feet in height. It was composed of terraced layers of whitish-yellow stone, similar to that which I have described as being found at the well-mouths; in some places tossed and tumbled in the wildest possible confusion. Dismounting from our horses, and leading them by the bridles, we proceeded to scramble, as best we could, down the cliff, being often obliged to hold on by the tamarisk bushes, and at last reached the shell-strewn beach below. Following the strand in a north-easterly direction, we reached a ravine which pierces the cliffs in an easterly one. This was the spot of which we were in search. It is called by the Turcomans the Kukurt-Daghi, or Sulphur Mountain.

My friend commenced his search immediately, for there was not a moment to be lost. We were on dangerous ground, where the nomads were frequently to be found encamped preparatory to one of their forays in the neighbourhood of Krasnavodsk. Strewn around were fragments of black and red lava, and the entire place bore unmistakeable signs of a more or less recent volcanic disturbance. Lumps of sulphur were to be found in every direction, and here and there were nodules, embedded between the stone layers, and in the indurated beds of detritus. Though we found tolerably large 'pockets,' however, nowhere could we discover any real vein. There was no considerable deposit of the substance —at least, such was the opinion of my friend, the geologist. After an hour and a half's search, we mounted for the return journey, and I was not sorry to leave the spot. We took a new route on our way back, and, riding across a country exactly similar to that of which I have spoken, two hours before sunset we got into a sandy, undulating area. The tamarisk bushes grew high and close, and were even mixed with a peculiar kind of osier. This infallibly denoted the presence of water. We were, in fact, at the Ghoui-Kabyl, or sweet-water wells, the only place in the whole district where such a thing as really drinkable water is to be obtained. We washed the salt from our hands and faces, and then lay down to rest upon the soft, yielding sand, which afforded as comfortable a couch as the softest feather bed, for it adapted itself perfectly to the form of the sleeper. As usual, several camp fires were lighted, for the preparation of the inevitable tea, without which no true Central Asian or Russian can get through a day's journey. The fires smouldered dimly around us, for the Yamuds were too cautious to allow a blaze to be seen in such a place. They did not go to sleep, but sat crouchingly around the fires, chatting to each other. The horses, each secured by one fetlock at the full extent of its tethering-rope, ran round in circles, screaming at and trying to kick each other. I have remarked this peculiarity about Turcoman horses, that while towards human beings they are the gentlest and most tractable of creatures, among themselves they are the most quarrelsome that it is possible to imagine.

Notwithstanding the noise which the horses were making—and it was very aggravating, when after the fatigues of the past two days we were trying to snatch an hour's repose—I was sinking gradually into slumber. A calm seemed to come over the bivouac, and everything appeared tranquil. I turned over on the sand to make myself comfortable, when I became aware that an unusual agitation prevailed among the ordinarily calm and taciturn Turcomans. They were whispering eagerly together. I raised myself upon my elbow, and looked round. Some were hastily saddling their horses, and before I had time to demand the reason of this proceeding, several of them came hurriedly up to where myself and my friend lay. There was something wrong, they said. The horses were sniffing the wind, with necks outstretched towards the east. Either strangers were approaching, or there was some other encampment near, and if this latter were the case, the encampment could only be a Tekké one. We held a council of war, and decided that the most advisable course to adopt was to move on immediately. Sand was heaped upon the camp fires, horses were rapidly saddled and packed, and, like a party of spectres, we stole silently away. Several Turcomans, with the apparently innate perception of locality, even in the dark, which is acquired by the habits of life of their race, led the way. For myself I had not the faintest notion towards what point of the compass we were directing our steps. During half-an-hour we forced our path among the bushes, and gained open ground. Four Turcomans were thrown out to reconnoitre in the supposed dangerous direction, and, anxious though I felt over the situation, I could not help wondering how they would ever find their way back. In an hour, however, they managed to rejoin us, and reported a large camp to the eastward. They estimated the number of its occupants at some hundreds, and believed they could be no other than Tekkés.

The sun was well above the horizon as we sighted several hundreds of camels browsing, on a rising ground, on the scanty herbage, and tended by some scores of Khirgese nomads. We hastily communicated to them the news of the proximity of the Tekkés, and rode forward, as swiftly as might be, after our protracted journey, towards the Bournak post, which we reached about two hours after sunrise. We reported our intelligence to the Commandant, Captain Ter-Kazaroff, who took the necessary precautions for the safety of his redoubt. I had slept a couple of hours at the shady side of the captain's tent, and was in the act of making some notes of the day's adventures, when scouts came galloping up in a headlong fashion with the news that the Tekkés were advancing in force, and that not a moment was to be lost if the camels were to be saved. Notwithstanding that a border post like that of Bournak is constantly on the alert, the rapidity with which the men were got under arms was surprising. The captain rushed from his tent, the bugle sounded, and in less than two minutes after the alarm the first company was moving to the front at the double. In fact, so rapid was the preparation that the captain had not even time to load his revolver, and I lent him mine. At the same time the irregular Yamud cavalry, some fifteen in number, together with the Khirgese shepherds, were driving in the camels, which could not be forced to accelerate their usual slow and dignified pace; and, consequently, several of the shepherds were cut down by the foremost Tekké horse.

Within ten minutes after the departure of the first company, the second, in reserve, marched with the camels carrying the spare ammunition, leaving only half-a-dozen men to garrison the redoubt. The first company was scarcely five hundred yards distant from the parapets when the leading Tekkés appeared in sight, galloping along the summit of the long undulation of the plain, and in a few minutes many hundreds of them were in view. Some affrighted Khirgese drivers who came in said that the greater number of their companions had been killed, a large proportion of the camels taken, and at least two thousand sheep swept away. They reported that the Tekkés were at least two thousand strong, and that a large number of them were horsemen, the remainder being infantry mounted upon camels and asses. Firing had already commenced, and myself and my friend were sorely puzzled as to what course we should pursue. The position, for us, was an exceedingly difficult one. I much desired to go forward and witness the skirmish, but the condition of our horses, after two days' hard riding, with little or no food save the few handfuls of corn which we had in our saddle-bags, rendered it excessively dangerous for us to proceed into the press of combat, especially as it was as likely as not that the slender Russian infantry force would be compelled to retreat, even if it were not annihilated. In the latter case, and with our jaded horses, we were certain to be captured, and mutilation, if not death, would have been our portion. To await the result of the fight in the redoubt, with its few defenders, was equally precarious, so we thought it best to make good our retreat, while there was yet an opportunity, as fast as our fatigued horses could carry us. Our baggage was rapidly packed, and we retired as swiftly as we could. Half a mile to the south of the post of Bournak is another reach of ground commanding an extensive view over the plain, and from this, though at a pretty long distance, I could, with the aid of my field glass, follow the movements of the Tekkés. It was not easy, however, to make out which way the combat was going, for the entire plain was covered with groups of combatants, and it was impossible to detect to which side they belonged. Once outside of the protecting parapets of the redoubt, our most prudent course was to make the best of our way to Krasnavodsk.

Our worn-out horses took at least three hours to cover the eighteen miles which intervened between us and that town. The heat was terrific, and I was in a general state of weariness. We entered the rocky circle of hills which shuts off Krasnavodsk and its immediate surroundings from the plains, and as we debouched from one horrid gorge, with its gaunt cliffs of burnt red rock, we met General Lomakin, the commander of the town, advancing with all his available forces. I had a short conversation with the General, explained to him all I knew about the situation, and once more pushed on. A little later I met one of the Yamud horsemen who had formed part of the escort of myself and my Armenian friend. He gave it as his decided opinion that we must have been under the direct protection of Allah as we got off from the Ghoui-Kabyl that morning. Had we remained an hour longer on the spot, he said, we should certainly have been captured by the Tekkés. I was really very much knocked up by the expedition. The heat, want of sufficient food, salty water, and, above all, the absence of sleep, had quite prostrated me, and I find in my note-book the following entry, which is very descriptive of the situation :—'I am very ill, and my back is nearly broken. My nose is almost burned off, and my breeches are torn from hard riding. I must go to bed.'

CHAPTER IV.

Waiting to advance—Water snakes—Quaint humanity—Caucasian cavalry—Uniforms—Ideas and fashion—Punishment of the knout—An angler's paradise.

I REMAINED at Krasnavodsk up to the first of May, awaiting a definite move on the part of the expeditionary forces, and made a trip to Tchikislar on board the 'Ural' war-steamer. During this excursion I had a good opportunity of examining the island of Tcheliken, with its steep seaward marl cliffs, stained by the black flow of naphtha which has gone on for ages pouring its riches into the unprofitable bosom of the Caspian. On one of its highest portions is one of the tall, sentry-box-looking objects which stand over the petroleum wells worked by Mr. Nobel, the enterprising capitalist of Baku.

Tchikislar, which I understand is now almost deserted, was, at the time of which I speak, in all its glory. Several thousands of men were under canvas, the cavalry to the north, the infantry to the south of the original sand redoubt and signal station. The environs of the camp were in a filthy state, the Russians neglecting the most simple sanitary precautions. The hospitals were full, and myriads of flies filled the air. Nothing was being done, so on the fifth I again went on board the 'Ural' to return to Krasnavodsk.

I remained only ten days at this town, leading the accustomed life—*soirées* at the club, dinners at the governor's, and driving about the neighbourhood. During one of the last excursions I made along the rocky shores of the bay, I was struck by the immense numbers of water snakes which, leaving the sea, had gone long distances inland. I have met these reptiles between five and six feet in length, of a yellow colour mottled with brown, by threes and fours at a time, crossing the scorched gypsum rocks at least half a mile from the shore, and making their way to the water, into which they plunged and swam out to sea. From on board ship I have seen them in the waters of Krasnavodsk Bay—five or six knotted together—floating in the sun.

On May 15 I was sent for by General Lomakin, who informed me that General Lazareff desired to see me immediately, and accordingly, on the following day, at one o'clock, I started for Baku, where the Commander-in-Chief was temporarily staying, but only to reach it after a long and tempestuous voyage, for Baku certainly deserves the title given to it by the old Tartars, 'a place beaten by the winds.'

On the following day I had an interview with General Lazareff, who wished to obtain some unbiassed evidence about the affair at Bournak, in view of the complaints which had reached him from different quarters relative to the want of promptitude of General Lomakin in hurrying to the assistance of the two companies defending the camels. He asked me whether I believed it was not possible for Lomakin to have pushed on the same evening and followed up the enemy. I had no other answer to give than that I believed he had acted with the greatest possible promptitude. General Lazareff afterwards told me it was quite possible that we should have to winter in the Akhal Tekké, and he declared his intention not to return until he had accomplished his mission—the 'pacification,' as he was pleased to term it, of the district. Further operations depended upon eventualities. Should the Merv Turcomans take part with their brethren of the Akhal Tekké, he would be obliged to move against Merv, but at present he had no definite instructions in the matter. He concluded by saying, 'We must do nothing in a hurry; we have plenty of time before us.'

Baku is not at all an agreeable place to stay in, and I was not sorry to receive a notification from the Chief of Staff to go on board the 'Constantine' mail steamer, to accompany General Lazareff across the Caspian to Tchikislar, which place we reached on Monday, June 3, anchoring as usual nearly three miles off shore, and we had the accustomed difficulty in landing. The arrival of the Commander-in-Chief with his staff, and the presence of some additional battalions which had preceded us, greatly added to the liveliness of the camp.

One of the most peculiar characteristics of Tchikislar was the presence of very large numbers of Khirgese and Turcoman camel-drivers, and of muleteers from Baghdad, who, under promise of high pay, had been induced to abandon their ordinary track between the latter city and Meshed, and to come to the Russian camp for the transport service. There is a very wide difference between the appearance of the Khirgese and that of the Turcomans. The latter are of a more or less slim and wiry figure, with approximately European features. They wear the huge sheepskin hat, and make a very fair attempt at a regular system of clothing. The Khirgese is as quaint-looking, awkwardly-dressed a figure as one could find upon a Chinese porcelain dish—the same impossible eyes, long, narrow, and dragged upwards at the outer corners, genuine Cathay hat, and occasionally an umbrella, which would not be out of place in a procession of stage mandarins; finally, he has a shuffling, slovenly gait, more ungraceful than that of a ploughman. His ordinary garment is a kind of dirty cotton sheet, twisted anyhow about him, or at most a very draggled and tattered linen tunic. In a burning sun he wears as much furry clothing as an Esquimaux. On his head is a movable conical tent of felt, which falls to the middle of his back, and which towards midday he supplements by another, and perhaps a couple of horse-cloths besides. Seated on the scorching sand, with his stolid mien, peeping eyes, and strange headdress, his general appearance is that of one of those squatting Indian deities of a pagoda, clothed in rags and skins.

There were large numbers of Caucasian and Cossack horsemen, all in picturesque attire, and looking quite unlike anything we are accustomed to associate with the uniform of a regular regiment. Both Cossack and Caucasian wore tunic-like garments, fitting tightly at the waist, the skirt falling almost to the heels, and made of white, brown, grey, or black cloth. The breast was covered with one or two horizontal rows of silver or brass cartridge-cases, according to the rank of the wearer. They all bore the before-mentioned guardless Circassian sabre. The Russian officers serving in Asia for the most part affect this style of weapon instead of the regulation sword, carrying it by a belt slung across the shoulder, instead of girt around the waist. There is a very remarkable trait of character noticeable among the officers of Caucasian cavalry regiments, among the Kabardian officers especially, which is well worthy of a few words of comment. Each one feels bound to have both arms and belt mounted as massively and richly as possible with enamelled silver; cartridge-boxes, tinder-boxes, poniards, and other accoutrements being decorated with equal richness. Many, however, regard a new coat, or one that shows no sign of wear, as entirely inadmissible and unmanly, and altogether in *mauvais goût*. When the dilapidation of a garment compels the wearer to order a new one, he straightway deliberately tears the latter in several places, and with his knife frays the edges of the sleeve, in order to give it the appearance of having seen service; and so well is this peculiar taste recognised, that the tailor has been known to send home a new habiliment with the requisite amount of tatters, and with the lower part of the cuff artificially frayed. We had in the camp a band of irregular cavalry, formerly professional robbers and marauders from the neighbourhood of Alexandropol, who were told off for the special duty of harrying the enemy's flocks and herds. They were under the command of a well-known brigand chief named Samad Agha, a Karapapak. These also affected the same style of dress and arms as the Caucasians.

I saw at Tchikislar an example of what I had been led to believe was abolished in Russian rule—punishment by the knout. The Khirgese and Turcomans who had been hired, together with their trains of camels, to serve in the baggage train of the expedition, received a fixed sum per diem for the services of themselves and their animals, and in case of any camels succumbing to the fatigues of the road, or being captured or disabled by the enemy, the owner was compensated to the extent of one hundred roubles in paper for each camel—a sum then equal to about ten English pounds. Many of these people brought with them only the very weakliest of the camels in their possession, knowing that they would not be able to dispose of them at so good a price elsewhere, and took the first opportunity, when on a long journey, to abandon them in the desert. In cases of this kind they were required, in proof of their assertions, to bring in the tails of the camels which were supposed to have died. A party of Khirgese and Turcomans were despatched with material from Krasnavodsk, and directed to follow the shore to the camp at Tchikislar. They abandoned their camels on the way, having first cut off their tails, which they duly brought into camp. Lazareff's suspicions were aroused, and he ordered a party of cavalry to proceed along the track by which the camels had passed, and to scour the country in search of their bodies. The horsemen came upon the camels, which were calmly grazing over the plain, in as good condition as ever they were but for the absence of their tails. The evidence against the culprits was overwhelming, and in order to make an example, and prevent the repetition of this fraud, each was sentenced to receive, upon the bare back, a hundred blows of a Cossack whip. This instrument in no way answers to our idea of a whip. It is more like a flail. The handle is of whalebone or cane, with flat leather thongs plaited round it. The thong of an ordinary whip is replaced by a similar combination, and united with the handle by means of a stout leather hinge. The delinquents were bound, stretched upon their faces, a Cossack sitting on the head of each, and another on his feet. Their backs were then laid bare, and the hundred blows were inflicted. They were severely cut up, but notwithstanding the suffering undergone, not a single cry or groan escaped their lips. Each seized with his teeth some morsel of his clothing, to prevent his exclaiming, and doggedly underwent the punishment. Among these people it is considered very disgraceful to allow any amount of pain to wring from one of them any groan or exclamation, and I have been told that the man who exhibits such sign of weakness will not afterwards be able to find a woman to marry him. When I happened to observe to a superior officer that I had believed the punishment of the knout abolished in Russia, he frankly replied that it was, but that the General took upon himself to administer this summary chastisement, inasmuch as the men themselves would infinitely prefer it to being sent to prison in Baku, or perhaps to Siberia; and he was probably right.

During the three long months that I remained in the camp, waiting in vain in the hope that a move in some direction would be made, I took advantage of a hunting expedition organised by Prince Wittgenstein to visit the delta of the Atterek, up which stream I had already been as far as Chatte, the result being that, on comparing my own observations with those of others, I felt convinced that nothing worthy the name of a river comes within ten miles of the coast. The water is entirely absorbed by irrigation trenches or the great spongy surface of the marsh, whose shallows were alive with fish, so crowded as to be incapable of moving save by floundering and jumping over one another. They were chiefly, as is always the case in these waters, the *sefid mahee*, or large white carp. As we occasionally crossed the stream, our horses trod them to death by scores. In less crowded nooks huge pike were to be seen lurking under the bushes, but so stupefied by the foul water that the Cossacks took them in numbers by striking them with the point of the sabre, or simply whisking them out of the water by the tail. Owing to the condition of the fish, however, it was deemed inadvisable to use them as food.

CHAPTER V.

Sickness—The death of an old friend—Funeral at sea—General Tergukasoff—Notice to quit—A start for Persia—A slimy waste—A home for reptiles—Robber Turcomans—The faithful dog—A Jack-of-all-trades—Night alarms—An unpleasant welcome—Asterabad.

WHEN the charm of novelty wore off, time hung heavily on our hands in the camp at Tchikislar. Notwithstanding all precautions, I fell a victim to the prevailing malady, which was carrying off soldiers by the score. I allude to that curse of ill-regulated camps, dysentery. It is a disease which prostrates one almost immediately. Simultaneously the Commander-in-Chief had a virulent attack of carbuncles. In spite of his sufferings he sent an aide-de-camp daily to inquire after me, and I returned the courtesy by despatching my servant to ask how the Commander-in-Chief progressed. Some of the people in the camp said it was a race between us as to which should die first. The hour for the advance having come, the General was lifted from his bed into a four-horse vehicle, which was intended to carry him to the front. He reached Chatte, where the carbuncles were operated upon by the chief surgeon of the army. The General insisted upon pushing forward at four in the morning, but before he reached the next station he was dead.

The doctors had told me that to remain at Tchikislar was to incur a more than serious risk of death, and from what I knew of military operations I was aware that before definite hostilities commenced I should have time to recruit my strength in a healthier atmosphere, and amid happier surroundings. On August 22 I staggered from my bed, and was supported to the pier, where a man-of-war's boat was waiting to take me on board the 'Ural,' *en route* for Baku. During my voyage this vessel was crowded with barely convalescent patients from the camp, most of them, if not all, suffering from dysentery, and I had an opportunity of witnessing a burial at sea. An infirmary sergeant, ill with the prevailing disease, had postponed his departure to the last moment, and died after the first twenty-four hours. His body, sewn in a hammock, lay beside the gunwale, partly covered by the Red Cross Geneva flag. Close by the head of the corpse was a lectern, on which lay a Russian missal. One by one the comrades of the deceased approached the lectern, and read over in silence some passages or prayers devoted to the memory of the dead. Lieutenant Woltchakoff, an officer of the war steamer, was among those who read longest and most earnestly to the memory of his departed comrade-in-arms. In the afternoon all the officers of the ship appeared in full uniform. The great bulk of the invalids, soldiers from the interior of Russia, many of whom had seldom seen any expanse of water larger than a river or a lake, were horrified when they understood that their dead companion was about to be committed to the waves. They grumbled, and said it was scarcely worth their while to run so many risks and suffer such great privations, to be treated in such a fashion when they died. As the final hour approached, the small sacred picture which garnishes the cabin of every Russian vessel was brought on deck. The body was elevated on the shoulders of four seamen, and a procession, with lighted candles, was formed, the boatswain, bearing the holy picture, leading. The entire circuit of the deck was made. The corpse was then deposited alongside the opening of the bulwarks, some iron weights were attached to the feet, the Geneva flag was run up to the peak, and a twelve-pounder gun, ready charged, was run out close by. The whole ship's company uncovered. The body was slipped along a plank, and as it sank beneath the waters the gun boomed out a farewell to one of the many victims of the Akhal Tekké expedition. The grumblers at once took heart. Those who had felt so irritated at the prospect of being thrown overboard like dead dogs when they died, now thought how fine a thing it was for officers in full dress to stand by bareheaded while a cannon was discharged in honour of their deceased companion—a greater honour than any of them could hope for in life.

I reached Baku, after being delayed by storms and shortness of fuel, on August 29. Two days afterwards, the body of General Lazareff arrived on board the 'Tamar,' enclosed in a rough coffin of blackened deal. A day was occupied in the embalming, and it was then carried in procession to the Gregorian Church in the great square, borne on the shoulders of the deceased veteran's compatriots. His decorations, each one borne upon a cushion by an officer, were carried in front. There was no military music, but priests and acolytes chanted. From the chapel the body was conveyed direct to Tiflis, where it was interred with military honours.

On September 17, General Tergukasoff, the new Commander-in-Chief of the expedition, arrived at Baku, and on the 20th I accompanied him to Tchikislar. Almost immediately the General went on to Chatte, and thence to the extreme advance; but he would afford me no facilities, so I had to go slowly forward with some baggage-waggons as far as Chatte, where it was intimated to me by the Chief of Staff that military operations were at an end for the winter, and I was desired to return to Tchikislar.

There was nothing for it but to go, so I returned there; but a fortnight later the same officer intimated to me that I should be more comfortable at Baku during the dreary Caspian winter. I simply bowed in reply. 'When will you go?' said the Chief of Staff. 'Well, Colonel,' I replied, 'you know I have horses which I must dispose of; they are scarcely worth carrying across the Caspian; I don't want them at Baku, and I should like time to sell them.' With this diplomatic answer our interview terminated. At the end of the week, as one day towards two o'clock in the afternoon I lay upon the carpet which separated me from the moist sand, trying to forget the restless hours of the night, a Cossack entered my tent, and, shaking me by the shoulder, told me that Colonel Shelkovnikoff, then occupying the post of commandant of the camp, desired to speak with me immediately. I rose to receive the Colonel, who said, rather abruptly, 'I think Colonel Malama intimated to you that it would be better did you pass the winter at Baku, on the other side of the Caspian.' 'It is true,' I replied, 'but I have not yet been able to dispose of my horses.' 'Well,' rejoined he, 'horses disposed of or not, the orders of the Commander-in-Chief are that you quit the camp for Baku by the steamer which leaves at seven o'clock this evening.' At this I grew indignant. 'Colonel,' said I, 'I admit that the Commander-in-Chief has a perfect right to order me to quit his camp, or even Russian territory, but I deny his right to dictate to me the route which I shall take in so doing. I will proceed at once to the frontier, and thence to Asterabad, the nearest point at which a British Consulate is to be found.' With this we parted. I waited until the hour fixed for my departure was approaching, and then ordered my tent to be struck and my horses saddled. A heavy downpour of rain was falling, and stormy gusts were sweeping from the landward. I sent my horses outside the camp, and followed them, lest notice should be taken of me, as would probably have been the case had I left mounted, and with baggage in marching order. Outside the guarded limits, I and my servant rode swiftly away in the direction of the Atterek River, the line beyond which Russia claimed no jurisdiction.

Towards six o'clock in the evening, on November 10, 1879, after wading across many a rain-filled channel and muddy expanse, I reached Hassan-Kouli. In this place the chief was a certain Moullah Nourri, by whom I was hospitably received, especially as I was believed to be a person who was well able and willing to make an adequate 'present' when leaving. In the hurry of my departure I had forgotten to ask Colonel Malama for a passport declaring who I was and recommending me to the Persian authorities. However, halting for the night at the village, I gave instructions to my servant to ride off early in the morning to the Russian camp, and ask for the necessary document. It was a couple of hours after sunrise before my servant returned from Tchikislar, bringing with him the document kindly furnished by Colonel Malama, the Chief of Staff, which stated that I had been attached to the Russian columns, and recommended me to the Persian authorities at Asterabad. I immediately ordered my horses to be saddled, and my scanty baggage put in marching order. Though the Chief of Staff had been good enough to furnish me with the passport to which I have alluded, I did not feel quite sure that, Pharaoh-like, he might not afterwards repent of his decision, and send a squadron of Cossacks after me to fetch me back to the camp, and force me to proceed to Baku, which Colonel Shelkovnikoff had intimated to me was the desire of the Russian authorities. Our way lay in a south-easterly direction, across a slimy waste of mud, in which our horses' feet sank fetlock-deep, and across which our progress was slow and disagreeable in the extreme. Away to the eastward are seen the low, sedgy banks of the Atterek proper, before it merges in the lagoon, and, further off, vast forests of giant reeds, amidst which nestle countless myriads of sea-birds. Ducks, cranes, flamingoes, and many other waterfowl of whose names I am ignorant, crowd these marshy solitudes, or wheel shrieking above the waters in such incredible numbers as to seem at a distance like an angry storm-cloud surging before a whirlwind. Whole battalions of waders fringed the muddy shores, and the all but stagnant waters of the lagoon were white with acres of gulls. Pushing on further still in a south-easterly direction, we crossed some disagreeably deep tidal guts, where the water reached to our horses' girths, and made us very cautious in our advance. Then a sand-spit was reached, and, at its extremity, a canoe, hollowed from a single tree-trunk, styled here a *täimul*, and conducted by an elderly Turcoman and his son, a boy of some twelve years, awaited us. The saddles and other effects were placed within the canoe, in which I and my servant also embarked. For a hundred yards our progress was more like skating over a muddy surface than floating upon water, but gradually, very gradually indeed, the depth increased; our horses, whose bridles were held in our hands, stepped cautiously behind our frail bark, slipping and floundering as they picked their way over the muddy bottom. Gradually the water crept higher and higher along their limbs, until at length the animals were afloat. Horses in this part of the world take things like this coolly enough, and without the least hesitation they struck out, swimming close to our stern. Towards the middle of the channel the current was pretty rapid, and our flat-bottomed canoe heeled over in an alarming manner as it was paddled swiftly across the stream. A distance of fully half a mile had to be traversed before the horses lost their feet, and a third of a mile was swum across before they again touched bottom. Another half mile of paddling brought us again into excessively shallow water, where our old Turcoman and his son, stepping on to the mud, in which they sank nearly knee-deep at every step, proceeded to drag us in the canoe to what they called the opposite shore. Shore, strictly speaking, there was none; the point at which we landed, if I may be permitted to use the term, in this case being one in which we sank mid-leg deep. It was absolutely necessary to leave the canoe, so that it might be dragged still further across the horrid mud-waste. I do not recollect that such a hideous wilderness of slime and desolation ever met my eyes, and, as we painfully waded along pulling our *täimul* behind us, we bore no distant resemblance to reptiles crawling over the surface of some Palæozoic morass.

Long and painful as was our progress southward, we could not soon succeed in reaching ground sufficiently solid to enable us to disembark our saddles and baggage, which were placed upon our horses direct from the canoe itself, as they stood alongside of it. It took a good half-hour's diligent scraping to remove the blue-black slimy mud from our boots sufficiently to allow our feet to enter the stirrups, as we mounted from the back of our old boatman. Far and near stretched the desert solitude of marly mud, strewn with algæ and fish-skeletons. Then followed a long, dreary wading march, for the space of at least two hours. Nothing more desolate than these slimy wastes can well be imagined. It was a place where an ichthyosaurus might momentarily be expected to show himself, or some broad, dragon-winged pterodactyl come beating the wind heavily above one's head. Then the ground became firmer, and sparse tamarisk bushes and mossy streaks topped the scarped banks, while great heavy-winged vultures crouched lazily, gorged with their banquet of decaying fish. As the ground assumed a solider consistence, long coarse sedge began to appear, and great numbers of water trenches furrowed the ground.

At last signs of cultivation indicated our near approach to human dwellings, and after another hour's floundering among partially inundated marshy sedge-fields, we saw the beehive-looking *aladjaks* or huts of the village of Atterek itself, situated near the centre of the delta. The people of this village enjoy an unenviable reputation as thieves and marauders, and even among the neighbouring Turcomans, themselves not over-scrupulous in their conduct, they are known as the *Karakchi*, or robber Turcomans *par excellence*. Worn out with hunger, I stopped to make some coffee. Though I wished to have as little as possible to do with the inhabitants, in order to procure fuel I was obliged to enter into conversation with some hang-dog-looking shepherds who were tending a flock of scraggy goats and sheep. As I sat watching the fire they gathered round me curiously, evidently surprised to see two strangers venturing thus hardily among them. 'Were we not afraid to come there alone?' they asked. 'No,' I replied, 'what should

I have to fear?' At this they smiled. Doubtless the sight of my revolving carbine and pistol rendered them much more honest and hospitable than they would otherwise have been. As I was quite unacquainted with the district, and as there is no trace of a road, I resolved to push forward, still in a south-easterly direction, until I struck upon the telegraph line extending from Tchikislar to Asterabad. By following this I should take the most direct line to the latter town. Before I had gone many hundred yards I struck upon the main southern branch of the Atterek, which winds in the most confusing manner. It was in vain I tried, at twenty different points, to ford it, and only after a couple of hours' wandering did I perceive, far away to the left, the telegraph poles, towards which I directed myself. I was fortunately able, by following the track of some camels, which I noticed in the mud, to discover the regular ford. Beyond the river branch, and still to the left, rose a high earth cliff, where the stream had eaten away the side of a large escar-like hill. This is known as Goklan-Tepessi, the hill of the Goklans. On its southern slope was another village of *Karakchi* Turcomans, situated within twelve hours' march of Asterabad. As night was already falling, no choice was left me but to risk taking up my quarters for the night in this thieves' stronghold. Huge savage dogs rushed out to assail us as we drew near the *aladjaks*, and we were obliged to draw our sabres to keep them at a respectful distance. The inhabitants were assembled for evening prayers.

I stood beside my horses at a little distance until the evening orisons were completed, and then, drawing near a group of elders, requested hospitality for the night. They were evidently as much surprised to see me, accompanied by but one servant, venturing into their midst, as were their brethren of the village of Atterek, and for some time an ominous silence reigned among them. They were clearly trying to make up their minds whether they would accord me the sought-for hospitality, or proceed to confiscate my horses and other property, and it was with no small misgiving that I awaited the result of the conference. Presently, however, their better natures seemed to prevail, and an old, long-haired moullah motioned to me to follow him. I was conducted to the *kibitka* of the village smith. The furniture of this hut was miserable in the extreme, and denoted wretched poverty. Indeed, throughout the entire village the same was a salient feature. This is quite uncommon among the ordinary nomads, who as a rule are pretty well off—as well-being goes in these parts of the world—that is to say, they are well clothed, seldom, in their villages at least, lack adequate food, and the earthen floor of the *aladjak* is generally well furnished with carpets of no ordinary quality. After a while it struck me that the chief had relegated me to the smith's home to conceal his own incapacity for entertaining me in a proper fashion. It was with difficulty that a kind of tattered quilt could be produced, on which I was invited to be seated. At one side were a diminutive anvil, a couple of hammers, and two or three flat bars of iron, probably purchased at Tchikislar. A heap of charcoal, and a rude bellows composed of a sheepskin, lying beside the fire, completed the entire stock-in-trade of this desert artisan. He was termed the *usta-adam*, the nearest comprehensive rendering of which in English would be handy-man, or Jack-of-all-trades; for here there is no division into guilds, and one *usta-adam* acts in many capacities for the immediate population. He will make silver rings for the women, shoe horses, repair gun-locks, and even bleed a plethoric individual. A rude hand-mill was set in requisition, some coarse brown corn was ground, and a cake of bread was there and then got ready. This, with some rather salty water, was the only cheer which it was in the power of the smith to afford me. There was not even a *kalioun*, or water-pipe, amongst his household goods. It was with no little uneasiness that I lay down to sleep, as I was in some apprehension that the people of the village might compensate themselves for the loss of their cattle by annexing mine before morning; and more than once in the course of the night I rose and went to the door to see if they were still tethered where I had placed them. My host, to do him justice, seemed equally on the alert, and doubtless he had good reasons for being so. Each time that a horse neighed, or we heard a trampling of hoofs, as he rose to shake himself, we started to our feet, and, seizing our arms, rushed to the doorway. When morning came, however, matters turned out to be all right, and giving my entertainer the sum of five francs for the night's accommodation—a sum which he doubtless, poor man, seldom looked upon—I mounted, and, taking leave of the chief, rode away along the crest of the Goklan-Tepessi hill to have a look at the surrounding country.

I had a long dreary ride southward, following the line of telegraph poles, toward Asterabad, across the muddy plain. The ride was not without incidents: at times flocks of pintail grouse would scare the horses by rising with a noise of whirring wings like distant thunder. Their number in some flocks could not have been less than half a million. We passed the line of ancient fortifications known to the Turcomans as Alexander's Wall, where old gold coins have frequently been found; and at last, after eight hours' march, the country began to look more

AN UNPLEASANT WELCOME.

verdant, while flocks and herds were visible with musket and sabre-armed shepherds in charge. Another hour's ride brought us to the village of Giurgen, close to the river bank. Here, as is usual when approaching a Turcoman village, we were again furiously assailed by scores of gigantic wolf-like dogs, whose invariable custom it is to surround the stranger, who, if on foot, is often in serious peril. Riding into the centre of the village, I invited the Turcomans, who stood at the doors of their *kibitkas*, highly amused by the predicament in which I was placed, to call off their dogs, who were leaping savagely at my boots and my horse's nose, causing the poor beast to rear and kick furiously. One had seized by his teeth the extremity of the rather extensive tail of my charger, and, managing to keep out of range of his heels, held on like grim death. I drew my revolver and exhibited it to the Turcomans, assuring them that if they did not immediately call off their dogs I would make use of the weapon. To this threat they paid no attention, and I was obliged to turn in my saddle and fire fully into my assailant's mouth. As he rolled over on the sward, his companions, with the most admirable promptitude, withdrew to a safe distance; and the Turcomans, rushing out with sticks in their hands, proceeded to beat them still further off, though at first I supposed that the sticks were intended for my own person.

Next morning our way lay through cultivated fields, principally of rice; through elm and plane-tree groves; through brakes of giant reeds, twelve to eighteen feet high, the home of leopards and wild boars; and then we had done with the burning salt plains, the muddy delta, and were where our horses seemed beside themselves with delight, and could scarcely decide on which hand to choose a mouthful of succulent herbage, so great was the *embarras de richesses* around them. Ripe pomegranates dangled above our heads, and fell at our feet, as we forced our way along, till after about an hour's ride through this belt of jungle, rice-fields once more appeared. Then through the open glades we caught glimpses of the town of Asterabad, with its picturesque towers and ramparts gleaming yellowly in the noonday sun. Seen from a distance, one might fancy himself enacting the part of the Kalendar in the 'Arabian Nights,' and, after a weary wandering amidst trackless deserts, coming suddenly upon the enchanted city.

CHAPTER VI.

A Persian town—Wild boars—Sanitary features—The bazaar—Manufactures—Felt-making—A finished carpet—Persian costume—A storyteller—Persian pottery—A lost art.

ENDLESS are the objects of interest to the European traveller in this old Persian town, with its ramparts and towers of unbaked brick, thatched with reeds to keep the bricks from being washed away, and ancient causeway, now a jumble of blocks of stone amongst water pools and land sloughs. Within an arched guardway at each gate the semblance of a military guard is kept up, though nothing like a regular sentry is to be seen. The traveller, on arriving, perceives a pair of superannuated muskets leaning against the walls; and some loose-vested Persians, squatting on a raised platform of brick, and smoking the inevitable *kalioun*, represent the custom-house officers. The greater portion of the space within the walls is taken up, partly with gardens and bare open areas, and partly, especially at the corners of the town, with a wild growth of jungle and briars. Here, at all hours of the day, and particularly towards sunset, wild boars and their broods, jackals, foxes, woodcocks, and snipes are to be found. I have seen as many as eight or nine old and young wild boars burst away from the briar thickets as I approached, and have watched them careering across the rice and maize fields outside, until they found shelter in the dense forest growth along the water-courses south of the town. They occur in extraordinary numbers in the surrounding country, and, looking from the ramparts over the adjoining fields of springing rice and corn, one sees them dotted at intervals of eight or ten feet with the large black heaps where the boars have been at work, rooting up the soil. One might imagine that a detachment of sappers had been engaged in throwing up a series of rifle pits, or that the ground had been subjected to a heavy plunging fire of shells. Such is the devastation produced by the wild boars and their broods that it is found worth while to maintain a body of professional hunters, whose sole occupation is to destroy these animals. Enormous quantities are killed annually, but their numbers do not appear to be perceptibly lessened. The inhabitants never on any account make use of the flesh of the boar. Mr. Churchill, the Consul, whose kind hospitality I was at the time enjoying, was exceedingly desirous of obtaining some wild boar's flesh, but though he made repeated attempts to induce the hunters to bring him a quarter of one of the animals which they were killing every day, he could not succeed. At length, however, a man specially retained by himself to furnish him with game of different kinds agreed that as soon as he had shot a boar within a reasonable distance of the town he would give notice to that effect immediately, so that a portion of it might be secured before the jackals discovered and devoured the carcass. By these means a head, a couple of hams, and other portions of the animal were procured, and were conveyed with the greatest secrecy to the Consulate. The cook, by dint of lavish bribery, had been persuaded to prepare some of the flesh, but he only undertook to do so on condition of the affair being kept a profound secret between himself and the Consul.

However, his fellow-servants by some means discovered that wild boar was being cooked in the house, and at once entered a protest, and one day the whole of them, including the cook, appeared in a body before Mr. Churchill, and respectfully begged to state that they could no longer remain. The cook said that as he passed through the bazaars he was scornfully pointed out and jeered at by the merchants and passers-by as a cooker of swine's flesh, that his life was miserable, that even his own family avoided him, and that he could not endure such suffering. A compromise was arrived at, and the cook and other servants agreed to stay on condition that the object of their abhorrence, the remaining boar's flesh, be immediately thrown out, which was accordingly done. As regards jackals, the numbers in which they assemble at nightfall, yelping and wailing both outside and within the ramparts, are incredible. They are attracted by the dead bodies of horses, asses, and dogs, which are left lying in the more remote thoroughfares, and, passing at night by one of these carcases, one is pretty sure to see three or four jackals start away from their uncanny feast. The old ditches of the town are entirely choked up with briars and bushes, the haunt of every wild animal indigenous to the district, including the lynx and the leopard, but the latter rarely ventures within the ramparts. As is the case in most Eastern towns, the place is full of hopeless dirt and neglect. Rubbish heaps are outside every door, and are left to be trodden down; the only redeeming feature amidst the loneliness, desolation, and filth is that the tall mud walls are overtopped with vines, the branches of the plane tree, and the blossoms of the almond and plum, that grow within.

The bazaar consists of a labyrinth of narrow streets, lined on each side with the booths of the traders and artisans, in which the dealer arranges the commodities he has for sale, and behind which he sits, cross-legged, as a rule smoking the scarcely ever unlighted *kalioun*. The most numerous are the general dealers, who in addition to the orthodox tea, coffee, sugar, rice, and spices, also sell ink, paper, percussion caps, bullets, iron small-shot, gunpowder, brass drinking cups, salt, knives, sulphate of iron, pomegranate rind, alum for dyeing purposes, and an infinite variety of other articles. Turning a corner, we come into an alley where ropes suspended from housetop to housetop support numberless curtains of deep blue and olive-green calico. This is the quarter of the dyers, who seem to be, in point of number, the strongest after the *bakhals*, or grocers. They are to be seen working at their great indigo troughs, clad only in a dark-tinted waistband and skull-cap, their arms, up to the elbows, being of as dark a blue as the calico which hangs outside. A little further on, towards the outskirts of the bazaar, are the vendors of fruit and vegetables, whose leeks and lettuces, spread in front of their booths, are a constant temptation to the passing camels and horses. More than once I have had to pay for the escapades of my horse in snatching up a bunch of spring onions and incontinently devouring it under the nose of the merchant. There were great basketsful of pomegranates and oranges, for Asterabad and its neighbourhood are famous for both these fruits, especially for the mandarin orange. Our ordinary orange is known as the *portugal*, while the *naranj* is quite as sour as any lemon, and takes the place of that fruit in cookery or with tea. Near the centre of the bazaar is a long street devoted to the coppersmiths, who manufacture tea-pots, saucepans, and cauldrons, for almost every cooking utensil used in this part of Persia is of copper, tinned inside, the facility of working copper more than compensating for the extra price of the material; moreover, the old vessels, when worn out, can be sold for a price very nearly equal to their cost when new. Now and then are to be seen cast-iron pots of Russian manufacture, but these are much more in use among the Turcomans of the Atterek than in Persian households. The copper utensils are wrought by hand, and the din of hammering which salutes the ear as one enters the particular quarter of the smiths is perfectly deafening. By the sheer force of beating upon peculiar knob-like anvils, a hollow cylinder of copper, three-quarters of an inch in thickness, is made to expand to the most formidable dimensions. When finished, it is placed upon the fire, heated to dull redness, and a lump of tin is rubbed round inside.

Then there are the gunsmiths and sword-makers, who live in separate, though adjacent quarters. Here one may see every stage of the manufacture of a musket or rifle, from the forging of the barrel to the rude process for grooving it, and the fashioning of lock, stock, &c., all by the same workman. Asterabad enjoys a certain renown in Persia for the manufacture of gun-locks, and I have heard of a detachment of the nondescript soldiers who constitute the bulk of the Persian army being sent to this town, with their gun-locks out of order, so that they might be repaired. It is a singular fact that, neither in Persia nor among the Turcomans, even in the most remote districts, does one ever see a flint lock. They are invariably percussion. The locks are evidently exactly copied from a European model, even as regards the very carving and ornamentation; they have nothing whatever Oriental in their appearance. The operations of the dealers in swords are generally confined to the manufacture of new scabbards, and the rehabilitation of old blades, for there seems to be a glut of the latter, which has doubtless existed from time immemorial in Persia, so that the manufacture of new blades is seldom entered upon. There are half a dozen booths in which the jewellers and gold and silver smiths ply their trades. They are strictly operatives, and do not keep any stock on hand. If you wish for some article in silver or gold, such as a buckle, button, or sword-mounting, you must, when giving the order, supply the artist with gold or silver coin, as the case may be: He melts this down, and manufactures it into the desired object.

The most important, and, indeed, almost the only extensive manufacture carried on at Asterabad, is that of felt carpets and mats, and the quarter occupied by the makers of these articles is one of the largest in the bazaar. I had noticed the excellence of the felt in use among the Turcomans of Krasnavodsk and Tchikislar, and had purchased several carpets of that material for use in my own *kibitka*. Until I came to Asterabad I was sorely puzzled as to the process by which this material was manufactured, but there I had ample means of informing myself upon the subject. Instead of being mere rectangular spaces, opening off the thoroughfare, each felt-maker's quarters consisted of a room twenty to thirty feet in length by about fifteen in breadth, with either a boarded floor or one of perfectly level beaten earth or cement. The raw material—a mixture of camel's and goat's hair and sheep's wool well beaten up together, and varying in proportions accordingly as the felt was intended to be dark brown or white—was laid in a loose layer about four inches in thickness upon a closely woven mat of fine reeds, somewhat larger than the piece of felt was intended to be. This was then beaten down with heavy, flat pieces of wood, until it was reduced to half its original thickness, and had assumed a compact texture. The ornamentation, generally consisting of arabesques and rude flowers of different brilliant colours, was put on by loosely spun worsted thread, which was laid by the hand in the required form. A strong, warm mixture of size and water was then copiously sprinkled over the whole, and the layer of felt material, together with the reed mat, rolled concentrically into a cylindrical form. In such guise the matting intervened between the layers of felt. The whole was then bound tightly with cords, and three or four men, placing their right feet naked upon it, all pressing simultaneously, rolled it slowly and by jerks from one end of the apartment to the other. As the felt grew thinner and denser, the combination was rolled more and more tightly, being undone from time to time to allow of a fresh saturation with size. When the felt had assumed the proper dimensions, and was considered to be sufficiently kneaded together, it was spread out in the sun to dry, the coloured pattern being thoroughly incorporated with the substance of the newly-formed carpet. The solidity and durability of this felt is wonderful, as I have been able to judge from having used a square of it as a saddle-cloth for over twelve months without its in any way showing a breakage, or, even when exposed to heavy rain, becoming undone or at all loosened in the texture.

The main central streets of the bazaar are roofed over with brick groining, which has holes in the side of each cupola to admit light, but the majority of them are simply covered with a sun-screen composed of rude poles reaching from the top of one shop to that of another across the way, and loosely thatched with reeds and small tree branches. In some cases gourds and grape vines twine among the rough rafters, the fruit hanging pendulously above the heads of the passers-by. At street crossings, and through gaps where this roofing has fallen away, the blinding sunlight pours, throwing the adjacent portions of the bazaar into comparative obscurity by its contrast, and causing its inhabitants, half seen athwart the torrent of rays, to look like so many ghostly occupants of a haunted cavern.

This oval blue bundle, set on end, which comes gliding silently toward us, is a Persian lady, wrapped in the all-enveloping mantle of calico which shrouds her from head to heel, and is here styled the *feridgi*. From the summit of her forehead hangs a white linen veil, forming a point upon the centre of her breast, and concealing the face much more effectually than the modern *yashmak* of the Osmanli Turks. The copious trousers are gathered in at the ankle in numerous elongated plaits, and terminate in the stocking, which is continuous with the trousers. These grooved, inverted cones of cloth, seen below the edge of the *feridgi*, give the wearer the appearance of having substituted two old-fashioned family umbrellas for her legs. The high-heeled slippers have just barely enough of upper to enable their owner to bear them upon the points of her toes.

At the central point of the bazaar, whence branch off the main thoroughfares, is almost always to be found the Eastern story-teller—generally a wandering dervish. I recollect seeing such a public novelist at this point, seated upon a door-step, and holding a numerous audience entranced by the narrative which he was relating. He was a young man, of a rather distinguished type of feature, and long, glossy, raven hair flowed upon his shoulders. He wore a large Tartar hat of black sheepskin, carried a stout staff of about five feet in length, and had his calabash basket, for the reception of contributions, laid beside him. The exigencies of the story seemed to require that he should have some tangible object to address. He accordingly placed his great sheepskin tiara in the centre of the roadway, and apostrophised it with the most ludicrous earnestness, at the same time mimicking the replies which he was supposed to receive. It was evidently a humorous story, for the group of idlers and small boys standing round, and the merchants leaning over their wares, occasionally burst into loud and prolonged shouts of laughter. He shook his stick at the being that was embodied in his headdress, raved at it, implored it, and ended by weeping over it. The acting was of no mean order, and a story-teller who possesses histrionic powers to any creditable extent is always sure of a crowd of eager listeners.

In the streets of the bazaar are generally congregated a number of Turcomans from the outlying villages along the Giurgen, endeavouring to exchange sheepskins against the various commodities which the Persians offer for sale, or trying underhand to procure gunpowder and percussion caps, for the sale of these articles to the nomads is strictly forbidden by the central government.

The Turcomans frequenting Asterabad generally come to the town fully armed—sabre at side, poniard in belt, and double-barrelled gun at back, permission being accorded to them to enter the town thus equipped probably in recognition of the fact that they are subjects of the Shah. In other border Persian towns further to the east, and frequented on market days by the Tekkés, the latter were obliged to leave their swords and guns with the guard at the gate of the town, retaining only the poniard, or more strictly speaking the knife, which the Turcoman rarely parts with. The throng was occasionally varied by the grave, stately form of a Baghdad muleteer, with his diadem-like headdress of twisted camel-hair over the sombre-tinted mantle which protects his head from the sun and weather, and envelopes his whole person.

Very beautiful specimens of enamelled tiles and Persian pottery are to be met with here, the former being the decorative portions of the ancient buildings; but these have been much defaced, for the blue china and keramic craze had taken fast root in Asterabad among its European inhabitants, and what I was informed were priceless specimens of early Persian pottery were unearthed by the enthusiasts from the forgotten closets and dusty shelves of inhabitants in the possession of whose families they had remained for many centuries.

The peculiarity of this Persian pottery is that, while it has all the external appearance of the finest porcelain, it is really composed of delicate brown earthenware, somewhat resembling hardened Roman cement, and covered upon the outside with a thick creamy glaze. Some of the plates and dishes of large size present, on a white ground, patterns in that beautiful blue tint so much admired by the 'maniacs' at home, but the tinting is by no means confined to this colour. There is a peculiar kind of bottle, closely resembling in form those Indian water-bottles of porous clay, but of slenderer neck and far more graceful form, the body often presenting a series of lobe-like divisions similar to those of a peeled orange. These generally have that golden, purple, or amber gleam, with prismatic colours when seen obliquely, which is known to the initiated as *reflet métallique*. The colours seen when the surface is viewed by reflected light are exactly similar to those observed on the surface of still water over which is spread a slight film of tar. Some of these bottles are reputed to be of great age, dating back, it is averred, over eight hundred years. This conclusion is arrived at from the position and nature of the sites from amidst which they were dug up. The art of producing this delicate keramic ware in Persia is now entirely lost.

CHAPTER VII.

Rumours of Activity—A fresh venture—Another dismissal—A snowstorm—Severe losses—Fresh plans—General Skobeleff.

BANISHED from the camp at Tchikislar, I had come to Asterabad in order to be within reach of the Russian columns, and to have it in my power to know what was happening from time to time at the former place. Various rumours of unusual activity on the part of the Tekké Turcomans reached me, and though, owing to the hospitality of Mr. Churchill, I was exceedingly comfortable at Asterabad, I resolved to move out into the plain between the Atterek and Giurgen rivers as far as Gumush Tepé, a point which would afford me many facilities for ascertaining what was occurring within the Russian lines. Travelling over the intermediate country was rather a ticklish undertaking, in consequence of the near proximity of Tekké raiders, who pushed boldly forward towards the sea-board, and of the never over-scrupulous parties of Turcomans of various tribes, camped and wandering, between the Atterek and the Giurgen. I made my journey to my destination, however, in safety, and during the next three months I lived amongst the Yamud Turcomans, finding them hospitable, careful of the worldly goods of the sojourner in their midst, even to punishing the thieves who took possession of his property, and giving me ample opportunities for observing their domestic habits and customs; but as these greatly resembled those of their relatives, the Tekké Turcomans, in the Merv oasis, with whom later on I made an enforced stay, I need not dwell upon them here.

I had, then, been residing continuously at Gumush Tepé about three months, when some Turcomans who had returned with a lugger from Tchikislar brought me intelligence of the resignation of General Tergukasoff, and the appointment *ad interim*, to the command of the expeditionary forces, of Major-General Mouravieff. This change in the direction of affairs gave me some hope that I might after all be permitted to follow the operations of the Russian columns, and I determined to try my fortunes once more at the camp. I had considerable difficulty in inducing any of the Turcomans who ordinarily travelled to and fro between Gumush Tepé and Tchikislar with forage and wood supplies for the camp to allow me to accompany them, as they knew that since my last visit to the Russian lines I had lain under a ban, and that if I again essayed to return I should in all probability be summarily expelled. By dint of great persuasion, however, and the use of a good deal of diplomacy, I succeeded in making them believe that it was necessary and permissible for me to have an interview with the new general, and, aided by the efforts of my Yamud host, Dourdi, I at length managed to discover the owner of a *lodka* who agreed to convey me along the coast to the Russian encampment. After a rather unpleasant night journey I reached the camp, and, as soon as I could obtain an audience, I presented myself before my old friend Colonel Malama, the Chief of Staff, who still occupied the position he had held under General Lazareff. He looked much aged and worn, short as was the time since I had last seen him, and I was not surprised at it, considering that he had been through the disastrous affair of the first attack on Geok Tepé, and had borne his full share of the responsibilities which the precipitate retreat from before that stronghold entailed. I asked him to tell General Mouravieff that I had come to make application to be allowed to remain at Tchikislar, and to follow the operations of the column, and he promised to do as I desired as soon as the General was visible. It was scarce daybreak on the following morning when I was aroused by a loud knocking at the door of the little alcove in which I slept. The major of a battalion, with whom I had formerly been on very friendly terms, accompanied by the chief of the camp police, a certain Timour Beg, a Mussulman lieutenant of cavalry, made their appearance, bearing an order from General Mouravieff that I should immediately quit the camp and return to Gumush Tepé, or any other place to which I might choose to proceed, provided I left the limits of the Russian lines. I asked permission to remain until I had eaten my breakfast, and then, accompanied by the same officers, I departed for the shore, where a *lodka*, specially retained for my transport back to Gumush Tepé, was lying, and on which vessel I embarked.

I did not like the appearance of the sky as we entered the mouth of the Giurgen. There were meteoric-looking clouds athwart the sun, and that angry glare over the waters which in this part of the world heralds a tempest. The wind again fell, and a dead calm ensued. The lugger had to be rowed and poled almost the entire distance between the mouth of the river and the village. A fierce yellow storm-light was on the *lodka* masts, and angry red streaks shone over the looming snow-clad Elburz. The leaden waters of the Giurgen slept 'stilly black,' the sun went down, and the call of the *muezzim*, like that of some storm demon, arose upon the ominous silence pervading land and sky. I had not been more than a few minutes on shore when the scudding mist-drift made its appearance along the western horizon, and before long the tempest was upon us. It was fortunate for us that we got on shore so soon. The storm struck the village with greater force than I had yet seen. The cattle galloped wildly about, the camels straggling here and there with their awkward run, stiffly brandishing their tails. Ere long it was pitch dark, and general confusion reigned throughout Gumush Tepé. The naphtha torches flared in every direction. Ropes and poles were hurriedly brought into requisition, and the universal hubbub, mingled with the noise of the storm, gave the place the appearance of being the scene of some unearthly combat. This storm, unlike the others which had occurred during my stay in these parts, was not of short duration. It continued with unceasing violence during the greater part of the night. Towards midnight it was accompanied by hail and a heavy snowfall. When I looked out in the morning the sun was shining brightly over a vast gleaming expanse of virgin snow.

Finding that my last chance of again being allowed to take up my quarters in the Russian camp had departed, I decided to return to Asterabad, there to consult with my friend Mr. Churchill as to what course I ought to pursue, and I took advantage of the setting out for the same place of a Turcoman who had been acting as agent for the British Consul at that city, and who was going in with his usual fortnightly report of the movements of the Russians. On our way across the plains we met with plenty of traces of the violence of the storm. The villagers had hastily constructed rough shelters for their flocks; but these precautions had apparently come too late, to a great extent, for on every side were strewn dead and dying lambs and sheep.

SEVERE LOSSES.

Men with long knives were going from one prostrate animal to another, cutting their throats to see if blood would flow. In case it did, however slightly, the carcass was taken to the village to be consumed as food; but, if no blood came, the flesh was abandoned to the village dogs, and to the wolves and jackals, who would invariably make their appearance as the sun sank below the horizon. The number of animals who perished in this snow *tenkis*, or storm, to judge from my observations of the limited space over which I rode, must have been enormous.

I remained some days at Asterabad, enjoying the kind hospitality of Mr. and Mrs. Churchill at the British Consulate, and endeavouring to recuperate my energies after the Turcoman *régime* to which I had so long been subjected at Gumush Tepé, and I then undertook an expedition to the Persian border fort of Ak-Kala, on the banks of the Giurgen. Here I was pleasantly received by the Persian officer in command, and after a short stay I crossed the bridge over the river Giurgen to return once more to Gumush Tepé. It was amongst the gigantic reed-growths of this district that I had the first opportunity since my arrival in Persia of seeing a wolf. He was feeding upon the carcass of a sheep which had either been killed by the late storms, or which he had himself carried off. His head was buried in its entrails, but, looking up as I approached, he eyed me savagely, his muzzle smeared with blood. I fired, and apparently touched him, for I could see the fur fly from his back, whereupon he charged me fiercely. My horse trembled with fright, rendering it very difficult to aim. On the second shot the enemy turned tail, and ran to a distance of about a hundred yards, where he seated himself, and, licking his bloody jaws, gazed at me as though he would say, 'When you think fit to go, I will resume my meal.'

Old Dourdi, as well as everyone else, was surprised to see me back again at Gumush Tepé so soon. I noticed considerable uneasiness on the part of my host, and was quite at a loss to account for it. Several times over he seemed about to communicate something to me, but on each occasion he checked himself, so that I did not press him to tell me what was on his mind. My stay was not protracted—principally because everything seemed stagnant at Tchikislar for the time being, and also because I had no fresh observations to make in the village. For, despairing of obtaining permission to accompany the Russian columns, and tired of the inactive and unprofitable life that I was leading, I determined to remain no longer, but to return once more to Asterabad, and thence try to make my way along the southern bank of the Giurgen through the Goklan country as far as the Kopet Dagh Mountains, and to cross them to the Akhal Tekké country. I knew that such a journey would be fraught with the extremest peril, but I was resolved to risk everything rather than continue to spend my time as I had been, during the preceding five months. I only waited until one of my horses, which had become slightly sore-backed, could get quite cured, before I put my intention into execution. On the evening previous to the day which I had fixed for my departure old Dourdi took me confidentially aside, and disburdened himself of the secret which had been weighing on his mind since my last arrival at the village. He said that the military authorities at Tchikislar had repeatedly made inquiries of Turcomans who had visited the camp as to whether I still remained at Gumush Tepé, and that that same evening a message had been brought to the effect that if I did not at once withdraw from the *aoull* (village) Cossacks would be sent to bring me a prisoner to Tchikislar.

On the morning of April 20, 1880, at earliest dawn, I once more rode out into the plains that separated me from Asterabad. Forty miles are but little to those who have locomotives to carry them, but forty miles on a horse carrying at the same time all one's worldly goods constitute a much more serious distance, especially when, owing to spring floods, a river of more than twenty feet in depth intervenes. I made my journey, however, in safety, and upon reaching my destination I had a long talk with Mr. Churchill about my proposed ride into the Akhal Tekké country; I also learned that General Skobeleff was on his way, if he had not already arrived, to take command of the Trans-Caspian expedition. After mature deliberation I resolved to proceed to Teheran, and there solicit the friendly offices of Mr. Zinovieff, the Russian Minister at that capital, believing that he might be able to procure for me the permission to accompany the Russian columns which had been denied to my own direct application. I had met this gentleman at Krasnavodsk, at the house of General Lomakin, and from his great courtesy on that occasion I entertained hopes that he would interest himself in my behalf. Mr. Churchill was about to leave for Baku, *en route* for Palermo, to which Consulate he had just been appointed, and as he intended journeying *viâ* Resht, through which town lay my easiest and most expeditious route to Teheran, I resolved to accompany him.

CHAPTER VIII.

Persian Boatmen—A Persian river—Sturgeon and silkworms—The ice torture — Venomous serpents — A ghastly burden — The 'Bite the Stranger'—Effects of a bite—The kanots—The Shah's capital—His Majesty's servants—Court splendour—Flower-scatterers.

AFTER several delays, due to the badness of the road to Kenar Gez—the so-called port of Asterabad—for which place our little English party started on April 26, 1880, and the dilatory way in which the steamers make their runs in the South Caspian, we reached Enzeli, where I parted from Mr. Churchill, his son remaining to be my companion to Resht, and from thence across the mountains to Teheran. What follows after your statement of intention to land at Enzeli is an illustration of the law of natural selection. A 'free fight' ensues, during which the strongest succeed in getting nearest to your person and effects. The Prophet Ali and the twelve holy Imams are called upon in fervent tones to bear witness to the iniquity of the man who has laid hold of your saddle-bags, by the others who have been unsuccessful in trying to do the same. Yells and threats are interchanged, and the traveller is ultimately hustled along the deck and over the side into one of the high-prowed launches, to reach which he has had perhaps to skip over a dozen others, springing from gunwale to gunwale as they toss and heave and bump together in the long Caspian swell. Amidst cries and execrations we force our way through the press of boats, and then the crew, raising a loud shout of 'Allah, Mahomet ya Ali!' bend to their odd-looking oars, and we sweep away to the southward, skirting the low-lying wooded shore. Entering the mouth of the Moredab, an extensive backwater into which fall the Piri-Bazaar and other streams, we come alongside a fairly constructed quay, and are rewarded with a sight of the Shah's yacht, which is about the size of a Thames steamer, and painted of a dirty white yellow. The Shah's palace on the western shore is also one of the objects that meet the traveller's eye.

Our way up to Piri-Bazaar was through a reedy-shored lagoon where the silence was broken only by the plashing of the oars, the shrill cry of some startled sea bird, or the scream of the fish-hawk. Then we entered the narrow channel of the river, varying in breadth from fifteen to twenty paces, the banks thickly covered with jungle and forest growth. The surface of the water was thickly strewn with the inflated swimming bladders of fish, coming from the curing establishment higher up the river. Large numbers of water snakes, too, were to be seen gliding by our boat. Great black 'snags' stuck out from the water like marine monsters watching for their prey, and water-logged tree trunks clung among the roots projecting into the sluggish stream. Once we were well within the regular river channel, the crew, with the exception of one who remained to steer, got out on the right bank, where a narrow pathway ran close to the edge of the water, just inside the tall bushes fringing it. A towing rope was fastened to the top of the mast, and the boat was thus drawn along, the five men in Indian file proceeding at a run.

Piri-Bazaar is the farthest point southward to which a boat can go, as here a fishing weir crosses the stream.

If I can trust the accuracy of the information I received, the capture of fish at the weir is enormous, fifty thousand of one kind or another being the amount taken daily. The principal fish taken are the *sefid mahee* (carp); the *soof*, the *somme* (four feet long); the salmon and salmon trout, besides the sturgeon, are caught in the brackish water lower down. The flesh of the sturgeon is but little used save by the poorer classes—the sterlet, a smaller species, being the only kind usually served at table, and generally used only for making soup. The sturgeon taken here measure from seven to nine feet long, the isinglass and *caviare* being the only portions utilised. From this place to Resht there is a fair road through the dense forest, in whose clearings are at frequent intervals odd-looking structures with high-pitched roofs, the eaves projecting and supported by wooden props. The thatching is of reeds and brambles of a brown colour, the whole resembling a very pointed haystack supported on low pillars. These were the *tilimbars* or sheds for rearing silkworms. Silk has been for a long time one of the staple products of this province, but diseases amongst the silkworms nearly ruined the cultivators, and of late tobacco seed from Samsoun on the southern Black Sea coast was sown, and the flourishing crops which resulted have done much to restore prosperity to the district.

Resht itself is a scattered kind of place, largely composed of two-storey houses built of unbaked brick, and roofed with red tiles. The minarets of the two mosques are of quite an unusual style. They are stout towers of red brick tapering slightly, and crowned with flattened cones of tiles, the cones projecting so much as to give the structure the appearance of an overgrown mushroom. During the three days I remained here I heard sad tales of misgovernment and extortion on the part of the local authorities. There seemed to be no regular system of taxation, the governor paying a certain amount to the Shah annually, and having delegated to him apparently unlimited power to squeeze as much as possible from the native merchants and peasantry. I was informed on unquestionable authority that a very short time previous to my arrival a trader had been imprisoned and buried up to his neck in the floor of his dungeon. Ice was kept constantly applied to his head to torture him, with a view of forcing from him a large sum of money. He stood this cruel punishment so long without yielding, that the stock of ice in the town was quite expended, and the governor was forced to adopt a new system of torture through sheer incapacity to continue the old.

As yet post-horses are the only means of rapid travelling in Persia. When a postal service of the kind is well conducted one can get along pretty well, but when, as in that country, the utmost mismanagement prevails, travelling post is the most exquisite torture it is possible to conceive. It was close on midday before I was able to get away from Resht, mounted on a very fair horse. I was accompanied by Mr. Harry Churchill, and we had with us a *gholam*, or courier, belonging to the British Legation at Teheran, and the usual postman to take back the horses. The stations are from twenty to thirty miles apart, and the road over the mountains at times is frightful, while the accommodation to be obtained often consisted of the bare boards for our resting places, and our saddles for our pillows. Travelling over such roads in the dark is most trying to the nerves. The horses, endeavouring to scramble up or down the steep ascents, many of them having an incline of forty-five degrees, slipped and stumbled at every step. The faintly-seen rocks seemed swimming around in the gloom. The horseman suddenly finds himself girth-deep in a torrent of whose existence he only becomes aware by the flash and roar of the waters. Huge spectral cliff-faces loomed in the faint dawn-light, and the white expanse of the surging river gleamed out, far down the precipice on the verge of which the road wound. No barrier of any kind existed to prevent man or beast from going over the edge.

At Mengil, where a long stone bridge spans the river, I had an opportunity of witnessing a curious phenomenon peculiar to the place. At the moment the sun shows above the horizon a violent wind commences to blow, continuing without interruption till evening. This wind blows at all seasons, and is sometimes so violent as to render crossing the bridge dangerous, especially for laden camels, the great surface exposed to the action of the wind sometimes causing the animals to be blown over the parapet into the torrent. This portion of the valley is remarkable for the great number of venomous serpents by which it is infested. When the Roman army, led by Marc Antony, came here, the camp had to be moved from the valley on account of the great quantity of vipers. I give this on the authority of His Majesty the Shah, who makes the statement in his published diary. A short distance beyond Mengil I came up with a small caravan going in the direction of Teheran. For some time I had been noticing a most unpleasant odour, which I was at a loss to account for. So strong was it that I supposed that a number of camels or horses must be lying rotting in my vicinity; and I urged my horse rapidly forward to get clear of the stench. However,

A GHASTLY BURDEN. 75

the further I pushed on, the stronger became the smell, and I was quite at my wits' end to account for its persistency, when a glance at one of the caravan conductors gave me an inkling as to whence it proceeded. The man was trudging along behind a small grey ass, on whose back was an oblong white case, which I at once recognised as a coffin; especially when, on nearing it, the stench became overpowering. It was a caravan carrying dead bodies to be interred at Kerbella in holy ground. The driver of the ass looked deadly pale, and had swathed his mouth and nose with cloths to avoid the pestilential effluvia emanating from the putrid corpse which his ass was carrying. He had been several days on the march, and I am not surprised that he looked sick and pale, considering the atmosphere which he breathed. I understand that Government orders have been issued prohibiting this system of corpse caravans; but though the traffic is much diminished, it still exists to a certain extent. Pushing on with our journey we reached Pood Chenar, a posting station where no horses were to be obtained. Then, after wearisome delays, onward past mountain and stream and Kurdish camps towards the tremendous Kharzon pass. To describe its passage would be only to multiply tenfold what I have already written about breakneck roads and dangerous precipices. Towards the higher portion of the pass, some twelve thousand feet above the sea, we came upon pyramids of loose stones, the pious offerings placed upon the burial-place of a saint.

At last we reached Masrah. When starting from Resht I had received many warnings from experts to look out for an exceedingly venomous insect which infests this neighbourhood. Strange to say, this place alone of all the entire district is so infested. I enter into details on the subject, as it is one which cannot fail to interest naturalists. I had been warned, on the peril of my life, not to sleep here, because here was to be found the *garrib-gez* (literally, 'bite the stranger'). The effect of the bite was described to me as being on the whole much worse than that of the black scorpion. Our horses could carry us no further, and, nathless the dread which I had of these creatures, I was obliged to make a halt of half an hour at the station.

One of the first questions which I asked of the stable attendants was whether they could show me a specimen of the 'bite the stranger.' After a few minutes' search, the man brought me out half-a-dozen in the palm of his hand. The largest was not over the third of an inch in length, and resembled in form what is vulgarly known in England as the 'sheep-tick.' It was of a silvery grey appearance, and had, as I carefully remarked, eight legs, four on each side. Its sting is productive of the worst results. A small red point like that produced by the ordinary flea is at first seen. Then follows a large black spot, which subsequently suppurates, accompanied by a high fever, identical, as far as external symptoms go, with intermittent fever. In this it is like the bite of the tarantula or *phalange* of the Turcoman plains. The only difference is, that the fever produced by the sting of this insect, known scientifically as the *arga Persica*, and locally as the *garrib-gez* and *Genné*, if neglected for any length of time, is fatal. It is accompanied by lassitude, loss of appetite, and in some cases delirium. There is a general belief that, when once a person has been stung, the 'Persian bug' is harmless against the same individual, and this seems to be borne out by fact; for the people living in the village of Masrah laughed at my fears as I carefully perched myself on the top of a rock with a view of keeping out of the way of the local bugs, while they held them with impunity within the palms of their hands. Some Austrian officers going to Teheran in 1879, happening to stay at this hamlet of Masrah, were stung by the *garrib-gez*. All of them fell ill, and one narrowly escaped with his life. Numerous cases of death can be cited as the result of the sting of the *arga Persica*. A Persian medical man informed me that it was the custom, when any important personage was travelling through a district infested by these insects, for his attendants to administer to him without his knowledge one of the 'bugs,' during the early morning, concealed in a piece of bread. The sting acts as a kind of inoculation, and the local physicians believe that the poison, taken through the stomach, is administered with equally good effect as if received directly into the circulation. A leading European member of Teheran society told me that he had simultaneously received seventy-three stings from these insects, the bites having been counted by his servants. The result was an extreme amount of fever, winding up with delirium on the fifth day. Violent emetics, followed by doses of quinine, were given without effect; and it was only after taking large quantities of tannin, in the form of a decoction of the rind of the wild pomegranate, that the patient recovered. For a great part of my information on this subject I have to thank Mr. Sydney Churchill, of Teheran, a young and rising naturalist, who has devoted much of his time and talent to the entomology of Persia. I need scarcely say that, finding myself in contact with this abominable 'Persian bug,' I was in a feverish hurry to get out of its dominions; and more than one severe objurgation rose to my lips before the half-hour's chase after several stag-like horses on the hill-slope was completed.

I was contemplating in a melancholy mood the skeletons of seven horses lying close by, without doubt the victims of overwork and little food, when our new steeds were driven in from pasture on a bleak mountain side, to commence a run of twenty miles at post speed.

Descending from the mountains we passed villages whose strong walls and towers told of the neighbourhood of the dangerous Turcomans. The gateway of each stronghold was a little fort in itself, and Biblical descriptions came forcibly to my mind as we saw the white-robed elders smoking their water-pipes, seated on either side the entry with a more than patriarchal solemnity, the attendants in robes of Oriental brilliancy, raising their heads to stare at the unholy Giaours dashing by as quickly as their poor weary, sore-backed steeds would permit. In riding over this plain I discovered the solution of a problem which had often puzzled me. I had seen small earth-mounds ranged in a symmetrical row reaching for miles and miles. I now discovered that they were composed of the earth thrown up from numerous shafts during the construction of what are called *kanots*, or underground watercourses, leading from the mountains to the plain below.

Kasvin, the birthplace of the sage Lockman—and for a brief space the capital of Persia—was our next halting-place. Then the road to Teheran began to improve, for, as a rule, a ride across the natural country would be better than the apology for a roadway along which we had to journey, matters being made worse by the wretched condition of the post-horses. Hissarek was our next changing-place, and at last, nearing Teheran, we rode over a dry hot plain, whose unattractive aspect was made more *pénible* by its thick dun-brown dust, while we could see the giant Elburz mountains towering up seemingly within hand's reach, all white with snowy caps—long silvery streaks coming down claw-like along their sides, the delicious aspect of coolness making one feel doubly hot and thirsty. On approaching Teheran the town presents not the slightest striking feature. Were not one advised beforehand of his approach to the place, he would never guess that he was in the proximity of the capital of Persia. I found it a strange mixture of the Eastern and Western styles: quaint buildings and bazaars, and close at hand modern avenues and gas lamps, while in one or two places the electric light had been established. The Shah is evidently anxious to follow the examples of Western sovereigns, and hence he has had European officers to drill and train his troops as well as to establish a system of police. I visited the bazaar with similar impressions to those I had received at Asterabad, and during my stay I had an opportunity of seeing the Shah proceed in state to visit his First Minister. From the door of the house where the Shah was staying to the mansion of this official, a distance of over a mile, the thoroughfare was lined with troops. Though these soldiers had taken up their position at six in the morning, the Shah did not appear until nearly twelve o'clock. About half-past eleven, sundry old-fashioned carriages, drawn by a pair of horses each, and driven by nondescript-looking coachmen, who to all appearance might have been royal scullions in undisguised professional costume, were seen moving outside the ranks of the troops, in the direction of the Minister's residence. These vehicles contained some of the principal harem favourites, and were preceded by a crowd of men in ordinary Persian civilian costume, beating the air and the ground with long osier rods, and vociferating to the bystanders to 'be blind' and to turn their faces to the wall, lest by any ill-luck they might catch sight of any of the 'lights of the harem.' The arrival of the monarch was heralded by a number of mounted policemen, who dashed along the ranks in an altogether unnecessarily impetuous manner. These police wear black tunics, with violet facings on collars and cuffs, and a stripe of the same colour down the dark trousers. A small black cylindrical shako and long boots complete the costume. The foot police carry short sabres made on a European model, those of the mounted men being longer. After the police came thirty horsemen bearing large silver maces; and, behind these, about a hundred others armed with sabres and having double-barrelled fowling-pieces and old-fashioned Persian muskets slung at their backs. All these people were dressed very plainly in sombre-coloured civilian costumes. To these succeeded some fifty oddly-costumed persons, proceeding at a trot on either side of the way. They were the King's running footmen. When I first saw these royal acolytes, I took them to be street mountebanks. Half-a-dozen were sitting down on the kerbstone near the royal gate. Knowing that in the East such people always seek out Europeans as victims, I hastily went round a corner, lest one of them should stand on his head for my benefit. Each of them wore a rather long-skirted red tunic, ornamented with a few scraps of gold lace sewn horizontally on the breast; a pair of dark knee-breeches, white cotton stockings, and shoes with buckles and rosettes. The oddest part of the costume was the hat. It was of black glazed leather, and something like a fireman's helmet developing into a lancer's casque, or the head-dress worn by the eccentric pencil-merchant in Paris some years ago, who drove about the streets in a carriage selling his wares. From the centre and forward and rear ends of the tall, straight crest, rise three bunches of red artificial flowers, made to resemble sweet-william blossoms. These are fixed on long stems, the centre one being the tallest, and all three nodding comically with every movement of the head of the wearer. When the Shah appears in public, he is invariably accompanied by these attendants, who run in front of, behind, and on either side of his horse or carriage. In the midst of them rode a group of forty or fifty of the highest dignitaries of the State, including the First Minister and the Commander-in-Chief of the army—the Hessem el Seltaneh, or 'Sword of the Kingdom.' All these functionaries were dressed very plainly. At their head rode the Shah himself, not as people are apt to figure to themselves the Shah of Persia—a perpetual blaze of diamonds—but if possible more plainly attired than the other members of the group. Had it not been for the crimson umbrella which he carried open above his head I should have been unable to distinguish him. As I saw him, he appeared a much younger and handsomer man than his photograph would lead one to believe. Perhaps this was the result of the glow cast by the red umbrella. Behind him came an immense concourse of horsemen, presumably belonging to the royal household, followed by a closed carriage resembling the Lord Mayor's coach, resplendent with plate-glass and battered gilding. Next came some led horses, splendidly caparisoned; and a body of police closed the procession, the oddest part of which consisted of the apes and baboons led along by their keepers, and intended to amuse the ladies of the harem. A new feature—new for Persia, that is—was introduced into the scene; viz. the scattering of flowers along the roadway in front of the Shah. One would have expected that children, or at least some tolerably good-looking persons, would have performed this graceful act. Instead, there were two ugly old men, whose ordinary avocation was to throw water from the leather bags which they carried on their backs in order to allay the dust when the Shah passed, and who, having first performed the more useful portions of their duties, were now hurrying about with articles resembling wooden coal-scuttles under their arms, scattering in a very business-like and unpoetical manner what looked like the sweepings of a nursery garden.

CHAPTER IX.

Important telegrams—Visit to a magnate—The Towers of Silence—Fortifications—Dwellers in the tombs—A false alarm—Beauty of villages – Bitten—A human churn.

HAVING more than ever in view my desire to get to the front, I called upon Mr. Zinovieff, the Russian Minister. I told him that I had been obliged to quit Tchikislar, and that on two subsequent occasions, when I ventured to return, I had again been summarily compelled to leave. I inquired whether he could use any influence in favour of my being allowed to rejoin the camp. He replied that the matter remained in the hands of the new Commander-in-chief, General Skobeleff, and advised me to apply to that officer. I immediately despatched the following telegram : 'Son Excellence le Général Skobeleff, à Baku.—Voulez-vous me permettre accompagner l'expédition de Tchikislar comme Correspondant du " Daily News" de Londres ? ' In two days I received a reply : ' O'Donovan, Teheran.—Ayant les ordres les plus positifs de ne pas permettre à aucun correspondant, ni Russe, ni étranger, d'accompagner l'expédition, il m'est à mon grand regret impossible d'obtempérer à votre demande.—SKOBELEFF.' This reply, dated from Krasnavodsk, was of course decisive. I telegraphed to Skobeleff thanking him for the courteous promptitude of his answer, concluding my message with the words 'Au revoir à Merv,' as I was resolved, if possible, to be there before the Russian troops could reach it. I then took measures to facilitate my journey to some point on the north-eastern frontier of Persia, from whence I could gain the Akhal Tekké region and Merv. I applied to his Highness Hussein Khan Sipah Salar Aazem, the acting Grand Vizier, for permission to go along the frontier, and if necessary to penetrate into the country of the Akhal Tekké Turcomans. I received a most courteous reply, to the effect that the minister was most willing to give me the necessary pass, but that he could not guarantee my personal safety outside the Persian dominions. He wound up by saying, 'Although you have been for a long time in Persia, and several days at Teheran, I have not yet had the pleasure of receiving a visit from you.' I was satisfied to take the hint as an invitation to visit his Highness, and went accordingly.

After a lengthened progress over ill-set pavements, and between high scorching walls of unbaked brick (*i.e.* mud), I arrived at an enclosure, amid which, high-reared, stood an unshapely mass of buildings with high gables. Broad bands of blue enamelled tiles stretched across the front; otherwise, and excepting the gates, it had no more pretence to architecture than any other building in Teheran. There were crowds of what we should term 'hangers-on' within the yard, to which a broken-down arch gave admittance. They seemed annoyed by my arrival, and evidently thought me a needless addition to their number, until M. le Baron Norman, the most courteous and courtier-like of secretaries, coming to meet me, ushered me into a vast hall, spread with rich Persian carpets. It was divided into two parts by a couple of steps reaching along its whole breadth. In the lower half was a large tank of water some fifteen feet by twelve. In a few minutes I was seated at a small table *vis-à-vis* with the person whom ordinary rumour, native as well as European, indicated as the ablest man in Persia. He received me most affably. He merely pointed out the great difficulties and dangers of such an emprise as I proposed to take upon myself, and said that the Turcomans of the Akhal Tekké and Merv were no better than they should be, after which we parted.

I duly received the written permission for which I had applied, one which purported to enable me to visit the extreme north-eastern limits of the Persian dominions. Dr. Tholozan, the Shah's physician, also gave me a letter of introduction to an influential border chieftain, the Emir Hussein Khan, governor of Kuchan, so that I was quite hopeful of successfully carrying out my intentions.

I now set about making my final preparations for journeying eastwards towards the long looked-for goal. I telegraphed to my servant at Asterabad, instructing him to start immediately for Shahrood, to meet me with my horses and baggage, hired another Persian servant, obtained the necessary order for post-horses along the road as far as Meshed, made some necessary purchases at the bazaar, and was at last ready to start for the borders of the Tekké country, my first point being Shahrood, two hundred and eighty-four miles away. In this long weary ride I shall merely mention the principal objects that attracted my attention, there being many things that, though interesting, would extend this narrative beyond reasonable limits.

Five or six miles from Teheran are the 'Towers of Silence' of the Guebres or Fire-Worshippers. These are certain low circular buildings, having at the top a grating, upon which are laid the bodies of the dead, whose bones, as decomposition advances, or the flesh is devoured by birds of prey, drop through the gratings into the tower below.

The posting stations presented the same miseries as I had previously had to encounter. At one place the post-master informed me, in answer to an inquiry, that the *garrib-gez* abounded there. I was consequently obliged to take up my quarters on the flat roof of the *bala hané*, or traveller's room, which during the daytime is too hot a spot for the 'stranger biters,' and at night too cold for their delicate constitutions. A horse-cloth spread on the roof, and a saddle, formed the only sleeping accommodation afforded. The *argá Persica* is, it seems, a parasite on all kinds of poultry in this neighbourhood, abounding wherever such are kept, and reducing them to a miserable state of leanness and toughness, as I discovered to my cost while endeavouring to sup off the cartilaginous hen supplied to me.

In all directions during my journey I noted the pains that had been taken for defence against the nomads of the desert. In the mountainous parts advantage was taken of the rocks; in the plains artificial mounds were raised upon which to rear fort or citadel. The castle of Aradan was the first of the kind which I saw in a perfect condition and in actual use. The mound is about seventy yards in length by fifty in breadth. Its sides are very nearly vertical, and almost in line with the walls of the fortalice which crowns its summit. The height of the entire structure cannot be less than seventy or eighty feet. Outside this place are whole acres of the places of sepulture, with a very slightly arched-in covering of earth. When rain and the feet of passers-by have worn these earth-crusts thin, it is exceedingly dangerous to ride over one of the spaces set out with this kind of ghastly pastry. Irrigation watercourses and well-built tanks were of common occurrence, at which groups of weary-looking men in long blue calico gowns were seen slaking their thirst—pilgrims these, on their return from Meshed—and scattered over the country were mud towers some two hundred yards apart, places of refuge in case of Turcoman attack. Here everyone goes to work with musket at back; and three or four men in one of these towers could easily hold out, even against a large force, until aid arrived from the neighbouring villages.

At Lasgird there is an extensive cemetery containing many large domed tombs. Passing by one of these, I was surprised to see lying around it a number of reposing camels, their burdens scattered about on the ground, and, within the tomb itself, in the vaulted chamber under the cupola, a couple of women, evidently of the better class, accompanied by three or four children. They had arranged their carpets and beds there, and were making themselves apparently as much at home in their somewhat lugubrious quarters as the most select party of ghouls or vampires could have done. I recollect once, in my youthful days, reading in the 'Arabian Nights' of a traveller who, arriving late in the evening at some unknown town, and finding the gates closed, took up his quarters for the night in a tomb near the city gate. I wondered very much what kind of a tomb it could be within which he could find lodging, my experience of such monuments up to that time being confined to flat stone slabs or tall obelisks.

Half a dozen miles beyond Lasgird, while riding along a narrow winding path between some sand-hills, I met with a somewhat startling adventure. Rounding the shoulder of a hill, I came suddenly face to face with a mounted Afghan trooper, in full uniform, and armed to the teeth. He wore a dark-coloured turban, one end of the cloth pulled up in front, so as to resemble a small cockade. His uniform was blue-black, and he wore long boots. A broad black leather cross-belt, with two very large brass buckles, crossed his breast. He had sabre, pistols, and carbine. He looked sharply at me as he passed, and immediately halted and entered into conversation with my servant, who rode behind. Next moment another horseman appeared, also an Afghan, thoroughly armed, and whose dress indicated that he was of high rank. He, too, took a good look at me, and, like the trooper, stopped to talk with my servant. Twenty yards behind him rode four more troopers, each one leading a laden baggage-horse. As I passed these I turned round, and saw the entire six halted together and looking after me. My impression was that they, having learned what countryman I was, were deliberating about attacking me, and, being now hidden from their view, I put spurs to my horse and dashed away at a headlong pace over the plain in the direction of a village some miles off. I hoped there to be able to get some aid, or at least to be able to use my revolver with greater effect from under cover of the loopholed wall. The ground was undulating, so that I could not see whether or not I was pursued until I reached the village. Arrived there, I swept the plain with my field-glass, and, to my intense relief, found that my apprehensions had been groundless.

Semnan I found to be in the midst of a very fertile and cultivated country, villages occurring all around at short intervals. The cupolas and towers of this place look remarkably beautiful, their bright yellow tints gleaming amid the verdant groves of pomegranate, willow, fig, and plane-tree, but on every hand were signs of apprehended danger. Each garden is a fortress in itself, the doors giving admission to it being barely two feet square, and closed by thick stone slabs turning on pivots. The house doors, too, were scarcely four feet high, very solid, and the locks invariably on the inside, while similar signs of the precarious life of people in these parts were to be seen as I passed the other stations that intervened between Semnan and Shahrood. The whole face of the country is dotted with towers of refuge, and strongly walled villages are on every hand. The land was well cultivated, but though figs, pomegranates, and the mulberry, both black and white, grow luxuriantly on all sides, the palm, olive, and orange, which one would expect to be equally common, are totally absent. Tradition says that the whole country between Asterabad and the Atterek was once an unbroken forest of palms; now not one is to be seen.

Few sights are more charming to the eye than the view of one of these fortified villages, with its walls topped by a crown of foliage, especially when the traveller approaches it after a long journey across the stony deserts. The hues which they put on in the evening sun are indescribably gorgeous. The clay walls glisten like gold in the slanting rays, and the flowers among the leaves of the trees above glow with gem-like tints till each village rampart, with its battlements and towers, and the patches of deep blue sky beyond and between, looks like a mural crown set with ruby and turquoise. Shahrood is one of the prettiest places along the entire postal route. There are several hundred gardens planted with apricot, fig, mulberry, and vine, the latter topping the earth walls, and hanging over them in graceful festoons. To keep them in this position one often sees the skull of a horse or camel tied to the branch, and depending on the outside of the wall. Water abounds at all times of the year, and the river from which the place takes its name, the Shah Rood, or Royal River, flowing down the middle of the principal thoroughfare, is, at the hottest part of the year, well filled. I here found myself suffering from the effects of a bite of one of the Persian bugs, received somewhere on the road from Teheran, notwithstanding all the precautions which I took to avoid such a contingency. On the day on which I arrived at Shahrood, I felt a slight soreness on the inside of the calf of my leg, and on examining the place found a small purple patch, surrounded by a dun-coloured circle. This gradually swelled until a very painful tumour was formed. Simultaneously I was attacked by strong fever, accompanied by headache and severe sickness. As I had been previously recommended to do, in case I should be bitten, I took purgative medicine and quinine, and soon almost recovered, with the exception of feeling queer pains in the joints like those resulting from rheumatism. Some people of the town, hearing of my illness, called to see me, and I was overwhelmed with advice as to the best treatment for my malady. By one I was advised to eat some clay of the place; another recommended making up a few of the insects themselves in bread and swallowing them; and a third counselled standing on my head frequently and then rolling rapidly on the floor. But the oddest remedy of all was that proposed by a moullah, or priest, who also practised the healing art. He brought with him a large net like a hammock, in which he proposed to envelop me. My head was to be allowed to protrude, and I was then to be hung up from the branch of a tree in the garden. When I had swallowed a large quantity of new milk I was to be turned round until the suspending cords were well twisted, and then, being let go, to be allowed to spin rapidly round. This operation was to be repeated indefinitely until sickness was produced, when other measures were to follow. I declined, however, to allow myself to be bagged in the proposed manner, especially as I had previously heard from my friend General Schindler, at Teheran, that he once saw this method of cure tried on an old woman, who, when taken down for supplementary treatment, was found to be dead.

CHAPTER X.

Female pilgrims—Dervishes—A strange escort—Joining the hadjis—A night march—A council of hadjis—A skirmish—A threatened massacre—Results of the fight—An awkward position—A weird procession—A dangerous ravine—A fresh halt.

ONCE a month Shahrood is enlivened by the arrival of a caravan of pilgrims from every part of Persia, on their way to the shrine of Imam Riza at Meshed. During my stay great throngs of hadjis poured into the town, arriving by the Teheran road. Shahrood is, it seems, the rallying point of the various parties. Eastward of this they all keep together, moving under protection of a military force; for, after leaving Shahrood, raiding parties of Turcomans are to be met with. The new comers were some on foot, some on horseback, and a very large number, too, on asses. There were very many women, who, when not mounted on asses or mules, were carried in *kedjavés*, hamper-like litters, slung one on each side of a camel or mule, and usually covered by a sunshade. Fully half the pilgrims—and I was informed that three thousand had arrived already—were Arabs from Baghdad, Basra, and other points in Turkish territory adjoining Persia. They filled all the caravanserais, and crowded every nook where refuge could be obtained from the intensely hot sun. The Arabs mostly camped along the edge of the watercourse, under the shade of jujube and chenar trees; and those who had women and children with them erected rough screens by means of quilts and mantles supported on sticks. Amidst all this moved a number of dervishes, those inseparable adjuncts of all gatherings of people in the East. Some were instructing groups of pilgrims in the formula to be repeated at the shrine of Meshed for the thorough accomplishment of the duties of a hadji; others related wonderful tales to an eager gathering of listeners; and others, the more numerous, simply went about pestering everyone for alms. These dervishes all wear their hair flowing on their shoulders like Russian priests, and a curious dome-shaped tiara of coloured stuff. Each carries some kind of an offensive weapon—a hatchet, lance, iron-headed mace, or heavy knotted stick, as the case may be. In addition to the three thousand pilgrims arrived, two thousand more were to come.

Immediately after the last batches of the pilgrims came the military escort, the like of which it would be difficult to find elsewhere. First came a herd of nearly one hundred diminutive asses, bearing an equal number of nondescript-looking men, dressed in garments of various fashions and colours. Each carried an old-fashioned musket. This first detachment was one of mounted infantry. Next came a body of about one hundred and fifty persons on horseback, each carrying a very lengthy Persian-made rifle, having attached to it a wooden fork, the prongs tipped with iron. This fork is stuck in the ground when the soldier wishes to fire. These appendages fold upwards, the two points projecting ten inches beyond the muzzle of the gun, and giving it at a distance the appearance of a hayfork. Whether when in' this position it is used in lieu of a bayonet or not, I was unable to ascertain. They were dressed with still less uniformity than their predecessors on the asses. In fact, in the entire cavalcade there was not even an attempt at uniform. Some wore long boots of brown leather, others had slippers turned up at the toes; and a considerable number had no pantaloons worth mentioning. Close behind these latter horsemen came the great element of the cavalcade, the artillery, represented by one brass smooth-bore four-pounder on a field carriage, and drawn by six horses; and at the immediate rear of this rode a man in a tattered blue and red calico tunic, blowing furiously on a battered bugle, painted red inside like a child's halfpenny trumpet. This four-pounder was evidently the *pièce de résistance*, and as it passed the bystanders gazed on it with awe-struck imaginations. Behind the gun came a *takderavan*, or large wooden box with glazed windows borne on two horses, one before and one behind. Then came mules, each bearing two *kedjavés* covered with crimson cloth. These contained the more opulent of the pilgrims, with their wives and families. About one hundred mounted men followed, a few of whom had, strange to say, Martini-Henry rifles slung at their backs, but to each of which the curious prongs had been appended. Another hundred horsemen came dropping in at intervals, some escorting tents, others in charge of cooking utensils. This mingled and motley throng of hadjis, troops, camels, mules, asses, and dervishes went streaming by for hours, each section of the column so completely resembling another that one fancied they must, like a stage procession, be only 'making believe,' and that they were simply wheeling round the corner to return again.

For two days I tried in vain to find a man with an ass or a mule to carry my tent, and accompany me along the road to Budjnoord. Twice I had men engaged; and twice the bargain was broken off, on the score that the road was too dangerous, and that Tekkés were to be found along it. I consequently changed my plans, and determined to reach Budjnoord by a circuitous route, *viâ* the town of Sabzavar on the Meshed road. From Sabzavar I could easily reach either Kuchan or Budjnoord across the mountains. Following this route would also give me an opportunity of witnessing the march of a hadji caravan. We started at a little before sunset, that being the usual time for setting out on a journey in Persia, so as to avoid the extreme midday heat. I had resolved to go as far as possible with the great monthly caravan of pilgrims, both because the road is better than the mountain one, and with a view of being able to describe a pilgrim-caravan on its way to one of the most celebrated shrines of the East—that of Imam Riza.

An hour before my departure, my quarters in the caravanserai were regularly besieged by dervishes of every description, not to mention beggars of the ordinary kind, and it was only by a liberal distribution of small copper coins called pools and shahis that I succeeded in buying myself off. On leaving, I thought I was rid of the mendicant and dervish nuisance, but I soon discovered my mistake. Taking short cuts across the fields, they had posted themselves at different points of vantage along the narrow path, from which they not only recommenced their importunities, but almost made use of physical force to arrest my horse. There were dervishes with beards stained of a fiery-red colour, and wearing queer conical hats, who, if they did not regularly belong to the howling sect of Constantinople, most decidedly showed themselves qualified for admission to it by the fashion in which they yelled, screamed, and groaned, exhorting me in the name of the blessed Ali, and the Imams Hassan and Hussein, not forgetting Haziret Abass, and many other holy people, to give them charity. Then there were the old, the blind, and the lame—men, women, and children—hanging on to my stirrup and seizing my bridle. Some were horribly deformed, and it seemed marvellous that they should have undergone such apparently frightful disasters as were necessary to reduce them to their then present mutilated condition, and yet continue to exist.

During our weary slow march of forty miles we had but one halt; and the only thing in the shape of refreshment, if I can give it that name, partaken of by the hadjis was an occasional smoke of the water-pipe. The manner of lighting this pipe on horseback is curious, and I don't recollect ever having seen it described. Some pieces of charcoal are placed in a small wire basket as big as a hen's egg, and attached to the end of a string a yard long. Some tinder is lighted with a flint and steel, and placed among the charcoal. The basket is then whirled rapidly round by means of the string until the charcoal is thoroughly ignited, and the pipe is then kindled. On a very dark night, when the road is very bad, the horseman lights his way by placing tow or cotton in the little basket, which, when whirled, gives light enough to enable one to keep out of holes and ruts, or from falling over precipices. All night long, as we wound slowly across the desert, the *kaliouns* might be seen gleaming at intervals in the dark column, sending meteor-like trains of sparks behind on every gust of the evening breeze. As the moon rose I was able to take a look at my companions. Very many, mounted on the most diminutive of asses, were fast asleep, their arms clasping the necks of the animals, and more than once we heard the 'thud' of some somnolent rider falling to the ground. Some laid themselves like sacks across the asses' backs, and thus managed to sleep comfortably. The march was a tiresome one, even to one mounted on horseback, and I dismounted more than once to stretch my legs. The pilgrims on foot kept up bravely, and generally led the van, though each carried all his travelling necessaries on his back. Just as the sun rose we came in sight of our halting-place, Maiamai.

I had the good fortune to secure the little room over the entrance-gate of the post-house. It was but ten feet square, and apart from the door were two windows of equal size, at opposite sides of the room, none of the three openings having any means of being closed. The Arab contingent of our party was camped close by. Owing to the great influx of pilgrims, food was very dear—that is, for the country—a very poor fowl costing over a shilling. Some butchers had found it worth their while to accompany the pilgrims for the sake of the amount of meat they could sell them; and shortly after our arrival half-a-dozen sheep were ready skinned and cleaned. Without this supply fresh meat would be unattainable, as the inhabitants of the place scarcely ever eat flesh.

A council of the principal hadjis was held, and it was decided to wait for the remainder of the pilgrims, the *thob* (cannon), and the troops, previous to venturing through a mountain pass about six miles further on, where caravans had been repeatedly assailed and plundered by Turcomans. Our escort was to arrive shortly, and to take post in the dangerous ravines. Then, when the moon had risen, the hadjis and the cannon were to come on. At midnight, just as I thought the starting time had certainly come, in marched the soldiers back from their strategic position. Some one had brought word that twenty-five mounted Turcomans had been seen hovering in the vicinity of the dangerous ground! Though we were two thousand strong, and had a company of soldiers with us, it was resolved to wait for the cannon and the remainder of the pilgrims, which would swell our numbers to over five thousand. This incident will help to convey a notion of the intense dread of Turcomans with which Persians are inspired.

The next day passed very much like the preceding one, save that the morning was enlivened by an incident which at one moment threatened to put an end to my further pilgrimage. About eight o'clock, as I was sitting cross-legged on my carpet, writing some notes, I heard a sudden and violent hubbub in the open space in front of my window, under the trees. The Arab contingent and a number of Persians were charging about, furiously belabouring each other with sticks. It appeared that some dispute had arisen between the Baghdad Arabs and the Teheran pilgrims, and that hot words had been spoken as to the relative merits of their respective countries. Each, in his quality of hadji, carried a staff five feet long and about two and a half inches thick at the stouter end, and the hadjis, having grown excited, were banging each other with their pilgrims' staves. At first I thought it was some rude play, a kind of 'baiting the bear,' such as I had seen practised among the Turcomans, and in which rather severe knocks are given and received with the utmost good humour. However, I soon discovered by the number of holy persons stretched on the ground that 'bateing' in a Hibernian sense was going on. Gradually the Arabs became very much excited, and behaved like mad people, jumping, dancing, and shouting the Arab war-cry. Matters were getting bad for the Teheranis, when the latter drew their swords and *handjars*. Notwithstanding this unfair advantage, however, they were scattered and beaten off the field, and forced to take refuge in every direction, some rushing into the *chappar hané* in which I was staying. The Arabs now assembled together, showing each other the stabs and cuts which they had received from the Persians; and they seemed to come to the resolution to pay them back in their own coin. They rushed off in search of weapons, and speedily reassembled. At this juncture my servant unluckily happened to go out in search of corn for the horses. He wore at his belt a large broad-bladed *handjar*, upon spying which an Arab woman cried out that he was one of the people who had used deadly weapons, and immediately hurled a large paving-stone at him. Then the whole crowd set upon him. He retreated hurriedly to the *chappar hané*, the doors of which were closed before the Arabs could get in. These latter then tried to smash in the door, shrieking out that they would massacre everyone within the place. The Teheran pilgrims within now showed themselves on the ramparts, and commenced abusing the assailants in unmeasured terms. The Arabs thereupon renewed their efforts to break the door, and showered bricks and stones on the ramparts, and also into my room. In a twinkling the floor was covered with missiles, mud fell in heaps with each concussion, and my servant rushed into the chamber, his face all bloody and disfigured from a blow of a great stone. I showed myself, thinking that my European costume would induce the Arabs to desist. I called on them to go away; but all to no purpose. I was made the target for over a hundred stone-throwers. The attack redoubled, and the assailants showed signs of being about to attempt an escalade. I felt certain that if they got in we should all be lost, so I sprang for my revolver and sword, and, posting myself at a loophole of a flanking tower, prepared to fire at the first who attempted to climb. Meantime, I cried out to some neutral spectators to run and fetch the Governor, and to tell him that our lives were in danger. This functionary arrived in a few minutes, bringing with him a force of armed men, who put a stop to the attack. Then the Governor, together with the Arab chiefs and about twenty of their men, came up to my room. I produced my pass from the Minister of Foreign Affairs at Teheran and complained that I had been attacked in my room without provocation. The Arabs responded by exhibiting their wounds, and horrid gashes some of them were. Notwithstanding the thick rolls of camel-hair, handkerchiefs and skull-caps, some of the scalp wounds were very deep. One man's thumb was nearly severed from his hand. 'And,' said one of the chiefs, 'the cowards drew weapons on us, who had only sticks in our hands; pretty Mussulmans these!' The Arabs now formally apologised to me for having thrown stones at me, stating that they did not know I was a stranger, but at the same time charged my servant with being one of the persons who wounded them. They swore that they recognised him, and one went so far as to swear by my beard, which he laid hold of in an alarming manner. 'By your beard, Emir,' he said, 'it is true.' However, we settled the matter peacefully, the Arabs promising not to bear any spite against the Teheranis. So ended a matter which at one moment threatened to conclude disagreeably enough. The Governor, Mahomet Khan, a little old man, requested me to give him a paper bearing my seal, stating that he had promptly and effectually suppressed the riot. This I did with pleasure. Shortly after his withdrawal he sent me, in true Eastern fashion, a present of fruit and bread, on a large silver tray, covered over with an embroidered cloth, and escorted by three servants.

AN AWKWARD POSITION.

At ten o'clock we were all in motion, but it was a good hour before we were clear of the camping ground. The artillery bugle sounded three times, to give us warning of the departure of the escort. Everyone wanted to be as near as possible to the cannon, so that nobody was willing to go forward or to hold back. As a result I found myself and my horse standing in a stream of water, jammed in between *kedjavés* full of women, mule-litters, and camels. Close in front of me was a collection of coffins, containing putrefying human bodies, fastened across the backs of asses, and smelling horribly. They were the remains of people who had left money enough to secure their being interred close to the sacred precincts at Meshed, and were being brought from heaven knows what far-off corner of Persia. Slowly and with difficulty I forced my way through the throng; for the ground was very irregular, and, though torches, lanterns, and fires blazed on every side, the press was too close to let one catch a glimpse of them. Outside the radius of the fire-light all was nearly pitch dark, for the moon had not yet risen, and the stars shed but a dim light in the flare of the fires. My horse had got out of the stream on to what seemed a narrow footpath. After a few minutes I felt myself getting strangely elevated above the people on each side of me. I halted until a light was brought, and then discovered that I was on the top of a mud wall four feet high. In a few minutes more I should have been twelve feet from the ground, on the top of a wall but two feet thick, a rather awkward place for an equestrian in the dark.

The entire caravan could not have covered less than a couple of miles of the rocky road, and a strange sight it presented as I rode as quickly as possible along its flank. The whole dark line resembled some gigantic train of waggons with blazing fiery wheels. The impalpable white dust boiled upwards in swaying columns like the steam of twenty locomotive engines. The hollow clang of the camel bells, and the fiendish groans of the camels, as they stalked swingingly along, laden with tents, boxes, and litters, joined in happy unison. Behind and in front of the gun, with its six horses, were two score of infantry, mounted on small asses. The men were rather big, and the asses the most diminutive that I ever saw. In the faint starlight their general effect was that of a number of four-legged men scrambling over the stones, and bearing long hayforks over their shoulders. A superstitious stranger, coming suddenly upon this weird-looking procession, might easily take it, with its unearthly sounds, flaming circles, and foully smelling coffins, for some infernal troupe issuing from the bowels of the sable hill hard by, to indulge in a Satanic promenade during the witching hours of the night.

As we drew near the dreaded ravines the greatest anxiety began to prevail; and the caravan drew into still closer order. Those who at first pushed forward valiantly now fell back upon the gun and its escort; the bugle sounded, and we came to a standstill. Just in front of us, at the entrance of the pass, was an old fort with tall curtain walls and crenelated towers. The half-waned moon was just rising beyond its crumbling battlements, shedding an uncertain light over the vast dim plain reaching away to the north. I could not help thinking of what would be the result if the merest handful of Turcoman horsemen swept down upon the straggling, unwieldy column. The gun, absolutely the most useless weapon among us, could do nothing, even if the gunners did not bolt at the first sight of the enemy. Besides, even with the steadiest artillerymen in the world, this gun, shut in by crowds of terrified, unreasoning pilgrims, would not be able to fire a single shot; and to fire with a small cannon in the dark at Turcoman cavalry whirling down in their usual loose order would be little short of absurd. It would be its first and last discharge. The few infantrymen, with their cumbrous old muzzle-loading rifles, which it would take five minutes to load, might also be set aside as practically useless, even if they had had bayonets, which, for some unaccountable reason, they had not. Anything like rallying the more bellicosely inclined of the pilgrims would, under the circumstances, be out of the question. It would be a thorough *sauve qui peut*, and the best thing that could be done under the circumstances; for to stay would be but to court certain death or capture. After a short pause we screwed up our courage and entered the defile, each man shouting and yelling as if possessed, in order, as I understood, to terrify the robbers. The confusion and din which prevailed during the hour which our passage of the ravine occupied cannot be easily imagined. The entire cavalcade became nearly invisible in the dust-cloud raised by its rapid progress. At ten yards one could barely distinguish the outline of a camel, like that of some shadowy, misshapen phantom gliding along in the moonlight; and one gasped for breath in the stifling atmosphere. The defile occasionally widened out, so as to allow easy passage for twenty abreast; but there were places where one camel only could pass at a time between the steeply-scarped rocks on either side. It was just at these places that the hadjis made desperate rushes, each one trying to be the first through. The result, of course, was a block and a dead stand-still. At last we heard cheering in the front. This was when the leading files of the caravan met with a party of returning pilgrims.

As we neared the eastern end of the pass we began to encounter long trains of camels from Meshed, laden with cotton. These trains were a welcome sight, for they showed us, as did the returning pilgrims, that the road was clear.

Dawn was fast brightening as we caught sight of the halting-place. It was an extensive caravanserai, the largest I had hitherto seen, and rose amid the solitude of the plain like some enchanted castle. It was named Miandasht, and here we made our preparations for passing the day.

CHAPTER XI.

The caravanserai—Flies and scorpions—A Persian residence—Offer of an escort—An act of lunacy—Insect pests—Fond of the sword—An awkward look-out—The Emir's palace—An Eastern dinner table—The Emir of Kuchan—A banquet—The following of a feast—Critical illness—After the fever—Abundance of fruit—Beauty of Meshed—Bazaar inmates—Persian officials—Ancient coins—My bedroom—Meshed water.

At sundown the scene and various preparations for starting from Miandasht were most picturesque. The amethyst hills showed indistinctly on the western horizon. A few taper clouds, like golden fishes poised motionless in the opal depths, alone broke the continuity of the vast silent arch above the desert. Around us, the boundless plain was one sheet of aërial purple. Far away to the south gleamed whitely the lonely tomb of some forgotten warrior or saint; and, further still, a solitary well, with its single straggling chenar tree—emblems of life in the wilderness. A tall dust column was waltzing solemnly eastward in the rising evening breeze, now breaking into viewless sand mist, now re-forming, bowing and caracolling like some sportive living creature, the very prototype of the *gin* of Eastern story, the enraged genius who came to slay the merchant that had thrown a date-stone into his son's eye. In the courtyard below the window of my lodging, people in every costume of the East were sitting or lying on the ground, under the horse-shoe arches of the arcades or on the terraced tank covers, smoking their water-pipes or drinking tea from their *samovars*. Others were performing their evening ablutions, a companion or attendant pouring water from a metal jug over their hands. These ablutions are little more than a matter of form, especially before prayers. For the feet, a damp hand is passed lightly over the instep; that is all. Other pilgrims were standing on their little carpets with their faces towards the *keblah* and their hands held before them like an open book, commencing their evening devotions. Some, similarly engaged, rose and sank during their orisons like the beam of a steam-engine in slow motion as they prostrated themselves. From tower and terrace a dozen self-appointed *muezzims* chanted their prayer-call, which echoed mournfully along the neighbouring plain. Camels and mules laden for the road, with their bells tinkling at every motion, stood around everywhere. The cupola and turrets of Shah Abass's caravanserai stood out boldly against the evening sky, and below, in the middle of the square, our cannon was conspicuous. As the sun disappeared slowly behind the horizon, and dim twilight settled over 'the level waste, the rounding gray' across which our path lay, the artillery bugles gave the signal for departure, and I had to scramble down the steep caravanserai steps and once more start on my journey.

This was through an alternation of uncultivated and cultivated plains, with scattered villages. Here and there were traces of the land having formerly been densely populated. In places the character of the region was shown by the traces of inundations in white deposits of salt. On crossing one stony plain during the prevalence of a strong sultry wind, which blew from the east, my horse's coat became most remarkably electrical, streams of sparks flying from his neck and mane wherever the reins touched them. I could draw sparks from the animal's ears with my metal-ringed riding-whip.

I journeyed on in company with the pilgrim train through Abasabad, Mazinan, and Mehr, to Sabzavar, where we parted company. The journey was unpleasant, but there was much that was interesting to a traveller: the halts in the caravanserais, the habits of the pilgrims, the poorer of whom had mostly something to sell, while others subsisted by cutting and selling fodder or firewood to the better off. It is surprising upon how little these people contrive to live. A piece of bread and a morsel of goat's cheese, with a handful of apricots, constitute their meal. The richer pilgrims only can indulge in the luxury of an occasional piece of chicken or spitted meat. All, however, drink tea.

At Sabzavar there are few inducements for a prolonged residence. Fruit was abundant, and there was a good supply of that unwonted luxury, ice, stored up in winter for summer use; but the furious west winds are almost unbearable. The swarms of flies add to the traveller's discomfort, and very large whitish green scorpions abound, stowing themselves in one's valise or in any garment laid carelessly aside for a few hours. Fortunately, mosquitoes are absent, but the flies and scorpions are quite enough. The town is dusty and burnt up in appearance, looking very like an immense brickyard. The houses, with their flat cupolas, from the top of each of which the smoke issues through a round hole, resemble so many brick-kilns, and the few trees that peep above the garden walls only intensify the dried-up appearance of the whole place.

I separated from the pilgrims without regret. The greater portion of them, having started on their expedition without any funds, had to depend on begging for the means of living, and so persistently did they ply their trade as to be a perfect nuisance on the road. Everyone who seemed to possess anything was remorselessly dunned for alms. But it proved easier to separate from my travelling companions than to pursue my journey to Kuchan. It was needful in the first place to call on the Governor, and discuss my projected journey, and the precautions necessary to make it safely. The people of this part of Persia are terribly in awe of their marauding neighbours, and a journey to a place so near the Turcoman frontier as Kuchan was looked upon as a most perilous if not wholly insane undertaking. To make my call on the Governor with due formality, I sent a messenger to announce my intended visit—an indispensable ceremony here, when the person to be seen is of any considerable rank. This preliminary over, I proceeded to that dignitary's residence, which, though fortified with flanking towers and bastions, was only built of earth. The guards at the gate seemed utterly astonished at my appearance, and I heard them speculating on my nationality. Passing the gateway and its guardians, I found myself in a bare courtyard with some dusty buildings on the far side. About a dozen persons belonging to the household were saying the evening prayer on a slightly raised platform in one corner. On the left was a one-storey building with folding windows, paper instead of glass being inserted in the openings in the sash. In front was a large tank of water full of weeds. A small side door gave access to a large court, containing some trees of mulberry, jujube, and willow, and partially paved. A number of the hangers-on, who are always to be found around the dwelling of a Persian grandee, loitered about the gateway. Immediately on my entry a carpet was brought and spread beside the tank, and two arm-chairs were placed on it, in one of which I was invited to take a seat.

The Governor, or Neyer el Dowlet, soon made his appearance. He was a handsome, sly-looking man of about forty, with large eyes, a slender aquiline nose, and a long drooping moustache of a heavy leaden black colour. His dress consisted of a long loose robe of lilac-coloured silk, and he wore the usual Kadjar hat of Astrakan. Like most Persians of the upper class, he was extremely courteous in his manners. I presented my letters from his Highness the Sipah Salar Aazem, and from the Shah's physician, Dr. Tholozan. Our conversation at first turned on the Europeans who had been in those parts during recent times, and I quickly found that I was the first newspaper correspondent who had come to the country. I then drew the conversation to the Akhal Tekkés, and inquired what reception I was likely to meet with among them. The Governor shook his head. The road across the mountains, he said, was pretty safe for armed persons travelling in company, as the governors along the Atterek kept strict watch against marauding parties from beyond the frontier and took heavy reprisals in case of damage to persons or property within the Persian territory, but the Tekkés were a bad lot. The Governor of Kuchan and Yar Mehemet Khan of Budjnoord would be able to give me more accurate information about them than he could. After some further conversation, he offered me an escort, but as I knew that this involved a heavy payment to the guard, I politely declined to accept it, trusting rather to my own revolver and sword and to the formidable appearance of my servant, who was fully accoutred with sabre, *handjar*, and pistols.

Two glasses of very strong tea, sweetened excessively,

were brought in at the commencement of our conversation, and immediately afterwards two highly ornamented water-pipes, which we smoked in silence for a few minutes. Two more glasses of tea were subsequently brought. This tea and smoking interlude, apart from the question of hospitality, has an important *rôle* in serious conversations in Persia. After some time I took my leave, promising to call again before my departure. Our parting was marked with all due formality. We rose and bowed profoundly to each other, and I then retired backwards, keeping an eye on the tank, and at ten paces from the carpet I bowed again and departed.

After this interview I intended starting as soon as possible for Kuchan, but was delayed by the difficulty of finding a guide. The first whom I engaged in that capacity lost his courage when it came to the moment of setting out, and declined to go unless I would ask for an escort. It cost me a couple of days to find another guide, and thus my stay in Sabzavar was prolonged until July 13, eight days in all. On the evening before starting I paid my visit of adieu to the Governor, and before sunrise rode through the bazaar as the people were unbarring their booths, on my way to the gate of the town. The tenants of the booths gazed after me with an air of astonishment, and evidently looked on my project of penetrating among the Tekké savages, which had got well published everywhere during my stay, as little less than lunacy. The last person to whom I spoke in Sabzavar, oddly enough, happened to be a man who had spent nine years in London as a servant of the Persian Envoy. His impressions, and the tastes he had acquired during his travels, were peculiar. He would like, he said, to return once more for the sake of eating corned beef and drinking bitter ale. He also had been highly pleased by the manner in which Madame Patti had danced the cancan at the Alhambra in Leicester Square!

The road to Kuchan runs in a north-easterly direction, and winds in and out among the hills for fifteen miles. I passed patches of mulberry trees—whose leaves formed the food of the silkworms—apricots, and a half-wild vine that bore a very small red grape. Hardly a soul was to be met with on the road, and passing Aliar and Aliak I came to Sultanabad, a fortified village, where there was a caravanserai. I established my quarters in a large dilapidated room on the ground-floor, and, having stuck my sword in the wall, and hung the linen Chinese lantern I carried with me to give light at night on the hilt, I spread a horsecloth on the floor, and, lying on my face thereon, proceeded to write my correspondence. Every now and then I had to cast a look around to guard against the advance of the various insect tribes.—beetles, spiders, ants, and others—which came in columns towards my light, and constantly sought to climb on my carpet and investigate the contents of the ink-bottle.

Starting at daybreak, I crossed a valley where the people were gathering in their harvest, and passing Kheirabad went on amidst hills of limestone and gypsum, mixed with rotten black shale, seeing enough in my ride to be convinced of there being valuable minerals in the locality, and picked up specimens of copper ore, hæmatite, and brown oxide of iron.

At length, after a weary ride, I reached the village of Karagul, where I succeeded in unearthing three witch-like old women, who were down in a cellar, engaged in boiling something in a pot. They must have taken me for a Turcoman, for on my appearance they fled away into inner recesses, from which they were only with difficulty induced to come forth. The head man of Karagul, a tall old man whose long beard was dyed with henna to the colour of a fox's back, became very friendly with me, after examining in succession my field-glass, revolver, sketch-book, &c. He advised me not to go through the Abdulla Gau Pass, as all the people there were *shumsheer adamlar,'* fond of the sword. He then pointed out a very high mountain, the top of which was shaped like a bishop's mitre, and recommended me to pass through the cleft between the twin peaks. However, I had had enough of mountain climbing already, and so preferred to risk the dangers of the road as it lay before me. Still, I was so impressed by the warnings he gave me that I determined not to pass through the village of Abdulla Gau in the dark, and accordingly I and my servant and guide camped out on a steep rock near that place and kept watch by turns all night. In the morning we boldly entered the suspected village, and found the people a sober-looking lot enough. One of them offered me some fine turquoises, from the mines of that gem on the mountains of Madane, at a very low price. Though much tempted to buy, I feared the offer might be a *ruse* to find out how much money I had, and I declined traffic. Then, passing through numerous villages, I reached Kuchan, beyond which rose the blue chain of the Akhal Tekké mountains, whither my course was directed.

I stowed myself and luggage in the den allotted to me in the caravanserai, and attempted some writing, but was disturbed by a sudden invasion of winged cockroaches, evidently drawn by my candlelight. These intruders resemble the common 'black clocks' of our coal-cellars at home, but fly quite actively. Small carnivorous beetles came in thousands during the night and effectually prevented sleep, disappearing with the daylight, to be replaced by clouds of flies.

Kuchan being an important point on the frontier, I had to spend some days there to prepare for the most perilous part of my journey, the expedition among the Turcomans. I wanted some information from the Governor, who rejoiced in the high-sounding title of the Shudja-ed-Dowlet Emir Hussein Khan, but that dignitary at the date of my arrival was absent on a pilgrimage to Meshed, though expected home at any hour. My purpose was to push on to Askabad in the heart of the Akhal Tekké country, and about eighty miles or more from Kuchan, beyond the mountain range which rose some nine or ten thousand feet straight before me. I was subsequently compelled by circumstances to change this plan, but at the time I am writing of I expected to find myself in a few days amongst the dreaded nomads. I hardly knew how I should keep up my communications with the civilised world across these mountains. Besides, I was quite uncertain what reception I should meet among the Tekkés in their own country. Should I fall into the hands of any of the roving bands of marauders usually to be met with I was pretty sure to be carried off *nolens volens* either to Merv or somewhere else, and there kept until I could procure a respectable ransom. If, on the other hand, I should run across the advancing Russians, I was certain of being sent under escort to my old quarters at Tchikislar and thence shipped across the Caspian to Baku.

Taken altogether, one seemed quite out of the civilised world here, especially as it meant a ride of nearly a hundred miles to send a telegram, but I met one

European during my stay in Kuchan. He was a curious character, some twenty-five years of age, with blue eyes and long yellow hair. He spoke Russian and German, but no other European language, though he said he was half French and half German. He had recently embraced Mohammedanism, and moreover he told me he was a Nihilist, but he would not tell the motives which had brought him to Kuchan. The people there set him down as a lunatic, and I have little doubt that they included me in the same category.

The Governor returned on the third day after my arrival. He despatched his chamberlain, an elderly and dignified personage, bearing a silver mace as the badge of his office, to notify me of the fact, and to invite me to dinner. Evening was falling as, accompanied by my two servants, I proceeded to the Emir's palace. The straggling booths of the bazaar were closed, and we stumbled through its narrow alleys in the dark as best we could, for the branch roofs overhead completely excluded even the twilight that remained in the sky. Dogs and huge rats scurried away at the sound of our approach, and more than once my guide had to lead me like a blind man through the labyrinth of holes and ditches of dirty water, a common feature of Eastern towns.

The Emir's palace has a large open space in front. The main entrance was in the form of a horse-shoe arch built of red brick, while the walls around were only mud structures. Squatting on the ground around were nearly a hundred people, many of them Turcomans. They were persons who had requests to make of, or petitions to present to, the Governor of Kuchan. Within the groined arch inside the horseshoe gate was a guard of men-at-arms. As I stepped into the guard-room I was met by the chamberlain, who, dismissing the crowd of unfortunate applicants, immediately ushered me into a courtyard measuring some fifty feet square. Passing by a doorway at the further side, I entered a still larger court, paved with square tiles, in the midst of which stood a large rectangular reservoir of water, in the centre of which played a fountain. Arranged in the middle of the pavement were flower-beds, planted entirely with the 'marvel of Peru,' that sweet-scented flower which opens its blossom to the sunset, and fills the night air with its perfume. It is a favourite with the Persians, whose banquets always take place after sundown. The scene which met my eyes was extraordinary. Ranged round the large courtyard were at least a hundred candles, burning in the peculiar candlesticks which Russia has made familiar to this part of the frontier. The candle, buried in the body of the candlestick, was forced gradually upwards by a helical spring, as in ordinary carriage lamps, the flame being protected from the wind by a tulip-shaped bell-glass. Shaded candles of the same description were placed around the border of the tank, between which and the main entrance of the Emir's residence a long table, draped in white linen, was laid out à la Franca. On the table burned half a dozen candlelamps.

At some distance from and at right angles to the table was a long-backed wooden bench. Sitting upon this, and attired in sober broadcloth robes, reaching to their heels, were a dozen individuals—brothers and cousins of the Emir, Hussein Khan, and who had been invited to do honour to his guest. A silver-mounted water-pipe, the head set with turquoises and emeralds, was passed from hand to hand. I took my place, as invited, at the right hand of the Governor, and we entered into the usual pointless conversation so characteristic of Eastern intercourse. We spoke of anything and everything except that which was nearest to our hearts or had reference to the situation. It was a kind of social fencing, for the Emir was not at all sure that I was what I represented myself to be. A servant brought in a silver tray, upon which were large glasses of the abominable spirit called arrack, each of which was supposed to be emptied at a draught. This tray was handed round with a frequency which led me strongly to doubt the orthodoxy of my Kurd host.

We were all slightly stimulated before a move was made towards the dinner table. When the Emir stood up, his kinsmen rose to their feet, and drew themselves up in line each looking the very personification of humility—their feet close together, their toes turned in, each hand thrust up the opposite sleeve, and each head slightly reclining upon the right shoulder. The Emir walked up and down the paved enclosure, talking rather wildly. He spoke of his friend Dr. Tholozan, the Shah's physician, who had kindly given me a letter of introduction to him. He stated that that gentleman had marvellously cured him of a malady of long standing.

For a wonder, there were chairs and benches, with which the immediate relations of the Emir and myself were accommodated. The remainder of the party, some thirty in number, sat upon long wooden forms. The table, a long one, was draped in faultlessly white cloth. In its midst was a great silver centre-piece, loaded with roses, and flanked on either side by a complete set of ornaments, including vases of opaline glass, decorated on the outside with gilt and ruby beads. These were Russian presents. The Emir supposed that the vases were goblets, and more than once in the course of the dinner they were filled with wine on the occasion of the different toasts which were drunk.

The *table d'hôte* was an unusual one. The candles flared around the courtyard, their lights glancing in the great reservoir. The air was heavy with the scent of the flowers. Around us were the ruins of the old palace, destroyed by an earthquake twenty years previously. The Kurdish Governor sat at the head of the table. I sat opposite to him. On either side were the colossal forms, gleaming eyes, and sombre robes of his relations. Before we commenced to dine, arrack was again served round. After each glass one took from a dish a kind of acid paste, the Kurdish name for which I have forgotten, and then very fair Bordeaux wine was served. Then there were roasted almonds and pistaches. While we were disposing of this preprandial repast, I remarked to the Emir that in Turkey we always drank mastic on such occasions. 'I know it well,' exclaimed he; 'did you bring any with you?' And he leaned eagerly across the table. 'I am sorry to say that I did not,' I replied; 'but if your Excellency wishes I shall take the earliest opportunity of forwarding you some from Constantinople when I get back there.' We had soup, and dishes *ad libitum*; and I could never have believed that the human frame was capable of absorbing such an amount of nutrition if I had not seen these Kurds eat. We were supplied with the excellent dry white wine of the country, and Château Margaux. The latter must have been brought at an enormous expense from Europe. It was probably a present from the expeditionary generals beyond the frontier.

Towards the close of the banquet, my host and his guests became rather excited by the alcoholic beverages, which they were consuming with a will. They talked at random, and spoke of their exploits in the field against the Tekké Turcomans. Later they fell to embracing each other in a more than brotherly fashion. I was sitting opposite the Emir's brother, and had got so far as making a pun, in the Kurdish language, about mushrooms, of which we were partaking at the moment, when the opposite form was suddenly upset, and Emir, chiefs, and generals rolled upon the pavement, locked in each others' embraces. They kissed each other with fervour, swore undying devotion, and seemed in no wise inclined to resume their positions at table. Later on, the Emir pretended to have need of exercise, and was promenaded from one end of the space to the other, a servant holding him under each arm—his feet in front, his whole body making an angle of forty-five degrees with the horizon. Suddenly he recollected himself, and, sitting upon a chair, asked, solemnly, 'Has the Ingleez gone home yet?' He evidently believed that, before proceeding further with his orgies, objectionable witnesses should be got rid of. I took the hint, rose, and, exchanging salutes as well as I could with the prostrate company, made for the door. The mace-bearer marched before me, accompanied by four men bearing lanterns, such as can only be seen in this part of the world. They were nearly as large as the bass drum of a military band, and were made of waxed linen, closing up like a concertina when not in use. The bigger the lanterns, the greater is supposed to be the dignity of the individual whom they precede.

An illness of three weeks' duration followed the Emir's banquet. After returning to my earth-walled chamber, and trying to sleep as best I could, for I was very tired, I took none of the usual precautions against the *shab-gez*. At four o'clock in the morning my arms and legs were covered with the tumid bodies of these pests. Two days later, virulent-looking pustules marked the bitten spots. I had felt inclined to doubt what had been told me in regard to the sting of these ferocious insects, but later experience proved how mistaken I had been. A high fever resulted. It had typhoid symptoms, all of which were aggravated by the foul air of the caravanserai, the bad food and water, and the anxiety of mind about my coming journey. For two days and nights I was delirious. In a lucid moment I discovered that I was suffering from one of the most dangerous complications of typhoid enteric disease. No one who has not been similarly circumstanced can imagine my critical position. Here I was, in a semi-barbarous town, with no one near who had the slightest idea of the nature of my malady, no medicine, no doctor. Had it not been for the intelligent devotion of a friend, a Tekké sheepskin merchant, I do not believe that I should now be alive. He sat by me during my delirium, applied ice to my head, and was the only one who understood me when I asked for camphor, the sole available drug. There was a moment when the enteric irritation was so severe that I felt convinced my last hour had arrived. I made up my mind to try a desperate remedy, and sent for opium. I took what for me, who had never tasted the drug before, was an enormous dose—a piece as large as the first joint of one's little finger. The effect was magical so far as the pain was concerned, and I then lost consciousness for nearly forty-eight hours. For once I can write the 'Confessions of an Opium-eater,' and I must say that my experiences of the visions conjured up would scarcely tempt me into a De Quincey's career. First I became chairman of a Russian Nihilistic society; then I was transformed into a black goat pursued by panthers on the mountains; then I was a raging torrent, dashing away to some terrible end; and then I remember no more. I woke with an intense feeling of dread and horror, and half a day passed before I could recognise the faces around me. When my senses were a little collected, I asked for some arrack, the odious, poisonous stuff to be had at Kuchan; but it was the only stimulant available. Diluting this with much water, I took it from time to time to combat the terrific opiatic reaction, and gradually I came back to my normal state. The pain was wonderfully relieved, but I was crushed and shattered like a broken bulrush.

Several would-be physicians wanted badly to prescribe for me, but as I knew that every one of them carried an astrolabe in his pocket, which would have to be consulted before he looked at my tongue, and also, in all probability, a brass basin in which to roast the fiend who had possession of me, I declined their aid with thanks.

My illness not only detained me in Kuchan, but had materially altered my plans. Before attempting the trip to Merv, I found it necessary to pay a visit to Meshed, hoping to find some needed medical assistance there, and accordingly, after a three weeks' sojourn in Kuchan, I abandoned the idea of taking the road to Askabad, and on the morning of August 10 started for the sacred city of Persia. I was much pulled down by my fever, and as I buckled on my revolver-belt preparatory to starting, my Tekké friend, who had nursed me so well, smiled pityingly. He evidently thought I was in little trim for wielding arms of any sort, considering my worn frame and tottering gait. Still I managed to get on horseback, though I could only bear the slowest pace of the animal. The journey to Meshed, usually made by foot-passengers in two or two-and-a-half days, occupied me no less than seven. Even so I was glad to leave Kuchan, with its horrid hovels and insect plagues, and to be on the road to more promising quarters.

Weak as I was, I endeavoured to keep a note of the road along which I was travelling, and which, though little known, is of the highest importance in relation to Russian designs in Central Asia. The road to Meshed is commonly said to be very dangerous; the trouble, however, does not arise from marauders, but from the peasants along the road, who eke out their ordinary gains by turning an occasional hand to robbery. The last six days of my journey differed in no material point from the first. All the villages were similar collections of cubical mud houses, with flat domes for roofs, huddled together without any streets, like so many wasps' nests. The food to be had was only round cakes so stale as to be like stones, with ill-smelling goat's milk and worse cheese. I managed to get half a dozen eggs, which I swallowed raw, as the state of my stomach would not allow of my attempting the other viands.

Within a day's journey of Meshed the cornfields began to be replaced by large melon and cucumber patches. In some places the tendrils of the plants are trained on slight trellis frames, so that their broad leaves form summer-houses to protect the watchmen of the gardens from the sun. Few prettier sights had met my eye than these fresh green bowers, with their broad yellow flowers, after the dusty and parched stubble fields through which I had been passing. Orchards, too, are found at intervals, from which the markets are abundantly supplied with grapes, peaches, apricots, and plums, all of delicious flavour. The dark purple plums are often as large as good-sized peaches. The ground is cut up with irrigating ditches in every direction, both open and covered with earth. The latter (*kanots*), when old, are a source of constant danger to travellers. In making them, shafts are sunk at intervals of from thirty to forty yards, like wells, and the sand and gravel from these pits is hauled to the surface in buckets and piled around the mouth of the pit in an annular heap. I have often seen skeletons of camels, with parts of the skin attached, wedged eight or ten feet down in these chasms, the animals having evidently fallen in and been left to perish there. On several occasions I should have met with a similar fate but for the instinct of my horse, whose look-out for such snares was often keener than his rider's. I have little doubt but hundreds of belated travellers must yearly find their graves in these horrible gulfs, which yawn in every direction, and certainly do not add to the comfort or safety of travelling in Khorassan.

It was late on a sultry afternoon, the seventh day after my departure from Kuchan, that I came at last within sight of the Holy City of Shiia devotion. In front, was a dark wide grove of tall trees, behind which the ochre-tinted battlements and ramparts of the town peered, while high over all towered the gilt dome and minarets of the mosque of the great Imam Riza. I had long learned to look with distrust on the external appearance of Eastern towns, so little in accord with their interiors, but I could not help being struck with admiration as I caught my first glimpse of Meshed. Except Stamboul, as viewed from the Bosphorus, nothing I had seen in the East could compare with it in beauty, and I could well realise the effect it must produce on the imaginations of the pilgrims who had toiled across the long dusty roads for, it may be, months together, when the sacred city reveals its glories to their devout gaze.

In the burning sun the golden dome seemed to cast out rays of dazzling light, and the roofs of the adjoining minars shone like brilliant beacons.

Entering by the western gate I found myself in a broad thoroughfare, down the centre of which flowed a canal, with kerbing of brick flush with the roadway. The canal was eight or nine feet wide and about five deep, but had only a few inches of filthy water at the bottom. In fact, it serves as an open sewer to convey the refuse water from the various dyeing establishments along its banks, and at times is entirely dry, when the water is drawn off for irrigation outside. A noble row of old plane-trees with large mulberry trees intermixed runs along one bank, and in places spring from the bed itself, nearly choking up the channel. The dirt and rubbish were the same here as in other Persian towns, and the streets as empty. In the narrow lanes you seldom meet a living thing except dogs and cats, but the activity displayed in the streets of the bazaar is in striking contrast. In the people that throng it the bazaar of Meshed differs most from that of the other Persian towns I have seen. Hadjis and merchants from all the neighbouring countries elbow the native Persians, and each nationality is easily distinguished. The Persian merchant is generally a clean well-dressed man with white silk turban, flowing robes, and long beard, unlike the officials, who generally affect European dress. This tall slight man, with delicately cut features, large dark eyes, and stately pace, is an Arab merchant from Baghdad. These two odd-looking little old men, with mouse-coloured faces, and red mark between the eyes, clad in dark monkish-looking gowns and sandals, are traders from Bombay, and, for the moment, the guests of Abass Khan, the native British agent here. They halt and salute.

me elaborately as I pass. Half a dozen Merv Turcomans, with calm, resolute air, and keeping well together, come next, with their usual sauntering step and upright carriage. They look as if they were taking stock of the goods displayed around them, and were meditating how best to effect a wholesale sweep of them. A little further on we meet some half-dozen jaunty-looking, handsome young men in dark tunics and sombre-tinted turbans, one end of the cloth stuck up cockade-wise in front, the other hanging upon the neck. One of them carries a small circular shield of iron, embossed, inlaid, engraved, and ornamented as the shield of Achilles. Held by the scabbard, and thrown carelessly over his shoulder, is an exceedingly curved Indian-looking sword, with wonderfully small, bulbous iron handle. He is an Afghan chief, accompanied by his friends. I am not acquainted with them, but they bow and smile pleasantly as they recognise my nationality.

The throng of passers-by give way to right and left, and a man appears, dressed in a garment half-frock-coat, half-tunic, of light snuff-coloured material. He wears black trousers of European cut, rather short, and shoes which allow of a view of his white stockings. On his head is the usual Persian black lambswool tiara. He keeps one hand upon the other, in front of him, as if he were handcuffed, and during his very slow walk sways his shoulders to and fro. Immediately behind him is a man bearing a large silver water-pipe; around him is a small crowd of persons somewhat similarly attired, and walking as nearly as possible like him. These are a Persian official and his attendants. He keeps his eyes on the ground, lifting them but occasionally, and affects an air of profound thought and pre-occupation, while probably he has not two ideas in his head. He is perhaps going to pay a visit to the Governor or some other high official. On such occasions the entire household turn out in their best array, and the silver water-pipe is as indispensable as the mace at a municipal state ceremony. In Persia, no one with any pretence to respectability would dream of stirring outside the door without at least four men walking behind him. My appearance with a solitary attendant—a factotum who looked after myself and my horses, and acted as cook into the bargain—created quite a scandal. The British agent was so terrified at the possible loss of national prestige that might accrue therefrom that he actually forced on me one of the soldiers who mounted guard at his residence.

The variety of coins current in this place would delight the heart of a numismatist. Besides the concourse of pilgrims who bring specimens of every Asiatic mint with them, 'finds' of old coins are frequently made in the ruins with which the whole country is filled, and contribute to the variety of the currency. Ancient Greek and Persian coins can be had here for little more than their bullion value, in abundance. I have little doubt but that rare and valuable coins might be found in the Meshed bazaar by a skilled collector. A friend of mine long resident in Persia told me that a gold coin of the time of Alexander might be found here, for a specimen of which twelve hundred pounds has been paid in Europe. I bought for two krans a Greek coin of the Bactrian kingdom, I think, as large as a shilling, with a well-executed head of Hermes on one side and a full-length figure of Hercules with his club, and a Greek inscription, on the obverse.

As I intended passing some time in Meshed, both for the sake of health and as affording me a point of vantage to obtain news from the Turcomans, I rented a house temporarily. It was a typical Persian abode. The entrance-door was set far back in a high mud wall, the recess having seats on each side, perhaps to let callers rest during the weary interval between their knocks and the opening of the door. A long passage led from the door to a paved courtyard about forty feet square, planted with a few flowers and shrubs. The side opposite the entrance was occupied by the kitchen and a large room adjoining, with five windows looking into the court. In this I took up my lodgings. It had, besides the windows on the court, doors on either side, communicating respectively with the kitchen, and with stairs on the other side. The room itself was about twenty feet wide and thirty in length, divided in the middle by two massive pillars, and the inner portion raised a few inches above the outer floor. There were deep recesses in the wall, serving as cupboards or closets. The whole interior was whitewashed. The outer part of the room between the pillars and the windows was nearly filled by a water tank with the kerb raised a few inches above the floor, and a stone pipe in the centre, from which a jet of water was occasionally played to cool the air: The tank was nearly five feet deep, and on several occasions I narrowly escaped an involuntary bath as I entered my room in moments of abstraction. The water supply of Meshed is very bad, and reeks with sulphuretted hydrogen, so that the presence of this tank in my bedroom was by no means an unmixed pleasure. Sometimes, indeed, when the water played at night from the jet and disturbed the lower depths of the pool, the stench was so unbearable that I used to have my bed carried out into the garden. Living fish were occasionally thrown in by the stream from the stone pipe, but they invariably died in a few hours, owing to the poisonous nature of the water. Besides the gases, which might readily be accounted for by the numerous cesspools through which the water supply passes in the town itself, the water seemed to be charged with mineral matters whose nature I could not determine. When I first arrived I wished to take a dose of Epsom salts, but on pouring the dose into half a tumbler of water it was almost instantly converted into a dirty white slag-mass like half-melted glass. The water had a thick and oily taste, and under ordinary circumstances would be quite undrinkable. This was all the more annoying, as hardly any other drink could be had in the place.

CHAPTER XII.

Persian obstruction—Opening communications—Turcoman heads—Persian ruins—Tarantulas and snakes—A strange drink—Kurdish castles—Beauty of mountains—A border chieftain—The Khan's kiosk—A Turcoman raid—Held to ransom—Brigandage.

I FOUND my stay at Meshed prolonged much beyond my original intentions by the action of the Persian Government. Either from fear of being held responsible in case of any accident happening to me, or out of complaisance towards the Russians, the authorities threw every obstacle in the way of my intended departure for the seat of hostilities. Immediately on my arrival, the chamberlain of the Prince Governor called on me and conveyed to me an order to proceed at once either to Shahrood or Seistan. I indignantly refused; whereupon a guard was placed over my house to prevent my setting out in any other direction. I wrote at once to Teheran to remonstrate against such treatment, and after considerable delay I succeeded, through the action of the British Minister, in getting the order revoked. No sooner was this done, however, than the principal Minister, Hussein Khan, was removed from office, and the Governor of Meshed declined to give me a passport for the frontier without receiving instructions from the new minister. This involved a fortnight's delay. At the same time I found it a very convenient place for gathering information respecting General Skobeleff's movements in the Turcoman country; and, besides, I needed rest after my illness. In spite of the continuous raids along the borders, Turcomans both of Merv and of Akhal Tekké came and went freely to and from the town.

From Shahrood I had already opened communications with Makdum Kuli Khan, the head chief of the Akhal Tekké and commander at Geok Tepé. He was much inclined to set me down as a Russian spy, as my character as a newspaper correspondent was a little beyond his comprehension, and I had taken care to repudiate all diplomatic character. A moullah, whom I got to write to the chief, mixed matters up by describing me as a major-general, and thus excited his suspicions. However, Abass Khan, the British agent in Meshed, having vouched for my nationality, the chief finally consented to meet me at Askabad, where he would judge, after a personal inspection, of the propriety of letting me advance any further. It was three months before my health had become sufficiently restored for me to think of visiting the Tekké country. I was by no means free from misgivings as to my safety among its brave but savage people, especially at such a time; but I felt too desirous of witnessing the course of hostilities around Geok Tepé to let such considerations keep me back. On November 8, I called on the Shah Zadé, as the Prince Governor of Meshed is styled, to take my leave, accompanied by Abass Khan. We traversed numerous corridors and endless arcades with only occasional signs of life in them, when the sleepy guards sprang up and presented arms with a noise apparently intended to make up for long inaction; and after climbing many of the extraordinary Persian stairs with steps two feet high, at length found ourselves in the audience chamber. Heavy purple curtains covered the entrance, but there was a superabundance of doors and windows all around the room. I never could understand how the Persians can bear the draughts from these numerous openings during the winter season.

The Prince entered a few minutes after our arrival, shoeless like ourselves, such being an essential rule of Persian etiquette. He was a handsome but somewhat heavy-looking man of five-and-thirty, and extremely courteous, as most Easterns of rank are. After a little conversation I mentioned my expedition, which the Prince treated as a piece of lunacy, but nevertheless he finally granted me the desired papers. I next asked permission to see some Turcoman heads which had been sent by the Governor of Budjnoord a short time before. His Highness carelessly replied that they were thrown around somewhere. I then backed out of his presence in Court fashion. Outside I renewed my request for a view of the heads, and was conducted to a courtyard where a company of soldiers were on guard. Some shapeless objects, looking like dirty lard bladders, were dragged out of a cellar. These were the skins of the Turcoman raiders' heads, stuffed with grass, four ugly gashes marking the place of eyes, nose, and mouth in each. I asked what had become of the noses, and a horse-laugh from the guard was my only answer. I said gravely, by way of rebuke, 'Our own heads in a few years will be in as bad a plight,' a remark which drew forth exclamations of admiration at its profound wisdom. When I had examined the heads they were tossed back into the cellar to rot or be eaten by the rats. As I walked away from the uncanny place, I could not help musing disagreeably on the signs of the times afforded by those heads coming from the direction in which I was about to set out. I felt sure that at night I should have visions of my own cranium stuffed with hay and minus the nose.

My Persian servants were greatly terrified at the idea of accompanying me among the Turcomans, and only one of them could finally be induced to come. It was with no small delight, after all these obstructions had been removed, that I ultimately left Meshed. My setting out was quite imposing. A Turcoman guide who was to accompany me to Derguez led the way; three soldiers, and as many servants, sent as a guard of honour by my friend Abass Khan, followed, after whom came my own people and horses. A dozen dervishes, and a crowd of beggars of both sexes, young and old, all bawling prayers and petitions for alms, brought up the rear. At the city gate I parted with my escort, military and mendicant, and rode away with a light heart on the road to Radcan.

Noting the peculiarities of dress as I entered the Kurd country, and how the grey felt eggshell-shaped hat of the Russian peasant gave place to black wool shakos, or turbans, worn low down over the eyes, I observed, too, how in this fertile valley the fortified villages were spread around in extraordinary numbers. As we journeyed on, it was to pass the ruins of Kakha, halting as I reached those of Toos, once the capital of North Persia, and notable for containing the tomb of the poet Ferdusi. The place is full of most interesting relics, portions of the destruction seeming to have been caused by an earthquake shock. Lying amongst the ruins I found numerous fragments of old, highly-coloured pottery, some of them displaying the *reflet métallique* so prized by the lovers of keramic ware.

I spent so much time examining the ruins of Toos that I could only ride four miles farther before darkness overtook me, and I passed the night at a small Kurdish village named Sarasiab, where a couple of rooms over the fortified gate were ceded to me. In one were sheepskins, bundles of wool, and a silk wheel; in the other were heaps of dried dung, intended for fuel, the rest of the floor being covered with cucumbers and melons.

The tarantula is very common in this valley, and, at the time of the year at which I was travelling, they are often as large as a half-grown mouse. They frequently make their way into the houses, especially at night, and, if a candle be left, a couple of them will generally be seen making their way towards it as if they were expected anxiously. They are covered with black hair, and have shining black fangs like a crab's mandibles, and about a quarter of an inch long. Their bite is considered more venomous than that of even the largest scorpions. Poisonous snakes, too, are found here. On the day I quitted Sarasiab, my guide killed one of a beautiful silvery white, with deep orange longitudinal stripes. The head indicated its poisonous character sufficiently. My guide considered the killing of this snake as a very happy omen for the day's journey. Eight miles from Sarasiab we stopped to breakfast by some rapidly flowing streams of clear cold water which form a small pond close to their source, and afterwards fall into the Keshef Rood. The pond is literally crammed with fish and fresh-water crabs. The latter are of a delicate purple colour, and exactly the shape of sea crabs. According to popular tradition these streams gushed from the rock at a touch of Ali's thumb. A native also informed me that the pond was unfathomable, though the bottom was plainly visible at a depth of ten or twelve feet.

The Kurds of this valley I found were very civil and

obliging. The great man in the town of Radcan gave quite a reception in my honour, entertaining me with tobacco and tea, during the repast displaying his knowledge of foreign affairs by informing his guests that an attempt had been made to blow up the Emperor of Russia with strychnine! My host was full of traditional lore touching the district. The old town of Radcan, the ruins of which stand about a mile to the south of the modern one, had been, he said, removed to its present site some hundreds of years ago, owing to an epidemic caused by certain foul drains and cesspools in the neighbourhood. One would have thought it easier to remove the cesspools than the town and population, but they do things differently in Persia. The old town, he further informed me, was the only one in the entire district which escaped the ravages of Zenghis Khan's army on its westward march.

During the dinner which followed I was introduced to a table drink quite as odd in its way as the Homeric draught compounded for the delectation of the 'divine Machaon,' which we are told was composed of a 'large measure of the Pramnian wine' flavoured with goat's-milk cheese and sprinkled with flour. The Kurdish beverage consisted of sour thick milk diluted with water, highly flavoured with salt and black pepper, and thickly strewn on the surface with finely-grated mint leaf. It was contained in a huge bowl of tinned copper, standing among the dishes, which were, of course, on the floor. Each person helped himself at pleasure by means of a large, curiously-shaped spoon of carved boxwood, which floated in the bowl, and was used in common by the company.

In the afternoon I rode with my host to visit an old conical roofed building that had taken my notice, to find the edifice most interesting in its nature. It had originally been ornamented with enamelled tiles of a beautiful deep blue. The building had been much injured by an earthquake shock; its original purpose I am at a loss to guess. My Kurd host was of opinion that it was the palace of an early Mussulman sovereign; the inhabitants that it was a hunting lodge.

Leaving Radcan, we began to ascend the ridge which separates the head waters of the Atterek from those of the Keshef Rood. I passed the night in a small village, where I was struck by the peculiar lamps in use. They resembled the chalices used in Roman Catholic worship, but were of copper tinned over, and filled with oil extracted from the *Palma christi* bean—the castor oil, in fact, of commerce. In the morning we resumed our way along the banks of the Atterek. At intervals upon the heights were the remains of old Kurdish castles, while one village, with its houses clustering round a fortified hill, seemed to take one back to the middle ages. Our journey was not without its scares, suspicious-looking horsemen watching us from a distance. The obstinacy of one's horses adds not a little to the difficulties of travelling in these mountainous countries. Once you are off his back, a horse considers himself his own master, and declines to be led. It takes no inconsiderable amount of trouble to make him proceed, especially up a mountain side. When one has been accustomed to much riding across plains, there is nothing so trying as going up a hill on one's own legs. The custom of the country is to hold on by your horse's tail, and thus get dragged over the mountain.

We overtook a caravan from Nishapur, of about fifty men and women, driving asses and mules. The men, with their voluminous turbans, closely resembled the Kurds of Kurdistan proper—much more so than those I had seen in the Meshed Valley. They have a very bad reputation, my guide told me. A solitary wayfarer, meeting such a caravan, would be certain of being pillaged, if not murdered. However, they let us alone, probably in view of our formidable armament, though they cast longing eyes at my saddle-bags, which their Oriental imaginations doubtless painted as crammed with gold tomans. Next morning, at daybreak as usual, we had to cross the Allah Akbar (God is great) range, which we got over after five hours' hard work. Near the top is a shallow valley, where graves are numerous, and the piles of little stones placed by the passers-by flank the road at short intervals. The graves are those of the murdered travellers who have perished during centuries.

From the mountain top the entire expanse of Persian border territory lay like a map at my feet. The summit on which I stood is, I think, about six thousand feet above the level of the sea. Twenty miles away was the ridge which divides the Derguez; far away to the right were the dim hills of Kelat, so far off that I should have deemed them clouds if not otherwise informed. The colours of these mountains were brighter than I had supposed possible in nature. The lights were all rose and amber, and the shadows of aërial lapis lazuli tint. Light and shade in the form of *chiar'oscuro* there were none. It was the opposition of colour. It made one believe in Raffaelle painting a red shadow to a roseleaf in sunshine. Backing up the view was a vast spread of vague distance reaching away to the horizon—the dim, terrible Turcoman waste over which lay my road. At the height at which I stood the scene was panoramic. Hill and dale, rock and plain, stood out with a stereoscopic distinctness which recalled the luminous image of a camera lucida. Camel trains wound like worms along the thread-like roads. Here and there buffaloes were ploughing; and parties of horsemen rode to and fro. There were all the evidences of life, save that of sound, as we gazed over the huge, silent expanse. As I rode down, my thoughts were not brightened by the appearance of two horsemen, each with a Turcoman's head slung at his saddle-bow. They were carrying their ghastly trophies to the Prince Governor of Meshed, as a present from the Khan of Derguez. Evidently the Turcomans could hardly be more ferocious savages than the people among whom I was sojourning. Riding across the plain in this frame of mind, I reached Muhammedabad, the capital of the Derguez, that evening.

I was courteously received by the Khan, who in conversation laughed at the notion, entertained by many of the peasants, of a Turcoman invasion of the Derguez in case the Russians should be defeated at Geok Tepé. He seemed to think he and his people were quite capable of protecting themselves against any force the Turcomans could bring in this respect. 'Pshaw,' said he, 'with five thousand of even my own cavalry I would undertake to sweep the Akhal Tekké from end to end.' The Khan, though nominally an official of the Shah, was constantly engaged in lifting the cattle and capturing the heads of his Tekké neighbours, though these amenities seemed to make no serious obstacle to the intercourse constantly going on between his subjects and the nomads. Small parties were continually sent out to plunder, and a large part of the Khan's income was derived from these expeditions. Heads to be sent to Teheran, much as wolves' heads were sent to the old Saxon kings of England as an acceptable tribute, and prisoners to be held for ransom, were booty as eagerly sought as the cattle and sheep of the Tekkés.

A few days after my visit I was invited to accompany the Khan on a pleasure excursion to an enclosed garden of his, some distance from the city. A crowd of servants were sent to escort me, in Persian style, to the place of meeting at the city gates. I found the chief riding slowly outside the walls, escorted by about thirty men. I soon learned the importance of this precaution, which seemed at first a mere formality. The Governor had also several led horses with him, all wearing heavy silver collars set with blue and red stones, to distinguish them as being reserved for his own mounting. The ornament lavished on the trappings of his horses was in striking contrast to the plainness of his own dress, which was hardly distinguishable from that of his principal attendants, external show being considered womanly. After riding round in the plain for about an hour, we made for the Khan's grove. There was a kiosk in the middle, in which a carpet was spread, and the Khan, some of his brothers and nephews, and myself, sat down. Excessively strong green tea was served to us, according to the invariable custom. The requisites for the meal, like the ordinary travelling equipage of the chief, were carried with us by one of the servants in two cylinders, slung at each side of his saddle like kettle-drums, and covered with embroidered crimson cloth. A round case of the same colour, slung on his back like a Kurd buckler, contained the tin plates and dishes. We amused ourselves for a while in the kiosk by scanning the country with field-glasses belonging to the Khan, and by inspecting the fire-arms, of which he had a most miscellaneous collection, picked up I know not how or where. Shooting at a mark was also tried, and the Khan made half-a-dozen very good shots at about a hundred yards distance.

We were riding leisurely homewards, after dinner,

when a mounted trooper dashed up and announced that the Turcomans were out and sweeping off the cattle from the plain. We immediately noticed peasants driving their cattle with frantic haste towards the town, and presently we were able to make out the raiders, who numbered about a hundred and fifty, wheeling in scattered groups and circling round like falcons. The nearest were not a mile from us. The Khan issued a few rapid orders, and sent half-a-dozen messengers to carry them in different directions, and then we pushed briskly towards the city. In a few minutes beacon columns of smoke were shooting up from the watch-towers around, summoning all the scattered retainers of the Khan to mount and ride to the city at once. Within an hour about six hundred troops were gathered in the town. I could now understand the meaning of the endless field-towers and walls which I had thought extravagantly numerous at first sight. The Khan despatched between three and four hundred men after the marauders, who had swept off sixty oxen and over a hundred sheep, and were on their way to the desert with their spoil. The Tekkés, however, had a good start, and while a few men drove the cattle off by short cuts impracticable for cavalry, the main body showed fight and covered their retreat successfully. The pursuers, finding small chance of anything but hard knocks, returned after some skirmishing, having captured four horses from the invaders. This was a large party for a Tekké foray, twenty or thirty being the more usual number in these districts. The Khan seemed to take the whole affair as an everyday occurrence, but it gave me a lively impression of the insecurity of life and property in this border territory.

Indeed, until I came to this district I had no adequate idea of the real state of things. Within a few days of my arrival three more or less successful raids were made by the Turcomans nearly up to the gates of the capital of the province. One can scarce venture half a mile, in some cases not even so far, from the fortified villages, without risking capture by the seemingly ever-present Turcoman bands. How grazing or any other kind of farming can be carried on passes my comprehension, even though herds and tillers be protected by the watch-towers which stand over the plain like ninepins in a skittle alley. Making and repulsing raids seemed the daily and never-failing occupation of the able-bodied male population on both sides. At the time of my visit there were in Muhammedabad half-a-dozen Turcomans, captured at different periods, and awaiting redemption. They were all heavily fettered, each having an iron collar round his neck, and a hoop of the same material encircling his waist. From both depended chains, composed of links a foot long, like those worn by French galley-slaves, and attached to the wrists and ankles. These irons are worn night and day. One of the prisoners, a stalwart young man, had been in captivity over two years, and although only thirty tomans (twelve pounds sterling) were demanded for his ransom, none of his people had come forward to pay the amount. Another, a native of the town, had been caught by the Turcomans many years previously, and had settled and married among the Akhal Tekké. In his capacity of naturalised Turcoman he had taken part in a foray into Persian territory, and, having been captured, was held to ransom like the others.

In conversation with the Khan, as to who was responsible for these forays, he did not seem to consider that any alteration need be made. He acknowledged that the Turcoman raids inflicted considerable loss on his own people, but he thought, on the whole, the latter managed to be quits by return expeditions. Just before my arrival in Muhammedabad, the Derguezli had made a sweep of about fifteen thousand sheep, which were being sold at eight or ten francs a head. In fact, one of the Khan's followers assured me that his chief would lose at least three thousand tomans of his income were this brigandage suppressed.

CHAPTER XIII.

A Persian passion play—The theatre—The drama—An apology for grief—A stage combat—A stirring scene—Sanguinary performance—A religious dance—Convenient pigtails—Doing penance—Displays of grief—The drama murdered.

WITH the month of Moharrem came the Mussulman services usually celebrated during that period; and every day a body of professional artists gave a public representation of the religious drama founded on the massacre of Imam Hussein, or, rather, of one scene of the play, the entirety of which extends over several days, every incident being acted in the fullest possible detail. By special favour, I received an invitation from the Khan to be present, as some extra acting was about to take place. Near the scene of the performance I was formally received by half-a-dozen *ferashes*, or palace servants, each bearing in his hand a long peeled stick, by whom I was conducted to the Khan. This official recognition was necessary, as otherwise offence might have been taken at my presence.

Crossing the open space which served as a stage, I found the Khan, together with his male relatives and principal officers, seated on a slightly raised platform of earth and brick at one side of the old town gate. The market-place outside, flanked by the caravanserai, constituted the theatre. Some three thousand spectators were present. To our left were the women, four rows being seated on the ground, and the remainder standing

behind, wrapped from head to foot in their mantles of
indigo-dyed calico, and looking like so many conventional
stage spectres when blue fire is lit at the wings. Opposite
them, and similarly arranged, were the men, for the
most part clad in the lemon-coloured sheepskin great
coat characteristic of the border populations. Here and
there were the red orange tunics of those who seemed
insensible to the rather chill air, and above all was a
sea of sunburnt bearded faces and huge grenadier hats
of black and brown sheep's wool. Still further back
behind them, perched on the top of the ruinous mud
front of the caravanserai, were about a hundred women
of the better class—among them the Khan's family.
Outside the open space were many mounted Turcomans,
gun at back, the prong of the forked rest sticking a
foot beyond the muzzle, and giving them the air of
mounted hay-makers. In the midst of the arena stood
two poplar poles, six feet apart, a stout camel-hair horse
rope reaching from one to the other at a height of four
feet above the ground. Close by was a heap of stout
osier rods, such as are used in administering the bastinado. At some distance sat a white-turbaned, long-
bearded moullah, on a tall throne approached by three
steps. There was a kind of wooden platform, such as
Easterns sleep on in the open air during hot weather,
on which stood a very prosaic-looking arm-chair. In
the latter sat a pompous-looking person, robed in
Cashmere shawls, and wearing an enormous turban of
the old Kurdish pattern, which may be seen to-day on
the heads of Sheik Obeidullah's followers about Bayazid.
A number of similarly attired men, and two boys of
about twelve years of age, sat upon a long wooden bench
opposite. With them was a man wearing female attire,
and closely veiled; but he had apparently forgotten to

take off a pair of enormous brown leather jack-boots. This was the third day of the play, and as I had never seen the text of it I was necessarily completely at sea as to the particular episode in the tragedy which was about to be acted.

The main idea represented was the struggle between what are now Shiia and Sunni— the justice or otherwise of the precedency of Omar to Ali in the Khalifat. As well as I could make out the sense of the dialogue, which was spoken in Jagatai Tartar, the man in the armchair on the platform was Hussein, and an individual in a spiked helmet was his standard-bearer and champion, and an upholder of Ali's reputation. He sang, or rather chanted, in a doleful tone, several lengthy expressions of his sentiments, finally ascending the platform and kneeling down to receive the benediction of the person in the chair, who knelt in his turn to receive that of the man in the helmet. Then the latter mounted a horse brought in to the rolling of a drum, and made pretence of departing on a journey, and Hussein withdrew from the stage. Meantime two new parties arrived on horseback, one of whom was evidently the typical Sunnite, and the other his chief executioner and right-hand man. The typical Sunnite issued several orders in a voice pitched like that of a field-officer commanding a battalion movement, and general dismay seemed to supervene, in the midst of which the helmeted champion returned from his journey and defied the executioner to single combat. Previously to engaging in the strife, he repeatedly embraces two small boys, who are apparently closely related to him. His remarks to them called forth universal expressions of regret from the audience. This constituted one of the most curious features of the scene. The women uttered short, snapping howls, which, coming from behind the closely-wrapped mantles of so many hundreds, produced precisely the effect of a burst of laughter on the part of the audience of a European theatre at some culminating burlesque absurdity. In fact, when I afterwards heard sounds of merriment from the same gathering, the vocal expression of opposite emotions seemed to be identical. The male spectators gave no audible sign of emotion, nor, apparently, did they feel any, though it was considered to be in good taste, not only as a tribute to the moral of the scene, but also as a compliment to the actors, to produce one's handkerchief and apply it to the eyes. The Khan had a large white damask napkin, evidently specially prepared for the occasion; but I caught him once, at an excessively tragical moment, and while holding his apology for tears in front of his face, making some remarks in an undertone to his brother, at which they both chuckled in a scandalous manner. While waiting for the conclusion of the long dialogue between the knight of the spiked helmet and the executioner, we were entertained with the spectacle of a man beaten to death with rods, the most curious element in which was that the men who made believe to whip the life out of the culprit were the very same who every day discharged such functions in reality; and the rods used were of the very same size and kind as those employed for the bastinado. This episode brought to the front a feature of Oriental manners which few Europeans have an opportunity of witnessing, viz., the manner in which a wife shows her respect and affection for her husband. The pseudo-female with the jack-boots turned out to be the wife of the man who was being beaten. Previous to his being tied to the whipping-post, she came forward and prostrated herself before him, her forehead touching the ground. Then she walked round him, kissing the back of his shoulders as she passed, again prostrating herself on coming to the front. There were some other examples of marital etiquette during the play, and in all of them it seemed to be the proper thing for the lady to make the entire circuit of her husband before coming to a halt before him. This, however, was mere by-play pending the advent of the great event, viz. the combat and subsequent execution.

The executioner, the villain of the piece, stood over six feet high, notwithstanding that his small head was, apparently in consequence of some spinal disease, set deeply between his colossal shoulders. He wore a pair of long buff leather boots, opening out in bell-fashion above the knee, and which in Europe would be considered as essentially 'stagey.' Here they form part of every-day costume. A red cotton handkerchief was tied around his head, not turban-wise, but rather as if it were applied as a bandage for some cranial injury, and coming down low on his beetled brows. Even without the circular brass Kurd shield and curved scimitar, he was as truculent-looking a person as I have ever seen on or off the stage. Shiia dramatic justice could not for a moment allow that such a person could be a match for a follower of Ali, so accordingly he summoned to his aid three other equally objectionable-looking personages, each very like himself, and thereupon a 'free fight' commenced.

One of the most interesting features of this scene was the illustration it afforded of the use of the small Kurdish buckler and curved scimitar in combat. Of Eastern races, I believe the Kurds are the most addicted to this rather primitive system of combat. Indeed, except among

L

the Kurds and some Afghan refugees at Meshed and Kuchan, I never saw the shield borne as an adjunct of actual warfare. We were treated to all the various arts and devices used in such combats, and merely as a specimen of attack and defence it was well worth seeing. Then there were various attempts on the part of the unarmed assailants of this champion of Hussein to trip him up with a rope, or entangle him in its folds by running round him. He ultimately vanished, as if by magic, below the surface of the ground, into a previously prepared hole which we had not hitherto perceived. This hole, I believe, represented a well, in which the real hero took refuge. Attempts were now made to smoke him out by stuffing lighted brooms with long handles into the cavity, but, this device failing, he was ultimately dragged out by means of ropes, and brought before the judgment-seat of the wicked individual, who, in no whispered tones, gave orders for his instant execution. The captive hero was thereupon bound Mazeppa-wise upon the back of a horse, and, having been led several times round the arena, ultimately arrived at the scene of punishment. Taken from the back of the horse, he was dragged by the heels a good fifty yards, to the gate of the caravanserai. On this occasion his coat of chain mail must have stood himself and his garments in good stead, the ground being in no wise like a skating rink, but, on the contrary, strewn with stones and broken earthenware. In a few moments he made his appearance on the top of the caravanserai among the ladies assembled there, surrounded by guards and accompanied by the executioner, and during a quarter of an hour pleaded for his life. This was excellently done, and drew forth a large amount of grief, as before, from the women, also bringing the men's pocket-handkerchiefs into requisition. He was ultimately thrown down, and we could see curved daggers brandished over him.

The system of execution here is to cut the throat with a dagger, and then sever the head from the body with the same instrument. The actors so managed that, while the body and legs of the victim were left in view, the head was just out of sight. The convulsive struggling of the limbs was admirably imitated, and then, the real man being drawn back, a lay figure was thrust forward, exhibiting the severed bleeding neck. This was immediately afterwards lowered to the ground by ropes, and dragged back to the centre of the ground—still struggling and kicking. Within the headless lay figure was a little boy, who gave the requisite movement to the limbs. The figure, still twitching in a most horrid manner, was hung up on the centre of the cord extending between the two poles fixed in the ground; and the climax of the entertainment, the disembowelling of the body, commenced. In the breast and stomach of the figure had been stowed away the lungs, heart, and entrails of a freshly-killed sheep. The executioner, with his dagger cut the figure open, and the still bleeding viscera were dragged out one by one with expressions of savage glee, and flung into the midst of the space. With this sanguinary performance the day's acting came to an end, and the spectators, who up to that moment had preserved the greatest order, rushed round, and I lost sight of the mangled remains. The acting was continued on the morrow, and during several succeeding days, but the whole of the lengthy play could not be performed, there being no one in the town rich enough, or at any rate disposed, to pay the expenses for any longer period. Up to that time the Khan had defrayed them.

Immediately on the termination of the acting, a still

more curious performance, in the shape of religious dancing, commenced. Twelve boys, varying in age from eight to fourteen years, clad in long tunics of clean printed chintz, and having dark-coloured handkerchiefs on their necks, which crossed upon the breast and were tied behind the waist, threw off their sheepskin hats, retaining only the little tight-fitting skull-cap. Some of these boys were wonderfully handsome. The expression of their faces was altogether feminine. In fact, dressed as they were, in printed calico frocks, they might easily have passed for so many pretty little girls. In each hand was carried a circular piece of wood, about four inches in diameter and two inches thick. Eight of them formed into a circle around the other four, who chanted something relating to Ali, Hussein, and Hassan. They faced slowly round one after the other, striking their pieces of wood together like Spanish castanets, and extending their arms at full length, now in front of the forehead, now behind the head, in cadence with the rhythm of the chant. In two or three minutes the chant quickened, and the boys commenced a kind of waltzing step, turning completely round in four movements, and accompanying each with a clap of the castanets. After completing the entire circle they again relapsed into a march, in due time resuming the waltzing, if I may give it that name. While the children were thus dancing close to where we sat with the Khan, further away the men had engaged in their own calisthenics. Some sixty had formed in line, each grasping with his left hand the waist-sash of the man beside him; his right hand remaining free. The chain thus formed started off in quick time, the man on the right flank leading. Each dancer made an oblique step with his left foot, forward and to the left, supplementing it with a hop on the same leg. Then came an oblique step with the right foot, forward and to the right, with another hop. At each step and hop the dancer smote his breast with his right hand, shouting 'Hussein! Hassan!' Each threw his body forward and appeared to be dragging the next one after him. The whole performance gave one the idea of a kind of mad can-can, in such quick time that the dancers could scarcely find breath to vociferate with sufficient rapidity the names of the two blessed Imams in whose honour they were thus exerting themselves. As each dancer became exhausted he fell out, but new-comers constantly appended themselves to the tail of the line that circled round the arena which had previously served as a stage. To all appearance the same set of men were dancing all the while, for the main phalanx remained unbroken for hours. Long after the sun had set, and I had retired to my lodgings, even at ten o'clock in the evening, rhythmic, muffled shouts of 'Hussein! Hassan!' smote my ear.

On the next day of the performance there was the usual quantity of tedious speechifying and doleful declamation, the great feature being the single combat between Abass, the standard-bearer of Hussein, and one of the enemy. Abass is supposed to lose both his arms during the fight, and continues the conflict holding the sword between his teeth. After the acting came dancing such as that already described. I omitted, however, to mention that the younger of the boys who danced had, reaching from the centre of their shaved crowns to the napes of their necks, slender plaited tails of hair, in fact, regular 'pigtails.' These, I believe, are the appendages by which the angel Gabriel will seize them should they in the journey from earth to heaven slip from the narrow path across the bridge of Al-Sirat, and be in danger of tumbling into hell. Among the elder boys this tail was not to be seen, being replaced by a bushy tuft of hair. The most peculiar portion of the after ceremonies consisted of the self-inflicted penance of some of the more devout members of the audience. Half-a-dozen persons, two of whom were powerfully built men, the remainder boys of sixteen or eighteen, drew close to where we were sitting, and, squatting in a circle, hastily stripped off their garments to the waist. Then, to the cry of 'Hussein! Hassan!' they commenced forcibly striking their breasts with their palms. In a short time a kind of frenzy seemed to gain upon them, and an instrument of torture was produced. It consisted of a short iron handle, terminating in a ring, from which hung half-a-dozen iron chains, each about eight or nine inches long. Each link of these chains was at least an inch and a half in length. The instrument was, in fact, an iron scourge. When the chant had become fast and furious, one of the men seized on the scourge, and, bobbing it a few times in front of his face, began to lash himself with it over the shoulders so quickly that the eye could scarce follow his movements. When each had borne as much of this self-infliction as he could he passed the instrument to his next neighbour, who repeated the operation. The shoulders of one of the youths were torn and bloody, from the violence with which he punished himself. All this is done by way of expressing sorrow for the death of the blessed Imam Hussein, who, together with Ali, seems, in the minds of the Shiia Mussulmans, to have thrown Mahomet completely into the background. This style of acting was carried to such an extremity that the Khan was obliged to give the signal for ending the play.

The last day being that in which, for Mussulmans, all the interest centres, the market-place in which the previous scenes had been enacted was quite inadequate to contain the concourse of spectators. Every shop in the town was closed, and men, women, and children flocked to a wide space entirely without the town walls, where the necessary preparations had been made. As before, the women occupied the left, the men the right hand of the small pavilion in which the Khan and his friends sat. These acts, to uninitiated eyes and ears, are all very much the same except in their main incident, which always seems to be illustrative of the killing of some person or persons. In this case Hussein and one of his children are the victims. The curious features of the scene are the introduction of the Frankish Ambassador, who pleads for the life of the Imam, and who is accompanied by a lion. The sensation produced is tremendous, and great bearded men weep in downright earnest over the woes of Hussein. In the course of the act the Khan had two fresh pocket-handkerchiefs brought to him wherewith to dry his tears. In very many instances among the men, it was easy to see that the expressions of extreme grief were entirely simulated; but there were many whose genuine emotion could not be doubted. Out in this far-off quarter the people have but little notion of what a Frankish Ambassador looks like. In this instance he wore ordinary Persian garb, qualified by a crimson sash across his left shoulder. With regard to the appearance of a lion, the stage manager seemed to be even still more astray. While the principal actors on horseback were caracolling to and fro, and declaiming the well-known phrases with regard to the reverence due to the grandson of the Prophet, I had been noticing an odd-looking object creeping about the centre of the arena on all-fours. It looked like an ape with a long white shirt on, who had fallen foul of a pot of red paint and smeared his garments with it. This object kept gathering up dust and throwing it on its head, in Oriental token of grief. I was on inquiry informed that it was a lion, which, together with the Frankish Ambassador, had come to be converted to Islamism by witnessing the sublime attitude of the Imam when about to die.

There is no question but that the tragedy is full of pathos and elevating sentiment, though in the hands of the wretched itinerant actors who travel out into these districts the drama is murdered as ruthlessly as is Hussein himself. Before this final act of the drama commenced, a scene was enacted which forcibly recalled to my mind what I had seen at home. The conductor of the theatrical representations, clothed in a long chintz gown, got up on a kind of table and addressed the assembled multitude, reminding them of the blessed Imams and of himself and his company likewise. The Khan had paid the actors the sum of twenty krans (francs) per diem during the ten days of the performances, but the audience were also expected to contribute their share.

CHAPTER XIV.

Fresh obstacles—Taken in ambush—Fall of Geok Tepé—The Russian advance—The Tejend swamp—Objects on the march—Skobeleff's contribution—Invited to Merv—The Russian agent.

On leaving Meshed all obstacles to my penetrating into the Turcoman country seemed to have been removed. I was in communication with Makdum Kuli Khan, the Akhal Tekké commander, and felt little doubt about overcoming any scruples he might still entertain about receiving me into his fortress. The Prince Governor of Meshed had given me a formal passport to proceed, and I fully expected to find myself, in a very few weeks at furthest, in Geok Tepé. Persian diplomacy, however, is hard to fathom, and Russian agents, who thought I intended to take an active share in the defence of the beleaguered fortress, raised up obstacles which kept me over two months in the Derguez. The Khan treated me with the greatest courtesy, and during my stay invited me to accompany him on a most interesting expedition to Lutfabad, the capital of the outlying Turcoman district of the Attok, situated on the edge of the great plain; but he refused to let me pass the frontier, and a guard was placed to watch my movements.

At last, however, I was allowed to start on my long-delayed journey. The secret of the matter was that the Russians had by this time completed the investment of the Tekké stronghold, and their agents were now perfectly indifferent to my arrival. I started from Muhammedabad about January 16, and proceeded to Durangar. News had come in of two sorties of the garrison of Geok Tepé on the 9th and 10th. The plans of the Tekkés had been betrayed to the enemy, and, in consequence, the first sortie was repulsed with loss. On the 10th, almost the whole Tekké force made a desperate attack on the advanced Russian works, and succeeded in storming three of the four entrenchments which had been thrown up in front of the gates of the town at about a thousand yards' distance. Two breech-loading field-pieces, and several prisoners, fell into the hands of the besieged, who cut the throats of the unfortunate captives shortly afterwards. This partial success, however, had no further results. Reinforcements were reported to be on the way to the front from Bami, where the bulk of the Russian forces were stationed, and it was evident that the final struggle was close at hand. Before the lines of investment were completed, a large body of cavalry had left the town, and were hovering about between Geok Tepé and Askabad. This force was not unoccupied in the meantime, owing to a characteristic event. The Khan of Kuchan, thinking the moment a favourable one for doing a stroke of business on his own account, while the Tekkés were occupied with the defence of their stronghold, sent out a *chappow* of a hundred horsemen to seize whatever corn, cattle, or horses they could find in the outlying Turcoman villages. The Tekké warriors outside, however, got notice of the intended visit, and ambushed their Kuchan invaders so successfully that not a man escaped, sixty being killed and forty made prisoners.

This affair, which took place two days after the sortie from Geok Tepé, of course did not diminish the danger of the journey before me, but it would never have done to turn back after having come so far, so I pushed on to

Kaltachenar, the last village acknowledging the Persian authority in that direction, and not far from Askabad. Not deeming it safe to trust myself in the plain, where I was equally liable to fall in with Russian scouting parties or Tekké warriors, I kept along the slopes of the mountain chain, though travelling there was very fatiguing to the horses. Besides my two servants, an escort of six or seven Derguez troopers accompanied me, but at such a time the utmost caution was needed. Early on the 24th we ascended the top of the Markov mountain, which towers some six thousand feet over the Tekké plain, and is not over twelve miles from Geok Tepé. With my double field-glass I could easily make out the lines of the Turcoman fortress, and the general position of its besiegers, but I was too far off to be able to make notes of details. I could plainly see, by the smoke of the guns and the movements of the combatants, that the attack had begun in earnest, and I watched its result with intense anxiety. The Russian assault was directed against the southerly wall of the fortifications, and, after what was apparently a desperate conflict there, it was evident that they had forced their way. A crowd of horsemen began to ride in confusion from the other side of the town, and spread in flight over the plain. Immediately afterwards, a mass of fugitives of every class showed that the town was being abandoned by its inhabitants. The Turcoman fortress had fallen, and all was over with the Akhal Tekkés, so we hastily turned our horses back to Kaltachenar. Crowds of fugitives from the captured town were already streaming in as I arrived, full of details of the struggle. Kaltachenar was evidently no safe place for me to stop in, nor was anything to be gained by remaining there, so with all speed we made our way on to Askabad on the following morning. This, however, was evidently no better, even had it offered any shelter. The Cossacks were scouring the plain in pursuit of the fugitives, and reconnoitring the country. I therefore hurried on at once, and indeed none too soon, for a Russian scouting party entered the place the same day.

At Lutfabad I learned that the scouting party which had entered Askabad so soon after my departure was composed of Yamud Turcomans, some two thousand of whom were in the Russian service as irregular cavalry. Though akin in race to the defenders of Yenghi Sheher, these Turcomans showed the utmost readiness to serve the invader against them. In fact they seemed delighted with the chance which General Skobeleff's campaign afforded them of paying off old scores with their hitherto independent neighbours. This place, however, was not left long without a more formidable Russian garrison than the Yamud scouts. A regular force of five thousand men, with sixteen guns, followed quickly, and not only occupied the town, but immediately commenced rebuilding it for permanent possession. This completed the conquest of the Akhal Tekké country, the fertile portion of which was now almost entirely under Russian domination. Makdum Kuli Khan, with the bulk of the fugitive cavalry from Geok Tepé, retreated towards the Tejend swamp.

Meanwhile the direst confusion prevailed throughout the country. The Tekkés who had escaped from Geok Tepé were everywhere robbing and murdering. The Russian pursuing parties were also active, and for me at least were scarcely less dangerous. Moreover, the moss-troopers of Derguez, and the Kurds from Kuchan, were abroad like flocks of sea-gulls in troubled waters, seeking what they could pick up, and mercilessly harrying the unarmed fugitives from Geok Tepé especially. There was no time to be lost, however, if I were ever to get to Merv, and I quitted Lutfabad on the day after my arrival there. I left my baggage behind, as I only intended to reconnoitre the road. My escort, as a matter of course, was furnished by the Khan, and I was to give them a message for him whenever they and I parted; they would not venture to plunder me, at least openly, though, as may be gathered from what has been already said, they were all trained robbers. We rode rapidly past a couple of villages, and reached Dergana, where the elders received us with the greatest deference. A large felt carpet was spread for our use, and we were regaled with a breakfast of bread, melons, and strong green tea. Leaving Dergana, we passed on through Abiverd to Kaka, from whence I made two journeys into the Tejend swamp, to find it a treacherous expanse haunted by wild boars and leopards, with an occasional tiger, and so dangerous that horses and men were often swallowed up in its depths while attempting its passage by night. Being convinced that it was useless to attempt a journey in that direction, I hurried back to Lutfabad, after two days' absence. Here I got my escort together, and, having stopped one night only, left at daybreak with all my baggage. I heard subsequently that Skobeleff and his escort arrived in the town the same day, so that my escape was again a close one.

Taking the same direction, and passing Shillingan and the Turcoman settlement of Makdum, we halted for the night at Kosgun, another Turcoman colony, in the ruins of an old tower. Early next morning we made for Kelat. The track lay along the foot of steep, almost overhanging earth-bluffs, under whose shade a wide stretch of gravel and large boulders showed the extent and violence of the winter torrents that come down from the mountains. The raised spots in the bed of the dry river, as well as its banks, were overgrown with thorns, huge reeds, and a high grass like the pampas grass of South America. At times the jungle was so thick that it was with much ado we were able to force our way through. Jackals and foxes started up before us in such spots, and once a leopard, or something very like one, showed himself for a moment. Snakes, mostly of a venomous kind, glided across our track every moment, and coveys of partridges were constantly springing up almost under our horses' feet. The red-legged partridge was the most common, but there was also abundance of the royal partridge, a bird equal in size to a small turkey, and occasionally we saw braces of a small ashen grey species, with yellow legs. No other birds were to be seen except very large black eagles, which soared high above our heads. Many of the tree-trunks along the dry river-bed were strangely transformed by the combined sun's heat and occasional moisture. The old trunks were literally charred, or rather baked, to the blackness and hardness of coal, while still standing erect. At first I thought they had been blasted by lightning, but on closer examination they showed no signs of splintering. They were lignite, formed in this place by the heat of the sun, and the fact may be worth noting by geologists, in connection with the theory of coal-formations.

In the deserted town of Khivabad, a city of ruins guarded by almost perfect fortifications, I found among the streets and houses a species of giant hemlock, with great bulbous joints on the stem. At those points where the broad bases of the petioles join them is to be found a quantity of snuff-coloured, clammy matter, which my guides informed me is eaten by the people of the locality, and produces an effect like alcoholic intoxication. It is probably the pollen of the flowers which has lodged at the joints of the stem and leaf. The town was built by Nadir Shah, and upon his death the inhabitants, by whom it had been forcibly colonised, went off *en masse* to their former homes.

Our next halt was at Archingan, and the next day we reached Kelat-i-Nadri, a place with its surrounding of snow-covered mountains and inaccessibility which recalled the Happy Valley of Rasselas. It is regularly garrisoned by a body of Persian troops, and contains a fort, the residence of the commandant. This place afforded me excellent opportunities for watching the Russian plans. I could hear of Skobeleff's movements, my information being supplied by Tekké refugees. Among other things I learned that he was forcing the Tekkés to return to their homes. He also, I was informed, ordered the women to deliver up their gold and silver ornaments as a war contribution. The Turcoman women, however humble, all possess an immense quantity of such trinkets, and a Tekké told me he had himself seen a pile of them heaped up on two carpets to a height considerably greater than that of an ordinary man. Whatever truth was in these statements—and they were confirmed by several witnesses—everything indicated that Skobeleff was determined to make thorough work of the conquest of the Akhal Tekkés.

My movements, I soon found out, were not left entirely to my own discretion in Kelat, any more than they had been in Meshed or Muhammedabad. The Khan politely invited me to lodge at his palace, where I was completely under surveillance, and I perceived quickly that he was by no means decided as to the propriety of letting me go. It was absolutely impossible to leave the valley without a pass from the Khan, as the two gorges which led from it were entirely closed by the forts at their entrances, and no ingress or egress was permitted without his order. About February 20, I was disagreeably surprised to see Dufour, the renegade Nihilist to whom I have already alluded, ride past the gate. He now appeared in the character of a Russian agent in Kelat, where he had formerly resided for some time. In this capacity, as I afterwards learned, one of his first steps was to ask the Khan to arrest me and keep me from going to Merv. The Khan declined, but promised, I believe, to keep a watch on my movements. Dufour left in the course of two days, and I determined to anticipate any measures he might take for having me arrested by following him at once. The Khan gave me permission to depart with an escort, which was in reality a guard, and on February 25 I started back to Kaka.

Before leaving Kelat-i-Nadri, Makdum Kuli Khan had sent me word of his intention to leave the banks of the Tejend with the forces he still commanded, and to fall back towards Merv, which, by the way, is not a city, but a collection of settlements. There, in conjunction with the Mervli, he proposed constructing a new stronghold similar to that of Yengi Sheher or Geok Tepé; and he invited me to the feast and ceremonies with which its foundation was to be celebrated. I was very desirous of accepting his invitation, but there were some important points to be first taken into account. It is the established custom among the Turcomans, on the arrival of a distinguished stranger, such as I should undoubtedly be considered if I accepted the chief's invitation, to overwhelm him with gifts of horses, rich carpets, and valuable weapons, entirely regardless of his own wishes. To refuse a present would be a deadly insult—enough to convert the would-be donor into an inveterate and implacable enemy. This would seem a trifling difficulty, but it must be remembered that in return for such generosity the givers expect, and, indeed, require, presents of at least equal money value to the highest market price of their own. Still, my mind was made up to reach Merv at any cost, and with an escort of ten horsemen furnished by the Khan I rode out of this strange valley.

At Kaka I found the Russian agent who had given me such annoyance already established, and engaged in buying grain for the detachments of Cossacks who were expected hourly. Luckily for me they had not arrived. He called on me soon after my arrival in the town, and endeavoured to dissuade me from proceeding; but finding I paid little attention to his remonstrances, he grew very insolent, and I had to order him out of the house. In the morning, however, he was again at my door, and by threats of the coming Cossacks he succeeded in terrifying my escort into accompanying me no further. He was ordering them to take my baggage off the horses on which it had been packed, when I heard the noise, and walked out with sabre in hand to demand what he meant by such interference with my affairs. He ran hastily into his house, and I ordered my servants to mount and start immediately. I was glad to be rid of my guard, with whom I should have found it difficult to get into the desert, and I at once improved the opportunity thus offered me of quitting Persian soil and its troublesome officials. Pursuit by the Cossacks was the chief immediate danger I had to apprehend, and to prevent this I avoided taking the direct road to Tejend, and pretended to turn back to Kelat to complain to the Khan of the treatment I had received. My two servants were now my only companions, and I felt at length really free.

M

CHAPTER XV.

Onward to Merv—Atmospheric deceptions—The Merv Tekkés—Taken for a spy—Insect torments—A meeting in the desert—Turcoman wigwams—A prisoner—The Tejend river—Boars and lynxes—A wet night.

The Russian agent had unwittingly done me a great service in ridding me of the very people who were charged not to allow me to go towards Merv. Both he and they thought I would never dare venture alone across the desert. Once, however, engaged among the first ravines and hill spurs thrown out by the great mountain chain, I turned my horse's head and rode swiftly in the direction of Merv, directing my steps by compass, and becoming involved in ground where it would not be easy to track me owing to the rocky and gravelly soil, and the number of mountain streams which intersected the way. There was no road or beaten track of any kind. Sometimes I plunged into deep ravines, densely grown with giant reeds and cane brakes. Pheasants rose by dozens at every twenty yards. Wild boars continually plunged with a crashing noise through the reeds, and now and again I caught sight of a leopard or lynx stealing away deeper into the jungle. The entire scene was one of primitive nature. Very probably I was the first European who had ever trodden that way. Indeed, except under such circumstances as those by which I found myself surrounded, there was small reason for anyone, European or native, to wander among those savage recesses. At length, the ground becoming dangerously swampy, I ascended the lower hill slopes in order to gain a firmer way, and at the same time to obtain a view over the plain, and take bearings for my future line of march.

From the summit of a grassy hill I had a fine view of the plain, reaching away northward and eastward. Although it was early in the year, the rays of the noontide sun were intensely hot, and the further reaches of the plain appeared of an aërial blue tint, such as in northern climes we are accustomed to associate with the sky rather than with the earth. Far and wide were scattered countless towns and villages—all deserted, their lonely walls and towers standing out, grimly desolate, in the white, mid-day blaze. Scores of ancient mounds dotted the plain. The vast expanse, marked with all these traces of vanished life, quivering and dancing in the mirage, had about it something weird and unearthly, that filled the mind with a sense of desolation and loneliness. I knew well that numerous parties of ruthless bandits were lying hidden among the ruins; and it may be imagined how carefully I scanned the ground with my field-glass as I decided upon which direction I should follow. It was not easy to make a *reconnaissance*, as, owing to the trembling, heated atmosphere, one could hardly tell whether an object at a distance of five or six miles were a look-out tower or a Turcoman horseman.

After a lengthened survey I decided on my course, and, descending the hill, rode straight towards the only inhabited place within reach. This was Dushakh, marked on maps as Chardéh and Charardéh, though the people inhabiting it recognise it by that name with difficulty. It was about twenty-five miles distant. The tract which I crossed on my way to it was a rich, loamy surface, where streams from the mountains run riot amid luxuriant growths of wild flowers and herbs, grass being of but rare occurrence. Dandelion, sage, foxglove, thistle, mints of all kinds, and a thousand other plants flourish, but a square yard of grassy sward is a rare phenomenon.

As I drew near Dushakh, dark, leaden-coloured clouds had come over the sky, and the sun was setting fiery red. To the left was a very large ancient mound, crowned by crumbling walls and towers. A long, low rampart enclosed an irregular rectangular space of about a hundred yards square. I now, for the first time, met the Merv Tekkés.

Uncouth forms were to be seen upon the ramparts, and curious eyes gazed at me as I galloped up at the head of my slender following. I was evidently taken for the tax-gatherer, coming to assess the newly-planted ground. When the rickety gate of unhewn tree-trunks was unbarred, and I stood within the quadrangle, my eyes fell upon a wild sight. Within was an irregular, muddy encampment, where pit-like hollows were half-filled with reddish-brown liquid of pestilent odour—the drainings of the camping-ground of camel, buffalo, and human being. Amid this stood what at first sight seemed to be gigantic stacks of corn, but which proved to be the huts of the inhabitants. They were composed of great sheaves of giant reeds, placed in lean-to fashion. A number of camels, looking as raggedly wretched as they usually do on these plains, groaned and grunted. A couple of hundred horses, none of them very remarkable for beauty, stood tethered around. Women with dishevelled hair and wild eyes, clad in long, flowing red shirts, which, with the long purple trousers, formed their only attire, gazed round corners at me with a guilty look. Fifty or sixty men, in colossal sheepskin hats and deep red robes, carbine at back and sword at girdle, came forward to meet me. The chief, Adjem Serdar, stepped out to give me welcome, notwithstanding the fact that he had not a very clear conception of who I was, or of the nature of my business at Dushakh. I was shown into the only habitation which was not a reed hut—a single chamber with earthen walls, partly excavated at the foot of the ramparts. I could barely stand upright beneath the rough roof of unhewn pine trunks. A fire of camel's dung smouldered at the upper extremity. The room speedily became crammed to suffocation by Turcomans, whose curiosity was little short of ferocious. They literally thrust their noses into my face, and seemed desirous of looking down my throat. The majority were of opinion that I was a Russian spy, but an active minority were in my favour.

An hour after my arrival, the Persian colonel commanding the garrison of Sarakhs, who was on his way to Derguez with a present of horses sent by the Prince Governor of Meshed to Mehemet Ali Khan, paid me a visit. Having seen a little more of men and things than had the nomads, he promptly declared that I was what I announced myself to be. I was, he said, a *Kara Russ*, or Black Russian, this being the description given by the Turcomans to the English, in contradistinction to the *Sari Russ*, or Yellow Russian, as they named Skobeleff and his co-nationalists.

Adjem Serdar came up to where I was sitting, and, in a whisper, imparted to me what he doubtless thought was a new and unforeseen piece of intelligence, viz., that the greater number of the people of his village were thieves, and that it was advisable to look very sharply after my horses. He had, he said, taken the precaution of chaining them together by the fetlocks, and he presented me with a collection of iron instruments, resembling small reaping-hooks and undersized crowbars, which I was informed were the keys of the padlocks which secured the chains. To make matters doubly sure, two trusted henchmen, made specially responsible for the safety of the horses, slept beside them.

After supper—a mess of greasy rice served in a great wooden bowl, and clawed up, ghoul fashion, by each one with his bare fingers—we lay down to sleep as well as we might in a place in which it is no exaggeration to say that all night long I could hear the huge black fleas springing and dancing around me. We were up an hour before dawn, for I had told the chief that it was possible a party of Cossacks might come that way two or three hours after sunrise, and I wished to be well away on my forward journey betimes. In the angry red dawn I rode out of Dushakh, with an escort of four men, in addition to my two servants, and a mounted musician, who was charged to lighten a mile or two of my way with the strains of a two-stringed guitar, on which he performed briskly.

Upon coming to a halt upon an immense ancient mound we made tea, after I had taken a good look round for Cossack patrols; and, upon talking of the route to Merv, my conductors exhibited scruples about the advisability of allowing me to go on, lest they should be held responsible for facilitating the advent of a suspected stranger to a place always jealously closed to travellers, and, at such a critical moment, when the immediate possibilities were so menacing, all but unapproachable. They did their best to dissuade me from continuing my journey, and, finding their eloquence thrown away, flatly refused to accompany me any further.

I told them that it was a matter of indifference to me whether they accompanied me or not, as in any case I was resolved to go forward. We then parted, and, steering by compass, I made the best of my way towards Ménéh.

I had been informed that this place was about sixteen miles away, but it turned out to be over forty, a fact my directors perfectly well knew. As we rode on my Kurd servant began to show marked signs of uneasiness, as the wide Turcoman desert opened before him. And now we more than once experienced false alarms. A party of horsemen apparently galloping towards us in the distance proved to be the ruins of a brick fort, the trembling of the heated layer of air giving to distant objects a singular semblance of life and motion. An hour or so before sunset there was a real alarm. Coming to the brow of a gentle undulation, I suddenly perceived a couple of horses some three miles off; and on drawing nearer two men rose from the ground, where they had been lying, mounted, and rode towards us. When within a quarter of a mile they unslung their muskets and laid them across their saddle-bows, in readiness for action—a movement which we imitated. At fifty yards we halted, and the new comers challenged with the usual salutation of the desert, 'Peace be with you!' This indicated that fight was not desired, at least for the moment. We approached to within half-a-dozen paces, each party eyeing the other intently for fully a minute before breaking silence. The horsemen proved to be two Merv Tekkés from the colony at Ménéh, roaming about on the look-out for prey. On learning who I was, and whither bound, they turned back with me, and we rode on far into the night before any signs of inhabitants were apparent. A little after sunset we came abreast of some ruinous old buildings crowned with crumbling cupolas, and styled the Imam Zadé of Ménéh. They lay about six hundred yards to our left, and my guides, galloping away in front, dismounted before the walls, and remained some little time in prayer.

During the last two or three hours we stumbled along slowly in the dark, splashing through flooded ground, and falling into deep irrigation trenches. We must have crossed some thousands of acres of cultivated ground before reaching a ruinous old mud-walled fort to which we were guided by some glimmering lights. The women and children, together with the cattle, were within the walls; the men, for the most part, inhabiting strange-looking wigwams without. By the blaze of the camp-fires I could make out some scores of Turcomans standing and lying about, their weapons tied in sheaves around wooden posts planted in rows. The huts were of the most primitive construction, consisting of oblong pits about six feet in depth, rudely roofed over with tree-branches and bushes, on which was piled the rough hay destined for the horses. A steep incline led to the interior, where a fire of brambles and cattle-dung gave out an uncertain light and stifling smoke. Saddles and other horse furniture were piled around. Here, in company with fifteen Turcomans closely packed together, I spent a thoroughly miserable night. At dawn the Turcomans went about their various occupations, and I had a little leisure to write. The task was no easy one, for the place swarmed with every kind of vermin, and, early as was the season, flies were present in myriads. They settled in clouds upon the paper, drinking up the ink before it could dry, and blotting the writing with their feet.

I had everything in readiness to start at midday, and only awaited the appearance of the escort and uides who had been promised me. While waiting, the chief brought in an Akhal Tekké Turcoman, heavily manacled at the ankles. He was a wretched-looking man—a fugitive from Geok Tepé, on his way to Merv. *En passant* he tried to do a stroke of business at the expense of his congeners at Ménéh, and was caught in the act of driving before him some of their sheep and cattle. Filled with virtuous indignation at this unseemly act, the Ménéh folk had set upon and ironed him, and I was informed that in compliment to my arrival he would be set free, and would accompany me to Merv.

The afternoon wore on, the sun rapidly neared the horizon, and yet I could see no sign of preparation for setting out. I felt very anxious, for, knowing the objections which the people at Dushakh entertained to my going forward, I feared that I was about to experience similar ones at Ménéh. I did not care to express my suspicions openly, for I knew that if they set their faces against my expedition it would be impossible for me to make my way thither across a vast, waterless space, with which I was utterly unacquainted, and in the midst of which I should probably perish with thirst, even if I were not cut down by the first party I should meet with on the way. Evening fell, and unable to restrain my impatience any longer, I asked why the day had been allowed to pass by without any move in the desired direction having been made. I said that I wished to set out at once, but was desired to wait a little longer. It was not safe to start during daylight. All kinds of marauding bands were sure to be abroad, who would espy our course from a distance, and waylay us. It was some time after sunset when I was told that everything was in readiness for our departure. I emerged from my semi-subterranean wigwam, found the horses saddled, and my escort of four mounted. The night was dark, for the slender moon showed but fitfully behind drifting clouds, and was but three hours from the western horizon. After that time the blackness would be dense, as it usually is, under such circumstances, out on these plains. There was certainly but little fear of anyone, friend or foe, detecting our whereabouts.

When all were mounted, we had the half-hour's pause, usual on such occasions, to smoke the water-pipe. At last we started, seven in all—myself, my two servants, and the escort of four Turcomans. I was not favourably impressed by the appearance of these latter, for each of them was as truculent-looking a fellow as I ever met with in any part of the world. The chief with half-a-dozen of his horsemen, accompanied us for a mile on our way, to see us off, and also to make sure that no evil befell his guests within his own particular jurisdiction. We picked our way with difficulty among the shallow pits which serve as granaries for the storage of the Turcoman corn, and then, after passing traces of old buildings and former cultivation, we rode on over the marly dust till my companions told me we were now getting very near the banks of the Tejend river, and must wait till it was daylight before it would be safe to cross.

It was but red dawn when I was awakened to cross the sluggish stream about fifty yards wide. Trees grew in abundance upon its banks. Birds of many kinds filled the bushes on either side, and from their whistling and chattering they seemed to be of a species with which I had not previously met. Huge water-rats scampered about, and I saw an animal, which I took to be an otter, plunge into the stream, which was barely fordable, and it was only by zigzagging in the most cautious manner, the horses feeling for the shallowest portion of the crossing, that we avoided getting floated altogether. To save our tea and sugar, the servants knelt on their saddles, carrying the saddle-bags over their shoulders. We crept up the sandy slopes of the river ravine—for the surface of the water is from twenty to twenty-five feet below the level of the surrounding ground—and out into the plain beyond. After an hour's ride we halted to make tea, and as we partook of our morning repast I noticed that the drifted hills of marly dust were covered with spring vegetation, amongst which was a remarkably beautiful species of lily with fleshy flame-coloured petals. Wild boars were plentiful, and while tea was being prepared some of my companions chased them.

We rode on over the intensely hot desert to Kizil-Dengli, where an obelisk marks the existence of a rain-water cistern, which proved to be dry, but we found water in a narrow track sufficient to assuage the horses' violent thirst. League after league of plain was traversed, no new features being seen. Marly dust in ridges or odjar bush were the only reliefs to the monotony of our ride. Part of this was continued in a hollow way that may at some former period have been a branch of the Merv river—the Murgab. This, my guides informed me, was a favourite place with marauders, but as we rode on in the darkness all we encountered were wild animals in our path. Some I knew, by their grunting, to be boars, which abound here in incredible numbers. Others, by their pattering trot, I recognised to be jackals, and a few that bounded away lightly were either lynxes or leopards. Here we watered our horses from a deep well of very brackish water perfectly unsuitable for man, but horses and camels drink it without hesitation. Once or twice during the heat and darkness I suggested a halt, but in whispered tones was informed that there was no knowing when *ogri* (robbers) might appear. This I thought rather good, considering that I was in the company of as select a party of thieves as could be found hidden in any desert bush or crumbling ruin. In the end, even the horses seemed incapable of going any further. The men appeared to be made of iron. We reined in for a consultation. It was decided to turn aside a hundred yards, and this we did, camping amongst the tamarisk bushes, where, in spite of lightning and heavy rain which soaked me thoroughly, I slept soundly till I was aroused in the dark to continue our journey.

CHAPTER XVI.

The 'Queen of the World'—My personal appearance—Reception by the Mervli—An awkward position—A sanguinary threat—First impressions of Merv—My residence—Under inspection—An eager audience—The Merv chiefs—Showy costumes—A Merv Israelite—The Ichthyar—Petty persecutions—A mischief-making servant—A formidable examiner—Result of the council—Held a prisoner.

It was a dismal morning when, after a halt in some grim ruins, we made straight for Merv, still distant sixteen miles. Our spirits were low; we were wet, tired, and hungry. Much of the ground we passed was under water through the action of the irrigation trenches, used in the cultivation of the ground, and altogether everything seemed depressing, when through the rain-mist beehive-shaped outlines were visible. They were the first *aladjaks* of Merv, and I strained my eyes eagerly to catch a sight through the fog of the domes and minarets which I expected to see looming athwart it above the embattled walls of the 'Queen of the World.'

Here came a pause. Some of my conductors suddenly entertained doubts as to my nationality, and my motives for visiting them in their inner *penetralia*. 'How could anyone know that I was not a Russian?' 'What will our friends say when we bring him among them?' 'Who knows but he has a brigade of Cossacks at his heels?' 'What is his business here?' Such were the words I heard pass between them. The more considerate said, 'Who knows but that they will kill him at the first village?' For two long, weary hours we sat on horseback in the driving rain, our backs to the wind, awaiting the result of this field council. Some of the party looked daggers at me, and seemed inclined to solve the matter by there and then finishing me off; but the better-minded majority seemed to get their own way. One of the latter rode up to me and told me not to be afraid—that all would yet be right, he hoped. He added, significantly, that if all were *not* right, I should have only myself to blame for coming there. A decision was come to at last, and we rode straight to the first huts, which we could see faintly, through the mist, a mile or two off. A number of bales of silk, with some tobacco, tea, and other merchandise from Bokhara, lay around, for a caravan which had come from the latter place was on the point of re-starting for Meshed. A crowd of wild-looking people of both sexes, who were busying themselves with packing the bales upon camels, left their work to stare at myself and my cavalcade as I rode up—the women, with their draggled locks and rain-sodden, witch-like garments, perhaps the most weird of all. We were at the Bakshih village of Beg Murad Khan—one through which the caravans passed to and fro.

There was new wonderment on all sides as to what kind of person I might prove to be, and all seemed to take it for granted that I was a prisoner. So far as my personal appearance went, I might have passed for anything. I wore an enormous tiara of greyish-black sheepskin, eighteen inches in height. Over my shoulders was a drenched leopard skin, beneath which could be seen my travel-stained, much-worn ulster overcoat. My legs were caparisoned in long black boots, armed with great steel spurs, appendages utterly unknown in Turkestan. A sabre and revolving carbine completed my outfit.

Some people may wonder that I openly presented myself in the midst of the Tekké population, among whom the nature of my reception was at best doubtful, in such a garb as this, and why I did not assume a style of dress more in keeping with the custom of the country. I had considered this matter carefully before deciding upon the irrevocable step towards Merv. I could speak Jagatai Tartar fairly well, and my sun-tanned countenance and passably lengthy beard offered no extraordinary contrast to that of an inhabitant, but my accent, and a thousand other little circumstances, not to speak of the indiscretion of my servants, would have been enough to infallibly betray me. To appear in Turcoman costume, or in any other which tended to conceal my real nationality and character, would, under the circumstances, have been to court almost certain destruction.

I dismounted at the door of a hut to which my horse was peremptorily led, and, in view of the attitude of the people, I for the first time fully realised the risks which at the commencement of my venture I had so gaily faced—at best, captivity for an indefinite period. Nevertheless, here I was, at last, in the heart of the Turcoman territory. Let the future take care of itself. The circular beehive house into which I was shown was instantaneously crowded almost to suffocation. Some one pulled off my wet riding-boots, after a prolonged struggle; another substituted a lambskin mantle for my drenched leopard-skin and overcoat. A bowl of scalding hot green tea, without sugar, and tasting like a dose of Epsom salts, completed my material comforts. I sat close to the fire, and warmed my shivering members. All the time, the assembled people were gazing at me with an eagerness of expression that no words could convey. They apparently thought that after all I might be somebody mysteriously connected with the events transpiring so near to them, and who had come among them on a friendly mission. This idea was evidently still further propagated by the volubility of my Kurd, who, in the last agony of apprehension about his own personal well-being, was pouring torrents of lies into the ears of his auditory, telling them what a tremendous personage I was, and what wonderful comfort I was about to administer as soon as I could get the ear of the Khan. As for my late escort, some of them simply stated that I had come from the direction of the Russian camp, and were sufficiently cowardly to shirk all responsibility, and declare that they knew nothing further about me, though on the road they had at times been quite enthusiastic about the advent of a friendly Ferenghi to Merv. They even went so far as to say that they believed me to be a Russian, and that I came to Merv as a spy. Their expression of opinion seemed to take effect, and I could see, by the thinning of the audience, that I was losing ground. Angry voices, reaching me from a hut, close by, told me in half-heard words that the general opinion was not in my favour. 'Who knows but he is a Russian, and come to survey the road, and we will have an *aleman* (hostile foray) on our backs in forty-eight hours?' Then a great fat man, with a mingled expression of ruffianism and humour, came in, and asked me plainly who and what I was. This was Beg Murad Khan, a gentleman whose more intimate acquaintance I subsequently made in more than one disagreeable instance. I told him as well as I could, considering that the language used was Jagatai Tartar, and that the Turcomans have not a clearly defined notion of the functions of a peripatetic literary man. I said that I could set myself right in a few days by despatching a letter to the British native agent at Meshed by the caravan which was about to start. This proposition was met by a general shout of warning not to attempt to write a single word, or my throat would be immediately cut.

Struck by the peculiarity of my surroundings, and wishing to chronicle them while they were still vividly impressed upon me, I once ventured to produce my notebook and jot down a few hurried items. At once an excited Turcoman darted from the hut with the news that the Ferenghi was writing, and I could hear the recommendation to finish me off at once repeated by many a lip. In came the humorous-looking ruffian again to assure me in a vehement manner that if paper and pencil were again seen in my hand I could only blame myself for the result.

Everyone save myself and my two servants was then ordered to quit the *kibitka*. A strong guard was mounted at the door; and I was left to ruminate over the possible outcome of a situation into which, my conscience whispered, I had thrust myself with a scarcely justifiable amount of recklessness. However, under the combined influence of dry clothes, a fire, and a meal of boiled rice, which was considerately sent to us, I speedily began to recover good spirits, and in a short time was sleeping soundly.

It wanted but an hour of sunset when I was awakened by the opening of the door, and the entry of a man whom I had not previously seen. My Kurd servant at once recognised him. He had often met him at Geok Tepé previous to its fall. The stranger was no other than the celebrated Tokmé Serdar, the chief military leader of the Akhal Tekkés, and the man by whose energy and ability the defence of the Turcoman territory and fortress had been so prolonged. He was slightly under the middle height, broadly built, very quiet, almost subdued in manner, his small grey eyes sometimes lighting up with a humorous twinkle. His features, though not at all regular, had that irregularity which is often seen in a distinguished *savant* of the West, and bore the impress of thought. For some time he said but little, being evidently engaged in examining me closely. At length he seemed satisfied that I was not a Russian, having probably had sufficient experience of Russians to enable him to form a sound opinion. We had a long conversation upon the political question of the Russian advance. Finally, he remained and slept in the same hut, going away early the next morning. A few days later he surrendered himself to the Russians at Askabad, and afterwards had an audience of the Emperor at St. Petersburg.

At ten o'clock on the following morning I was ordered to mount my horse and proceed to head-quarters —to Merv itself, the seat of the Tekké Government, that mysterious goal to which I had been so long looking forward. It was still raining, and the flat country presented a wretchedly dismal appearance. I was escorted by my fat acquaintance of the previous day, together with twenty other horsemen, and preceded and followed by over a hundred persons on foot. We rode in a northwesterly direction, crossing large and deep irrigation canals, roughly bridged over by tree-trunks covered with brambles and earth, and floundering a good deal through flooded spaces. Then the weather began to brighten somewhat, and I was able to look round.

On every side was an immense plain, here and there broken by extensive plantations of trees, and hundreds of groups of beehive-shaped huts, each group consisting of from fifty to two hundred dwellings. The villages were usually from one to two miles apart. The ground was everywhere well tilled, corn-fields and great melon-beds alternating. Another hour brought us to the banks of the Murgab, which I now saw for the first time. We crossed it upon a rickety bridge, supported on unhewn tree-trunks planted vertically in the river-bed, the roadway being four feet wide, and devoid of anything in the shape of a parapet. This structure was nearly fifteen feet above the surface of the river.

I soon after found myself in the midst of about two hundred huts, ranged in rows of two or three hundred yards in length. In front of one of the foremost waved a small red banner, from a lance-shaft lashed to the top of a pole. This marked the residence of Kadjar Khan the Ichthyar, or executive chief, elected by the leading persons of the entire Merv district. Five hundred yards distant to the northward loomed a long line of earth-work, forming a front of a mile and a half in length, and shutting out the prospect in that direction. A few yards behind Kadjar Khan's house was a tolerably large pavilion tent of a pale blue colour, intended, I was informed, for myself. It was part of the spoil captured from the Persians, and had evidently belonged to some ill-fated officer of rank. Within it I found a thick felt mat, covered by a Turcoman carpet. In a shallow pit near one end burned a charcoal fire. A decent-looking, white-bearded old man received me. He was the brother of the Khan, and a moullah. Kadjar Khan himself was absent at some distant village. While very civil, my new acquaintance was exceedingly reserved in manner towards me. Doubtless, he did not care to be too cordial with a person whose throat might have to be cut within the next twenty-four hours. During the first evening I was left comparatively tranquil, but early the next morning a change came over the scene. It was one of the two days of the week on which the people of the oasis assemble at the bazaar for trading purposes. On each of these occasions several thousand people come together. Long before the sun was well above the horizon a surging crowd had gathered around my tent, the interior of which was also crammed with members of Merv society, all eager to interview the mysterious stranger who had fallen among them, as it were, from the clouds. They were, as a rule, the same sort of dressing-gown-robed, sheepskin-clad, gigantic-hatted beings as the Yamud Turcomans whom I had met so frequently upon the Caspian shore. They invariably sat upon their heels in a kneeling position, their folded arms resting upon the fronts of their thighs, and gazed at me with the ludicrous eagerness which may be observed in baboons and apes when some unfamiliar object meets their eyes. I had been fast asleep, my head resting upon a heap of baggage, and my body covered over with a large sheepskin mantle, but these people waited patiently until it might suit me to let myself be seen, for it is an inviolable piece of etiquette among them never to disturb a sleeper.

I was somewhat bewildered by the events of the past few days. I sat up, rubbed my eyes, and looked around me, quite unable to understand the sudden and numerous audience who had favoured me with their presence. Words cannot describe their astonishment on beholding my unwonted costume. My short, black, closely buttoned tunic and cord riding-breeches seemed to fill them with amazement. They gazed and gazed as though they could never stop looking at the external appearance of the Ferenghi. Simultaneously, from without, scores of eyes peeped through every nook and cranny of the tent walls; and I could hear remarks upon my personal appearance and costume, winding up with a statement of the conviction of the observers that I was most unmistakably an 'Oroos'—a Russian. As the tidings of my arrival spread, relays upon relays of fresh sightseers thronged to the capital and besieged my abode. Sometimes the crowd was so terrific that the tent reeled and swayed around me, and I thought it was coming down upon my head—a thing which ultimately happened when the spectators, utterly impatient at not being able to get within reach of the peep-hole, or in line with the doorway, tried to lift up the edges of the tent and introduce their heads. This being done simultaneously, and all the tent pegs becoming removed, the thing actually subsided upon me, nearly smothering myself and the more select party inside. Then came a rush of *yas-saouls*, or local police (!), striking right and left with sticks, and shouting reproaches against the sightseers for their violent breach of decorum in thus inconveniencing a stranger guest.

All night long, even when I slept, the same state of things continued, both inside and outside the tent. During the first month of my residence at Merv I might be said to have lived in the interior of a much-patronised peep-show, in which I was the central—and, indeed, the only—object of attraction. At first the effect was maddening, but I afterwards fell into a kind of comatic stupor, and began to feel under mesmeric influences. One could not make a move but it was commented upon. The manner of washing my face and hands called forth loud exclamations; and the operation of combing my hair seemed greatly to tickle their fancies. More than once I asked the old moullah whether there were no means of getting rid of the persecution under which I suffered. He shook his head gravely, and said surely I was not harmed by being looked at. I had not seen the Ichthyar, Kadjar Khan, but I had visits from persons who proved to be of higher social standing. These entered and, gravely saluting me with much ceremony, took their seats beside me. The first was Kouchid Khan, commonly known as Baba Khan, the son of the old ruler of Merv. Baba Khan, as I will henceforward call him, was chief of the Toktamish division of Turcomans, those residing in that portion of the oasis which is situated to the east of the river Murgab. The second, Aman Niaz Khan, was chief of the Otamish, or western division; and the third was Yussuf Khan, a lad of fifteen or sixteen years, brother of Makdum Kuli, the Akhal Tekké chief, and hereditary leader of the Vekil, or extreme eastern division of the Merv Tekké. Baba Khan was a low-sized man, of cunning aspect. One eye was completely destroyed by *keratitis*, the ophthalmic malady commonly known by the name of 'pearl'; the other was of a deep black colour, actually flaming with vivacity and penetration. At least ten per cent. of the Turcomans seem to be affected by this disease, probably in consequence of the combined effect of the fierce sunlight reflected from the marly plain, the irritation produced by the dust-storms, so frequent in this district, and the smoky atmosphere of the huts. Baba Khan, while apparently speaking to me, was in reality talking at the crowd within the tent, and endeavouring to show his keenness of perception by sneering at my stout denial of being a Russian, and broadly hinting that he could tell my nationality from the very style of my long boots —which, by the way, were made in Constantinople.

Aman Niaz Khan was much more agreeable in his

manners than his brother chief, and was evidently more of a natural gentleman. His eyes were feeble and watery, and he had the sallow, downcast air which accompanies the excessive use of opium. His features were regular, but wasted. He affected an extreme humility, which I am quite sure he was far from feeling. He told me that his health was very delicate, owing to his excessive consumption of opium, by which, he said, he was gradually ruining his constitution. He could not give it up, he remarked; he had been used to it from childhood. Over his long, sash-girt robe of striped crimson silk was another, of similar material, variously and brilliantly tinted. The ground of the robe was white, and it was so woven as to present a number of irregular patches, or rather splashes, of bright red, blue, yellow, and purple. At a distance he looked as if wrapped up in a large Union Jack. Some of his attendants were similarly attired, the colours varying to green, vermilion, and purple, according to the taste of the wearer. In this respect Aman Niaz and his followers were in distinct contrast to Baba and his men, who were clad in very sombre garments. All wore the huge grenadier hats of black curled sheepskin characteristic of the Turcomans, and each had the usual long carving-knife-like dagger stuck in his white sash.

Young Yussuf Khan had the most Tartar-like physiognomy of the company—flat nose and high cheekbones, but his eyes were full and grey, and quite unlike the peeping, slit-like organs of the genuine Kalmuck. Out of reverence to his seniors, he said but little. He was seated on his heels, his hands clasped before him, and concealed beneath his robe of amber-coloured camel-hair cloth. He gazed steadfastly before him, as if lost in contemplation, expressing little or no curiosity about me or my belongings. This is considered *bon ton* in Turcoman society.

I spent a weary day, repeating the same answers a hundred times to the same never-varying, tiresome questions, and do not think that I ever talked so long before, in any language; and as that which I used to express myself was Jagatai Tartar, it may be imagined how trying the conversation was to me. One after another the chiefs withdrew, saluting me with ceremonious politeness, and again leaving me at the mercy of the inconsiderate crowd, who seemed to have no regard whatever for my privacy or convenience.

Towards evening one of the few Jews living at Merv, a merchant named Matthi, paid me a visit. He wore a long robe of cotton stuff, with narrow red and white stripes, and a dome-shaped tiara of yellowish-brown leather, bordered round the lower part with fine black Astrakan. His beard, tinged with grey, was of inordinate length and fulness, and he carried a staff of some five feet in length, but no arms. Thinking that, like most of his co-religionists in the Levant, he might speak Spanish, I addressed him in that language, but no word did he understand. He spoke Tartar, Persian, Hebrew, and some Hindustani. He brought with him a bottle of arrack, and one of reddish-brown wine from Bokhara. The arrack, coloured yellow with turmeric, was not altogether unpalatable, though it would have admitted of very considerable improvement; the wine was simply abominable—a treacly syrup of some vinous liquid. He told me that there were but seven families of his religious persuasion at Merv. They had resided there from time immemorial, and had not among them even a tradition as to the place from whence they had come previous to settling in the oasis.

It was only after sunset on the second day that Kadjar Khan, the Ichthyar, made his appearance. Owing to the excessive crowd in the tent, he had been sitting not far from me for an hour before I was aware of the fact; the intense democracy of the population, as well as other circumstances which became known to me afterwards, preventing the display of any of those external signs of respect usually shown to the chief magistrate of a State, however small it may be. He was in every respect a remarkable-looking man. Tall and gaunt, he was clad in simple robes of the soberest tint. His aquiline features were the exact counterpart of those of the bust of Julius Cæsar at the British Museum. The total absence of beard, save a few scarcely perceptible hairs upon the chin and upper lip, gave him the appearance of being closely shaved. His face was decidedly a fine one, though somewhat ascetic, and spoiled by an uneasy, vulturine expression of the eye, the pupil being quite surrounded by the white. His lips were firmly set, and the muscles of his jaws twitched and worked convulsively, as if he were under the influence of some strong emotion. He was over sixty years of age. For some time he spoke apparently to himself, his eyes fixed on vacancy. At first I did not feel at all comfortable beside him. I had seen his face before, but it was only when reminded that I recalled the fact of its being in Teheran the year before, when, with twelve followers, he had tried to come to an understanding as to the Turcoman relations with the Shah. He said but little, his observations being mainly confined to 'Inch Allah' (Please God) at the end of each of my sentences. At last he got up and went out abruptly, and I saw no more of him for two days. About sunset his brother, the old moullah, sent me a large wooden dish filled with broken bread, and mingled with some shreds of meat, over which mutton broth had been poured. Of this my Kurd servant and myself made our suppers. The Akhal Tekké servant had discovered his family among the refugees from Geok Tepé, and had taken his leave.

During the first fortnight I had not a single moment of privacy or undisturbed repose. I was closely confined to my tent, for whenever I tried to go outside the door I was followed by a number of persons, evidently told off to look after me, and to warn me that I should not go straying about, 'lest,' they said, 'the dogs might bite you.' It is true that these dogs were really dangerous, and a stranger, even though a Turcoman, approaching the place, ran imminent risk of being pulled in pieces unless the animals were called off by their proprietors. During the day the intense heat, within my abode, was stifling; and at times dust storms arose, drifting the powdered marl, and forcing it through every chink of the tent, until it filled one's ears and nostrils, and insinuated its way into the saddle-bags and among one's eatables. It was wearisome work, sitting there all day to be stared at, with absolutely nothing to do. If I attempted to read a page of one of the few books that I had with me, I was tormented by demands for explanations as to its nature, and I really believe that, unless relief had arrived in one form or another, I should have become demented.

On the seventh day after my arrival, advantage being taken of the assembly of people at the bazaar, a general *medjlis*, or council of the Merv chiefs and elders, was summoned to investigate my case, and to decide what my standing at Merv should be. When I received the news, my Kurd servant was lying in a corner, stupefied with the fumes of opium, which he had been smoking to deaden his fears of the possible result of the reunion of the redoubtable Merv elders. He was in the last extremity of fear, and had the conviction, which he more than once expressed to me, that we had not the slightest chance of escaping with our lives. This Kurd had done me a world of harm, and his action bade fair to place me in serious jeopardy. His name was Gholam Riza. To put himself under cover of some greater responsibility, he on all occasions gave out that I was a person of immense importance, going to Merv with the British flag in my pocket, which was immediately to be hoisted; and that I was about to summon from Kandahar endless legions of British troops. I repeatedly warned him not to make such statements, and told him that I would flatly contradict them; but, maddened by fear, he paid no attention to what I said.

Here I was, then, in a very awkward position. From hearing my servant reiterate the statements which had sprung from his own imagination, stimulated by his fears, the authorities had begun to attach some kind of importance to what he said, and to believe that after all I might be some kind of envoy, despatched to Merv by reason of the very critical position with reference to the advancing Russian forces. I had to dispel these illusions, and at the same time to make known the nature of my business among them—by no means an easy task.

The council of elders had been sitting for over an hour when I was summoned to attend it. I confess that it was not without a considerable degree of trepidation that I obeyed the summons. Issuing from my tent, I was led through a surging crowd to a wide waste space in the rear, where, on the marly earth, some two hundred persons were seated in a circle of twenty yards in diameter. An immense gathering of the public pressed around them; for at Merv the entire population, of both sexes and all ages and conditions, are privy to the important deliberations of the Council of State. Within the circle, and close to one side of it, was laid a large felt rug, on which I was requested to be seated. Then followed a dead silence. Everyone was scrutinising me and my garb. I cast a rapid glance around me when I was seated cross-legged on my rug. There were young and old, well-dressed and shabbily-attired men in the assembly. The general expression of countenance was far from reassuring; but there were some faces that gave me confidence, and many of the Turcomans present would very easily have passed as being of European blood. There was a general whispering for some time, and then, from the opposite part of the circle, I was addressed in thundering bass tones. The speaker was a man of colossal proportions and of advanced age, as the long white beard which swept his breast denoted. He was rather well dressed, in the fashion of the country, one which probably dates back to a very remote period. His formidable name, as I afterwards learned, was Killidge Ak-Saghal, or the Old Man of the Sword. He said, in the tones of one accustomed to send his voice afar in the tumult of combat, 'Who and what are you, and what brings you here?'

I said that I was a native of that part of Frangistan called England, and that my present occupation was observing and reporting on the progress of the Russian arms; and that, fleeing before General Skobeleff's advance, I had arrived at Merv. Then ensued a pause, during which my statement was discussed throughout the assembly. 'What proof can you give of the truth of your statement?' said the Old Man of the Sword. Hereupon I deftly produced my pocket-book, and unfolded the various documents which I possessed, some in English, others in Persian, testifying to my identity and occupation. The old man, who seemed tacitly recognised as the speaker of the assembly, and who furthermore possessed the rare accomplishments of reading and writing, not only his own language, but also that of Persia, gravely examined my papers, which he subsequently read aloud and translated into Turcoman idiom for the benefit of the assembly. A murmur of approval followed. 'But,' said the militant elder, 'how can anyone tell that you are not a Russian who has murdered some Englishman and taken his papers?' I said, gravely, that there were means of showing that this supposition was untenable, by a reference to the British agent at Meshed, and to the Minister at Teheran. Then followed divers queries from other members of the assembly. How long had I left England? What was my rank, &c.? During this questioning there was much jumbling together, in the minds of the speakers, of Hindustan and England, the Padishah and the 'Coompani.' I was asked to indicate the respective directions of England and India, and when I pointed to opposite portions of the horizon, the wonderment and astonishment grew greater. Who and what the 'Company' might be was discussed at length, and I was asked whether it could possibly be true, as was currently reported in the East, that the Padishah of England was a lady. In a little while I found that I began to gain ground, and could perceive the truth of the adage that 'we easily believe that which we wish.' This council of dignitaries concluded by convincing themselves that I was an Englishman, and had come to Merv for the purpose of doing what my Kurd had so industriously circulated to be my object. After an hour's discussion I was told that I might withdraw. I was led back to my tent, from whence I could hear the loud and eager debate which ensued.

While awaiting the final decision of the council, the moments were anxious ones. For all I could tell, sentence of immediate death might be pronounced upon me, and I endeavoured to steel my mind for the very worst. In half an hour I was again summoned. From the smiling faces around I knew that a favourable decision had been arrived at. The thunder-voiced old Nestor told me that I was not to be killed. 'But,' said he, 'you are to remain a prisoner until a reply can be received from Abass Khan, the English agent at Meshed.' Couriers were to be at once despatched to that city, on whose return another *medjlis* would be held. I then again withdrew, and the council broke up.

CHAPTER XVII.

My new home—A hut interior—The Turcoman costume—Merv fortifications—Captured cannon—Quaint ideas on artillery—The great earthwork—A weak defence—A tour of inspection—A naïve proposal—My purpose at Merv—My servant's departure.

A FEW days had elapsed since the meeting of the *medjlis* when I perceived an unusual movement towards the rear of my abode. On drawing aside one of the folds, I saw a number of Turcoman women engaged in the erection of an *aladjak* or *er* quite close to my tent. The new dwelling was destined for me, for I had several times complained about the dust and the extreme heat to which I was exposed in my canvas house. No one who has not resided in tents in a hot climate can imagine the great inconvenience of living under canvas. During midday hours the heat is unbearable unless the tent be doubled with felt or very thick coloured stuff. The erection, then, of the dome-shaped wicker hut, with its covering of reed mats and felt, was very welcome.

The furniture of these tents is very simple. The fire occupies the middle of the apartment, immediately under the central opening in the dome. The half of the floor remote from the entrance is covered with a *ketché*, or felt carpet, nearly an inch in thickness. On this are laid, here and there, Turcoman carpets, six or seven feet long by four to five in breadth, on which the inhabitants sit by day and sleep by night. The semicircle next the door is of bare earth, and on it chopping of wood, cooking, and other rough domestic operations are conducted. Round the walls hang large flat camel-bags, six feet by four, one side being entirely composed of the rich carpet-work in which the Turcoman women excel. Ordinarily, all the household goods are packed in these bags, for transit from place to place on the backs of camels. When empty they form a picturesque tapestry.

Besides the primitive horizontal hand-mill, or quern of our Celtic forefathers, and the *samovar*, which is in almost hourly requisition, for the courtesies of Central Asia require that every stranger be presented with a cup of tea immediately upon his arrival, nothing more exists in the way of household furniture. Hung on one side are the saddle and other horse trappings of the master of the establishment, along with his sabre and musket. The horses are tethered by the fetlock close by the door of the *ev*, and in cold weather are covered by the Western Turcomans with a great cloth of felt.

Within the roof, and near its top, hang a couple of lamb or goat-skins, turned inside out, and smoke-dried. The neck-aperture is kept widely open by four crossed sticks. These skins swing to and fro in the air current produced by the fire, and are termed *toonik*. I have repeatedly questioned the Turcomans as to the meaning of this. They evidently attached some mysterious importance to it, but were loth to explain. Near the doorway, against the felt wall-lining, is sewn a piece of linen or calico, four or five inches square, forming a pocket for the reception of the bounties of wandering spirits. This they call the *tarum*. A horseshoe, too, is occasionally to be found nailed upon the threshold. These are the principal superstitious usages of the Turcomans. I was surprised to find how few they were.

It was an unspeakable relief to me to abandon my old quarters in the tent for the comparative coolness of the *ev*; and I longed to be equally quit of my tormenting visitors, who continued to observe and catechise me with the same unflagging zeal as at the commencement. At last, perceiving that it must be my European garb which attracted their curiosity, I resolved to adopt the attire of the country. A native dealer from the bazaar waited upon me, and produced a store of choice garments. I selected the ordinary Turcoman costume—a long crimson tunic of coarse Bokhara silk, with slender black and yellow combined stripe. Over this comes a light brown flowing garment, of fine camel-hair tissue. I next purchased an embroidered skull-cap, a sheepskin hat, shirt, sash, wide white cotton trousers, and a pair of broad-toed slippers, of red stamped Russian leather. Stockings are rarely worn—never with slippers. When long riding-boots are used, the feet and ankles are swathed in a band-like wrapping. In severe weather the enormous great-coat styled a *kusgun* is worn. Sometimes this is replaced by a heavy mantle of woven sheep's wool. Thus equipped, though I was far from getting rid of the troublesome curiosity of my neighbours, I obtained much relief in this regard, and was enabled, in company with some acquaintances, to stroll about the village, generally with a following of not more than two hundred persons.

Shortly after procuring and adopting the Turcoman costume, a courier arrived with a letter from Meshed, from Abass Khan. In this letter he thoroughly testified to my nationality, and declared that I had no connection whatever with the Russian expedition. From the moment of the receipt of this communication I was placed at comparative liberty, though always subject to a certain amount of surveillance on the part of the Turcomans,

o

who took up a strangely mixed attitude towards me—partly that of hosts, and partly that of gaolers.

One day, old Kadjar Khan called upon me, and asked me to accompany him on a visit to the fortifications then in process of construction, and to the guns captured by the Tekkés from the Persians and others. When I arrived at Merv, the new fortress was but half-completed. As many as from seven to eight thousand young men worked at it daily. The rapid and unforeseen arrival of the Russians in the neighbouring oasis of the Akhal Tekké had given a great impetus to the work. Each subdivision of the people was forced to supply a certain number of workers, every able-bodied young man being required to give four days per month or to pay a sum of two francs for each day omitted.

The fortifications were of that kind which the populations of these Central Asian plains seem to have constructed from time immemorial, and the remnants of which one still sees scattered far and near. They consist of one huge continuous embankment, thirty-five or forty feet in vertical height, and sixty feet at the base. The summit of the embankment was sixteen feet wide, and the parapet on its top seven feet in height. The footbank to enable the defenders to fire over the crest was about two feet wide. The parapet itself, like the whole superstructure, was of well-kneaded and rammed tenacious yellow loam. The Turcoman is accustomed to the dead level of the plain in usual internecine combat. On the top of something lofty he considers himself invincible. He has no notion that his laboriously constructed cliff can be brought down about his ears.

The water supply is independent of the main river, and is much better in quality than that of the main stream below the dam, which is very foul, owing to the number of villages on its banks and the amount of filth discharged into it. Bubbles of sulphuretted hydrogen ripple its sluggish grey current; and after bathing in it I have retired with nausea and headache. Moreover, the people told me that, in case of an attack and siege, wells within the place would supply all their needs. Standing upon the ramparts, the eye ranges over a fair expanse of well-cultivated country. Corn of various kinds, and melons, seemed the only produce, if I except the apples, jujubes, grapes, and apricots of the frequent enclosed plantations. Away on the eastern horizon are frequent mounds, the remains of former fortalices; and just visible are the towers and cupolas of the ruined capital of these plains.

Later in the afternoon I went to see the cannon captured from the Persians, about which I had heard a great deal before my advent to Merv. Half a dozen of them were close by the hut which I occupied; the remainder were within the new ramparts. No sooner did I emerge from my dwelling in company with the Khan, than, as usual, I was surrounded by a crowd of some hundreds of persons pressing so close upon us that I was nearly suffocated. They seemed to treat me as some inanimate object of interest. Thus escorted, I visited the nearer half-dozen of guns. Three were still on their field carriages of rather ponderous construction; the other three lay on the ground, the broken woodwork of their supports rotting hard by, and the ironwork scattered around or still clinging to the fragments of the carriages. One was an 18-pounder, the others were six-pounders—all smooth-bore, and of bronze. The guns themselves were in fair condition, save that the vent-holes were inordinately enlarged, and of such irregular form as to lead me to think that when abandoned the guns had been spiked, and the nails subsequently roughly wrenched out. One of these guns was of Bokharan make, as the inscription on it told. The bores were, as a rule, so scraped, apparently by the passage of heterogeneous projectiles, such as gravel and horse nails, that at first sight the guns might pass as having been formerly rifled.

Passing onwards, a great gap in the ramparts was reached, and I stood within the interior of the *enceinte*. There were a group of *aladjaks*, and some young trees and bushes. This was the immediate dwelling-place of Baba Khan, son of old Kouchid. On a small open space —some on the carriages, some on the ground—were twenty-eight pieces of bronze ordnance. There were three or four 18-pounders, a dozen four-pounders, one chambered seven-inch howitzer, and two six-inch mortars. The Turcomans were very proud of their spoils, and took every pains to tell me all about the different guns. I said that, in view of the possible arrival of the Russians, I wondered that some pains had not been taken to mount the disabled pieces. 'Oh,' said the Khan, 'there are plenty of people who could do that in a couple of weeks. There is abundance of wood growing in the gardens. Most of the ironwork is on the spot; and I know where the tire of one wheel is—it fell off as we were bringing the gun across the river.' This was all highly satisfactory to the general audience; but I knew that in the whole of the Merv tree plantations not a trunk of more than eight inches in diameter was to be found. I asked whether any considerable quantity of projectiles was on hand. Thereupon the chief told me of several traders in the bazaar who had many, which they used as weights when selling corn. 'Besides,' he said, 'the Persians fired a great deal; and the old men who were looking on could easily point out where the shot fell, and we could dig them up when required.' As regards the gunpowder, there were Ali Baba, and Hussein and Hodja Kouli, and several others who knew what it was composed of; and, besides, there was every reason to believe that the Emir of Bokhara would not be backward in affording facilities for a supply if he had a good 'present.' The Khan further naïvely remarked that he hoped I should be of no small assistance in remounting the guns and founding the necessary projectiles. Having deciphered the inscription and date on each piece, I left the precincts of the Turcoman park, having impressed the spectators with the idea that I was consequently no small artillerist in my way.

While examining the guns, I was joined by Baba Khan and Aman Niaz Khan, each of whom arrived on horseback, attended by a large following, also mounted. They told me that they were about to make a tour of inspection of the works, and invited me to accompany them. The fortifications were under the immediate superintendence of these two Khans, in virtue of their separate jurisdiction over the two great divisions of the Mervli population—the Toktamish and the Otamish. We rode up the steep breakneck slopes of the incomplete ramparts, and at very considerable risk, as we trod upon half-finished parapets and terraces, following the line in a north-westerly direction. Parties of toilers were everywhere at work, the great majority creeping, ant-like, up the ramps specially provided, and bearing on their backs great bags of earth taken from the irrigation trenches in course of construction within the works, and from the surface of the ground outside. The contents of the bags of earth emptied on the summit of the embankment were levelled out, and beaten with rammers. One elderly man, doubtless having a repute for engineering skill, supervised the work of some fifty of his younger companions. It was a singular fact that the south-eastern extremity of the enclosure was almost entirely open; what would be termed in field fortification a musketry trench alone closed it. I inquired the reason of this, and was told that from that direction little danger was apprehended, and that the points most likely to be immediately attacked were being put in a state of defence. My informants seemed to imagine that an enemy would dash himself against the first point of their defences with which he came in contact, and would not seek any easier access to the interior of their fortress.

During our promenade, which lasted some hours, I was struck by the great respect shown to the two hereditary Khans, and the careful attention with which their instructions were followed after they had pointed out anything which seemed to them at fault. We sallied out by the north-eastern gateway, and, turning to the left, wended our way towards a collection of huts and buildings of earth, surrounded by luxuriant groves of trees, and situated half a mile distant from the northern angle. This settlement was a curious one in its way, being chiefly composed of several Jewish families. They seemed by far the busiest and most flourishing of the Merv communities which I had hitherto visited. Bales of merchandise lay in the vicinity of every house, awaiting transport to Bokhara or Meshed. In one respect the houses were very different to the majority of those scattered over the plain; for, instead of dwelling exclusively in *aladjaks*, as the Tekkés for the most part do, tower-like buildings of unbaked brick, plastered over with fine yellow loam, had been constructed, giving the place a fortified appearance. The settlement was not entirely made up of Jews. There were in it some Kurd families, who, years before, had been carried away from the Persian frontier, and had settled among the Tekkés. At this point, too, was the *medressé* or college, presided over by a Turcoman much renowned for his erudition, and named Khodja Nefess. His academy, a large and not unpicturesque edifice of loam, was surrounded by a grove of pomegranate, jujube, peach, and willow trees. I never had an opportunity of meeting this worthy. He studiously kept aloof from me, doubtless lest his sanctity might be impaired by contact with a giaour, for he had a great reputation for holiness—whether deserved or not I am unable to say.

It was evening as we turned our horses' heads towards the 'capital,' and rode along the Murgab to the seat of government. Our way lay across a cemetery, which, as is usual in most Turcoman countries, lies in very disagreeable propinquity to the habitations of the living. As on the Persian frontier, the graves are very shallow, and the hoofs of the horses broke through the slender mass of earth which covered the bodies. A couple of dismounted guns lay among the graves, and I was told that a few others were scattered among the villages of the oasis, the inhabitants of which, having taken a leading part in their capture, wished the trophies of their prowess to remain near them.

Baba Khan left us to proceed to his own village, but Aman Niaz accompanied me to my house, which, on our arrival, was filled by a very numerous and disagreeable crowd. Among them was an individual of considerable note—the *ustá adam*, one of those universal artists or Jacks-of-all-trades of whom I have already spoken. He could work in silver and gold, repair gun-locks, shoe horses, and perform all manner of skilled labour. He was introduced to me with great ceremony, and evidently looked upon me with no small amount of awe, as he appeared to think that, in my capacity of Ferenghi, I must be his superior in all manner of arts. His object in coming to see me was ludicrous enough. The Turcomans had had a sore experience of Russian breech-loading cannon during the siege of Geok Tepé, and the desire of every heart was that the Merv artillery should be converted into *Susana thob*. He wished me to draw him a plan and section of one of these modern implements of destruction, and also sought my co-operation in the work of altering the pieces on hand to the newest form. I asked him what tools and apparatus he could command for the purpose. From beneath his robe he produced an old rasp, such as is used in these parts for finishing off the hoofs of newly-shod horses. It was considerably the worse for wear. Along with it he had brought a hand-saw, probably manufactured by himself, for each tooth pointed in a direction different to that of its neighbour. With these two implements, and my aid, he purposed to effect the wished-for transformation of the cannon. Aman Niaz became quite enthusiastic, and was already verbally laying out plans for the construction of a large factory close at hand, of which I and the *ustá adam* were to take the direction. He graciously added that I should have command of the pieces in action, at which condescending intimation I rose and bowed profoundly. I felt that if I had to follow Kadjar Khan's hint about remounting the guns on carriages sawn out of trunks of apple and peach trees, and, moreover, to convert the guns themselves into breech-loaders with a hand-saw and a horse rasp, I might safely accept the position of artillerist-in-chief without in the least compromising my national neutrality. All this will serve to convey an idea of the extremely primitive notions of the people among whom I found myself, in regard to artillery at any rate. In some other matters they were shrewd enough. However, notwithstanding the disagreeable circumstances immediately attending my arrival, and the manner in which I had been kept in custody, I managed to make some progress towards securing the good opinion of the Turcomans.

At this time, my object was to make as perfect a survey as possible of the Merv district, to become fairly acquainted with the manners, customs, and government of the people, and their general tone of mind, and then get out of the place as quickly as possible. The same evening, I took the first step towards effecting my release —one of many which ultimately proved successful. I wrote a letter to Abass Khan, explaining my position, in which I confined myself to asking him to emphasise the fact of my being a British subject by immediately sending me a communication stating that my presence was instantly required at Meshed, and expressing the hope that he would see me there shortly. The more to impress those around me with the genuineness of this communication, and especially as I was not sufficiently master of Persian orthography to convey in that language all I wished to say, I wrote to Her Majesty's Minister at Teheran asking him to make the desired communication with the Meshed agent. This letter to the British Minister was naturally calculated to show the genuineness of my statement as to my nationality.

I found a ready messenger in my Kurd servant, Gholam Riza. That personage had been wandering about the village in a state bordering on distraction, engendered partly by fear, but to no small extent by excessive indulgence in arrack and opium. Notwithstanding all my injunctions, he had gone on reiterating that I was an emissary of the British Government, and that immense importance attached to my mission. Sometimes I did not see him for days together. My horses were neglected, and I had to shift for myself. Kadjar Khan called upon me, and inquired whether I had any objection to Gholam Riza being sent away from Merv. 'I do not think,' said the Khan, 'that he is a proper attendant for you. I have to send men to look after your horses, while he receives the pay. Besides, he goes round to all the *evs* at meal-times, and eats up all the food, a thing which would be highly improper in itself, for the people of Merv have not too much to eat, and cannot afford to support a stranger.' A caravan was leaving on the following day, and it was agreed that Riza should go with it. When he came in that night, he was overjoyed to hear of his release; and as in due time he started with the party, I found myself entirely alone among the Turcomans.

CHAPTER XVIII.

The waterworks—Holding the stirrup—The guest-chamber—How to show gratitude—Delights of a siesta—A generous host—The Benti dam—The sluice—An awkward crossing—A dainty dish—Porsa Kala—Snakes in the desert—Hunting a runaway—Glimpse of the old cities—Homeward bound.

THE water system of Merv is the key to the entire territory. It has its origin at the great dam of Benti, some twenty-five miles to the south-eastward of Kouchid Khan Kala. Without this dam the present cultivated area would be reduced to a condition as bleak and arid as that of the plains which surround it. Owing to the extreme flatness of the plain, the manner in which the water channels are concealed by the growing crops, and the accidents of the ground, slight as they are, it is impossible, even from the commanding heights of the ramparts, to form any idea of the direction in which these watercourses flow. I was extremely anxious to pay a visit to the starting-point of the irrigation canals, and to visit the old Saruk fortress, which, prior to the coming of the Tekkés, constituted the central stronghold of Merv, and protected the waterworks. The Turcomans being themselves rather curious in the matter of ancient buildings, they seemed thoroughly to appreciate my wish, and I was told one evening that on the following morning Baba Khan would show me the works.

A little after daybreak on May 2 I found an escort of fifty or sixty horsemen drawn up before my door, and

Baba Khan, in riding costume, came in to say that he was ready to go with me. We consumed several bowls of green tea together, and, as usual, chatted a good deal about Frangistan and its people. Finally, about eight o'clock we mounted and started on our journey. Four or five miles to the north of the Kala, after traversing a considerable number of villages surrounded by luxuriant groves of various fruit trees, we passed, on our left, an extensive sepulchral monument standing alone in the plain. It was the tomb of Kouchid Khan, the last great ruler and autocrat of Merv—a kind of rude mausoleum, ten or twelve feet in height, surrounded by an embattled wall. Some pomegranate trees grew within the enclosure. My companions halted, and, turning their horses' heads towards the tomb, inclined over their saddle-bows and prayed for a few moments. This was a tribute to the greatness of the departed. Then we turned to the east, and reached an extensive village called Baba Kalassi. Here we dismounted, for the sun was becoming exceedingly hot. · The elders of the village advanced to meet us, holding our stirrups as we dismounted, and uttering the stereotyped phrases of welcome—*Khosh Geldi* ('You are welcome'), *Safa Geldi* ('You are the bringer of good fortune'). This holding of the stirrup is not the mere token of respect which one would be likely to suppose. For me, at least, it was an absolute necessity. Easterns do not generally tighten the girths of the saddle, lest, as they believe, it might interfere with the lung action of the horse. Consequently, when the weight of the body is thrown upon the left foot in dismounting, the saddle is apt to turn under the animal, and the rider to receive an ugly fall. In this ceremony of reception the right stirrup is tightly grasped by the host, so as to prevent such an accident. This service is usually performed by one's attendant; when it is performed by one's host, it is a polite method of expressing that he is at your service. The Turcomans, in spite of this slackness of girth, have a knack of getting in and out of the saddle without help, but I could never manage it.

Before we were allowed to stir from the sides of our horses the indispensable water-pipe was presented to us, after the usual indulgence in which we were led into the interior of the village, several men armed with long sticks laying about them furiously at the dogs, who, according to their wont, rushed savagely at us. In each village of any extent there is generally a house, belonging to the chief, but not habitually used, set apart for the reception of visitors of distinction. That to which we were conducted was an *ev* of more than ordinary dimensions. It was comfortably carpeted, and the walls were hung round with embroidered camel-bags, and adorned with sabres and muskets. Special carpets, of small size, were immediately laid for Baba Khan and myself close to the lattice walls, from which the felt covering had been temporarily stripped in order to admit a current of air. The carpets were laid as remote from the door as possible, that being the position of honour in an Eastern dwelling. In a kneeling posture, and sitting upon our heels, we uttered the muttered compliments, lasting for more than a minute, which are the invariable prelude to talking about the matter in hand. I was the chief object of attraction. The Khan, having taken upon himself the responsibility of showing me round, seemed also to feel the necessity of maintaining the genuineness of my character as much as possible. He told our hosts that I was a *sahib* from Frangistan, who had travelled much, and who had been driven by the Russians to take refuge among the Merv Turcomans.

A quarter of an hour after our arrival large circular wooden dishes of *gattuk*, or coagulated and slightly sour milk, were laid before us. In each dish was a coarsely carved wooden ladle, with a handle eighteen inches long. A rather dirty-looking piece of coarse cotton stuff was unrolled, disclosing three or four cakes of smoking bread, twenty inches in diameter and an inch and a half thick. On these viands we regaled ourselves with as good an appetite as we could muster, for Turcoman good behaviour requires that when food is laid before a guest he should simulate, even if he do not possess, a voracious appetite.

Our repast finished, we all said grace. Turcomans never by any chance, whether at home or in the desert, neglect this ceremony. Holding our joined hands before us, in the fashion of an open book, we prayed in muttered tones. What the terms of the prayer were I was never able to catch, but I muttered away as well as the best of them. Then, separating our palms, the elbows resting on the hips, we each exclaimed with unction, and in subdued ones, 'El hamd Lillah' (Praise be to God). Then we stroked our beards, with the right and left hands alternately, and looked cautiously over our shoulders, right and left, lest Shaitan (the devil) might be lurking nigh us. A deep, heavily-drawn sigh, by way of expressing the stomachic oppression which we experienced from the completeness of our meal, and eructations, natural or forced, were polite and indispensable recognitions of our host's hospitality.

I remember that when upon one occasion I had ridden a long distance since the early morning, and was worn with fatigue and hunger, halting with my companions at a village, dishes of newly-made *gattuk* were laid before us—a preparation which, when fresh, is really delicious. It needed no adventitious politeness to make me devour it, and I emptied my huge dish of coagulated milk in a manner which charmed my host. Another was set before me, which I devoured with equal zest. I had even surpassed my companions in voracity, and from time to time I observed my grey-bearded entertainer turn to the assemblage, and, with a look of genuine pleasure lighting his countenance, say, alluding to me, 'He is a good man; he is an excellent man.' Occasionally, a few hours after gorging in this manner, I have been compelled by circumstances to set to again, and, in following the dictates of Central Asian politeness, have rendered myself incapable of mounting my horse for the next twelve hours.

After this eating match, bolsters, six feet long and two in diameter, were brought forth. The general audience retired, and myself, the Khan, and a few chosen associates lay down to take our siesta. This is an established institution in Merv, even on the war path, unless immediately pressing circumstances supervene. It was delicious thus to shelter from the sultry blaze outside, gently fanned by a comparatively cool breeze which swept across the flooded fields, and to sink into forgetfulness. We remounted at three in the afternoon, and bent our steps in a south-easterly direction, more or less parallel to the watercourse which irrigates the interior of Kouchid Khan Kala. Towards five o'clock we struck the main eastern branch of the Murgab, passing to the right of two ancient mounds of considerable size, entirely bare of vegetation, and staring yellowly in the sun-blaze. We meandered a good deal among irrigation canals, and ultimately turned our horses' heads due south, along the main eastern canal, arriving at a rude bridge of poles covered with brushwood and packed earth. At this point the canal was nearly twenty feet wide, and the current flowed rapidly. Five hundred yards eastward was a village of the Beg sub-division of the Toktamish, under the jurisdiction of Murad Bey, the maternal uncle of Makdum Kuli Khan. Here we halted for the evening, though we might well have gained our destination before the darkness set in ; but Baba Khan seemed to delight in halting, and thoroughly to enjoy the eager hospitality pressed upon us. Murad Bey was one of the most respectable Turcomans with whom I came in contact. He was free from that grasping covetousness which is an unfortunate characteristic of the large majority of his compatriots. While he entertained us with the most lavish generosity, he firmly, though courteously, refused the half-dozen pieces of silver which I offered him. He was, as I afterwards discovered, one of the richest men of the community. At daybreak we were off again, Murad Bey, his son, and a troop of horsemen accompanying us for a time.

We recrossed the bridge, and pursued our way southward along the western bank of the canal. As we progressed, the banks became steeper, until at length the water lay far below us. The ground which we were traversing was so elevated above the water-flow that irrigation was impossible. It was arid and barren. Thistle and dandelion, with other and similar herbs, grew sparsely over its surface, which was staring white. To our right was a long embattled line, with many a bastion square and round.

Baba Khan was in too great a hurry for his breakfast to permit me to examine the old position just then, and we rode on a little farther to the south, to the dam itself. As we neared it, the ground became still more arid than before, rising steeply. The traveller approaching Benti would imagine that he drew near some extensively fortified position. There were bare earth surfaces, heaped wildly here and there, groups of men crowning their crests. Away to the right, half seen among the undulations of the accidented ground, were some hundreds of *evs*. I was in rather an ill humour as we drew near this spot, for the superior officers of our numerous escort were continually urging me to the front. I was not then sufficiently accustomed to Tekké manners to know whether they meant me to keep abreast of the Khan, that being the position of honour. I was rather under the impression that they did not wish me to stay behind, lest I might disappear, and make my way to the Persian frontier.

When within four hundred yards of the dam, the Khan halted, to allow me to come up with him. He said, 'This is the point upon which all Merv depends.' The words sprang to my lips—I could not repress them, for I felt exceedingly annoyed, out of temper, hot, and thirsty. 'If this be your vital point, why have you pitched your fortifications twenty-five miles away from it?' He said nothing, but his solitary eye glowed brighter.

We rode on abreast. A subdued roar of waters, growing louder as we advanced, struck my ears. In ten minutes we were upon a bare ridge of newly turned earth. Around us were a number of sun-shelters, a couple of stakes in the earth supporting a cross pole, from which depended a rude mat of plaited rush. The sun was fiery hot. In the scant shade crouched dozens of men, bronzed to the tint of Moors. As the cavalcade drew nigh they rose to their feet with a respectful air— at least a hundred of them. To the south-east was a stretch of ground, covered with waving reeds, across which

P

flowed the broad, level expanse of the upper Murgab. It was the first time I had an opportunity of seeing the main stream which gives fertility to the oasis. As far as eye could reach in the same direction stretched a wild jungle. Notwithstanding my colossal sheepskin hat, which warded off the sun's rays, I was glad to throw myself upon the proffered carpet, in the scanty rim of shade which the sun-shelters afforded. Green tea was served. The bronzed workers stood by with folded arms, waiting for the Khan to tell them to be seated. Then they sat down with the stoical repression of curiosity characteristic of North American savages. They refrained from asking about me, though news of me had already reached their ears. They waited till the Khan should condescend to inform them. Presently he said, 'This is the Ferenghi who has come to Merv, and I have brought him here to show him how we cultivate our grounds.'

We reposed for an hour, and then Baba Khan proposed a visit to the dam. A broad stretch of calm waters, eighty yards wide, lay in a south-easterly direction. Along its banks were thickets and reeds, and right and left were sedgy plains. Just at the point at which the dam was placed the river expanse was suddenly constricted. For twenty yards on either side the river bank above the dam was revetted with stout fascines of giant reeds, solidly lashed to stakes planted in the bank to prevent the friction of the current, as it neared the dam, from washing away the earth surface. Huge masses of earthwork closed the narrow gorge by which the stream found exit to the lower level by a passage scarce ten feet wide. The waters rushed thunderingly through this narrow gap to a level eight feet below their upper surface. The passage was some fifty yards in length, and, like its approaches, was lined with reed fascines.

AN AWKWARD CROSSING.

The object of this dam was to enable lateral canals to be thrown off, which would water the high lands above the level of the main stream northward of this point. The rush of water was tremendous, and nothing but the most assiduous care could prevent the narrow outlet from being widened to an extent which would have brought the water level with the lower reaches. One hundred men are incessantly employed in care of the dam and its sluice, and their best energies are continually exerted in replacing the fascines washed away by the heavy rush of the torrent. As I stood on the summit of the earthwork two dozen men, waist deep, were lashing new fascines into their places, while others were ramming earth behind them.

At last Baba Khan said, 'I think dinner awaits us.' Our horses were led up, and we trod the yielding, shifting slopes of the newly-thrown earth. We neared the dam itself, below which thundered the current from the upper surface. Baba Khan's horse went first, but he curvetted and pranced as his rider forced him towards the shaking pathway that spanned the current. He reared, and nearly threw his rider. He had never crossed the bridge before. I rode a powerful grey animal from the Caucasus, used to the torrents of his native mountains, and he stepped upon the bridge without a moment's hesitation. It was little if at all over three feet in breadth, and my steed trod mincingly as the brambles and earth gave way beneath his feet. The sounding torrent roared beneath us, and the spray, caught by the passing wind, wetted my face and clothes, short as was the time of passage. When I had crossed, the other horses followed uneasily.

We were received by the Kethkoda, or hereditary chief, of the village of Benti, a place of about seven hundred huts, and the usual number of bowls of *gattuk* were produced. Immediately after these came the *pièce de résis-*

tance. It was contained in an enormous wooden dish, and consisted of mutton fat, melted down on the previous day. The great heat of the weather prevented it from becoming actually solid, and it was in a pulpy, semi-crystalline state, and of a greyish-green colour. These Turcomans invariably keep their meat, before consuming it, as long as the very hot climate will allow. In fact, they prefer it when its odour has become what might be styled 'gamey.' This dish was placed in our midst as we sat, cross-legged, in a circle. Each person dipped in it a morsel of bread, and proceeded to eat. The first mouthful was enough for me. The nauseous taste of the unsalted fat, combined with its abominable odour, made it quite impossible for me to repeat the dose. I had largely partaken of the *gattuk*, and made pretence of going through all the little pantomimic arts which obtain in the country with a view of showing that I had eaten enough, and more than enough; and though I felt that I was scandalising my host and companions by not dipping further into the dainty dish, I was obliged to run the risk of their displeasure. I withdrew from the circle, and threw myself upon a felt mat, feigning sleep. In an hour I was aroused by Baba Khan, to accompany him on a further inspection of the waterworks and dam. In one part a number of Turcomans were bathing, and I remarked that in swimming they never adopted the system commonly in vogue among Europeans. Instead of swimming fully abreast, and striking simultaneously with both arms, they kept one shoulder forward, and struck hand over hand.

Above the dam the two principal canals, the Novur and Alasha, form as nearly as possible a right angle, the former flowing north, the latter west; and from these the land obtains its principal irrigation, the branches naturally diminishing in volume as they grow more remote, till in certain portions of the year they are almost dry. The greatest length of irrigated territory is from fifty to fifty-five miles, measuring from the southward of the dam in a north-westerly direction. Its greatest breadth from east to west is from thirty-five to forty miles. For a short distance below the dam the main stream of the Murgab is available for irrigation, but seven miles or thereabouts to its northward the channel of the river is too deeply cut to allow of the waters being conducted over the surface. Within this point, however, it is largely available, and, apart from irrigation, the streams are used to turn a very considerable number of rude turbine mills for grinding corn.

Two miles to the north-westward of the great dam of Benti, and close to the northern bank of the Murgab, stands the old city of the former occupants of the oasis —the Saruk Turcomans—Porsa Kala, once the military and political capital of the oasis, but now deserted and replaced by Kouchid Khan Kala. After having observed the watercourses, and gained as much information as I could from my guides, I rode away early next morning with Baba Khan and his following towards this place. Seen from a distance of a mile, Porsa Kala exhibits a long line of parched yellow walls and towers, rising from the summit of a slightly raised bank-like rampart similar in construction to that of Kouchid Khan Kala, but of not more than one-half its vertical height. Thirty years ago the place was thronged with its Saruk inhabitants: you can still see the roof-trees black with the hearth smoke, and water pitchers stand idly in the corners. So strong is the remaining impression of former life that one momentarily expects to meet a stray former inhabitant, and almost fancies he hears the soft muffled tread of the camel, when it is only the stifled throb of some choked stream which once gave birth to a turbine mill. The Saruks were apparently of much more gregarious instincts than their successors, the Tekkés. While dwelling here among the latter I saw no approach to anything like a permanent place of residence.

The sun was nearly vertical, and the sky wore that purple hue which belongs to mid-day hours in this part of the world, as I left my companions asleep in the scanty shade of the roofless walls, and sauntered out to take a look at the ruins. All around was an expanse of yellowish brown. No trace of vegetation could be seen on the burned-up expanse. Here and there lay a leaden-tinted snake with unfolded length, a veritable image of lethargy had not its diamond-like eyes denoted its sleepless vigilance. I have not a Turcoman's religious mania for killing snakes, but I have a terror of finding one curling around my ankle; and I fear that incessant vigilance in this regard made me lose much of the melancholy, solemn impressiveness of the once inhabited waste around me.

When my companions had aroused themselves from their siesta, we mounted, and made towards home. Our way, as before, lay along the left bank of the Novur canal, up to the point at which the branch which feeds Kouchid Khan Kala diverges to the westward. Here, crossing the rude wooden bridge, we halted for a brief space at the headquarters of Murad Bey. On proceeding northward by a group of villages occupied by a subdivision of Turcomans, known as 'Sore-heads,' an amusing incident occurred. A Turcoman dismounted from his horse, a white one. Animals of this colour are rarely seen in this district, an evil repute attaching to them. The horseman wanted a draught of water, and incautiously loosed his hold of the bridle. The steed started incontinently to gallop across the plain. A runaway horse is a serious nuisance in a country-like this, and everyone feels it to be his duty to aid the master of the fugitive beast in recovering his property. The whole of us, sixty in number, strove to head off the truant. For a couple of miles we rode in a straight line, but the runaway, unencumbered by weight, and having a good lead, gave us a long chase. Then the irrigation canals shifted both our courses, and we doubled and turned, sometimes heading away towards the desert, sometimes back upon the cluster of villages. At moments a Turcoman rider galloped close on either side of the riderless steed, and tried in vain to grasp his bridle, and I saw one attempt the daring expedient of springing from his own saddle into that of the horse which we pursued. He met, however, with a sad overthrow. Backwards and forwards over the vast plain we went, for a space of not less than an hour and a half, and, though we were joined by extra parties from the villages, who tried to turn the contumacious horse, we could not succeed in catching him. I was completely tired of the matter, and, besides, knowing that we had a long journey before us, I did not care to blow my horse any further, so I drew up on a slightly rising ground and watched the hunt. From what I saw of the remainder of it, I am of opinion that Turcoman horsemen would scarcely do well 'across country,' for though they will hang alongside their horses, stand in one stirrup, and sling themselves under the belly at full gallop, they do not care for leaping. I saw many a one come to grief at the broad irrigation trenches. The country is so flat that the horses are never taught to jump. At length it was decided to abandon the chase, and the proprietor of the wayward animal borrowed a horse to ride home upon. He issued orders that the fugitive should by no means be allowed to escape, and that if he could not be captured he should be shot. This was quite in keeping with the spirit of Turcoman ideas. They would much sooner liberate a captive without ransom than tolerate his running away from them, and in the same way the instructions to shoot the horse, and not allow him to run wild at his own discretion, were given.

Journeying northward we came to numerous villages of the Mjaour Turcomans, at one of which we halted to give our horses to drink, and to refresh ourselves with a draught of *yaghourt*. While waiting, I mounted a small sepulchral earth mound which stood hard by. From its summit I caught my first glimpse of the old cities of the plain—the ancient capitals of Margiana. A long line of walls and turrets, dominated by some towering domes, broke the line of the horizon some eight miles away to the north-east. I could scarcely express my anxiety to proceed there and then to this mysterious spot, concerning which so much has been written and so little known. Half-way between me and the ruins lay a large, shallow sheet of water, where unused irrigation trenches expended their supplies upon an uncultivated plain. Black ibises, wild swans, storks, cranes, and a hundred other varieties of aquatic birds waded in or swam upon the silent marsh. I begged again and again that my conductors would turn their steps in that direction, but was told that the day was too far advanced; that the neighbourhood of the ruins bore a very bad repute; that there were ghouls and divs, and various other kinds of evil spirits to be met with;

not to speak of the Ersari robbers from the banks of the Oxus, who from time to time lay in wait to plunder passing caravans. They promised, however, that if matters went well I should very shortly pay a special visit to the old cities, and with this I was obliged for the moment to be content, and nothing was left but to turn my horse's head homewards. Riding as swiftly as we might across the flooded plains, we arrived at Kouchid Khan Kala on the evening of May 5, having been absent just three days.

CHAPTER XIX.

Makdum Kuli Khan—Promised gifts—A doubtful ruler—Another present—Small jealousies—Signs of the times—A Russian prisoner.

Two days after my return from the dam of Benti and Porsa Kala, I received a visit from a person whom I had long been desirous of seeing, viz. Makdum Kuli Khan, the redoubtable chief of the Akhal Tekkés, who, in co-operation with Tokmé Serdar, his principal general, had long and successfully held the Russians at bay before the walls of Yengi Sheher. He had arrived at Kouchid Khan Kala on the previous evening, but had not been allowed to see me at once. As I afterwards learned, they feared that he might assist me in effecting my escape, and it was with the greatest difficulty that the Akhal Tekké chief at length obtained permission to call upon me.

I was quite alone when he entered. I was surprised at his youthful appearance. He did not appear to be more than twenty-seven years of age, though the total absence of beard and the extreme slightness of his moustache might have made him appear younger than he really was. Makdum Kuli Khan is over the middle height, slightly made, with very regular features, large hazel eyes, and a somewhat ruddy complexion. His costume was that of a well-to-do Turcoman—a long, striped crimson tunic, girt with voluminous white sash knotted in front; a long-sleeved camel-hair robe of light brown, thrown across his shoulders, and bound at the edge with the broad, peculiarly marked ribbon, striped diagonally yellow and red, indicating the Tekké division to which he belonged. Thrust in his sash was the long poniard which the Turcoman always carries, the handle of embossed gold, set with turquoises, and enamelled in the pommel. This was the only occasion on which I had seen a Turcoman, chief or otherwise, bearing gold-mounted arms. As a rule it is rare to see even silver used for this purpose.

Makdum Kuli saluted me gravely, and seated himself after the fashion of the country—kneeling, and reclining upon his heels. We exchanged the usual formalities required by Turcoman politeness, and he then told me of the difficulty he had experienced in obtaining permission to visit me. Kadjar Khan, he said, was very jealous of my being visited by any person except himself. In the conversation that followed he spoke with some bitterness of the defence of Geok Tepé and the small number of the Mervli who had come to his assistance. He said he had been offered the most favourable terms on condition of returning to Yengi Sheher, but had steadily refused to accept them. It was the intention of himself and his staunch followers to fight to the last should Merv be invaded, and, if beaten, to retire into Afghanistan. If not well received there, they purposed asking an asylum within the frontier of British India.

Our conversation was but brief, for Makdum Kuli Khan evidently feared lest Kadjar Khan might suspect him of concocting plans with me. He promised to see me again shortly, and reminded me that in one of my letters to him, written from Derguez, I had promised to make him a present of a field-glass, a revolver, and a signet ring. He inquired if I had these articles about me at the moment. As the two former were in full view it was not easy for me to deny having them. It is true that I had promised him the gifts mentioned, but I had done so with a view of inducing him to enable me to penetrate to Yengi Sheher; and, seeing that very little was to be gained at the moment by giving away what were to me almost indispensable articles, I should have been glad of any excuse to put off the Khan. On second consideration, however, knowing that his brother's district adjoined the ruins of the old cities of Merv, which I intensely desired to see, I thought it well to gratify his desires. He was delighted with the double telescope, and expressed his admiration of the Smith and Wesson revolver. Before leaving Meshed I had had made a very heavy gold ring, of Oriental pattern, and bearing an oval blue stone of the kind known in that part of the world as Solomon's seal, and engraved in full with his name and title. This I also presented to him, and he took leave of me, very well satisfied.

After Makdum Kuli's departure, my *ev* was crowded with visitors, anxious to know what the Akhal Tekké chief had been saying to me. Something was evidently on the *tapis*; and, apart from the hints which I received, the anxious and earnest conversation among the Kethkodas who visited me indicated that it was a matter of no ordinary importance. Rather broad hints were let drop that Kadjar Khan, the chieftain whom I had hitherto regarded as the Ichthyar, or supreme ruler of Merv, was not altogether what I had supposed him to be, and that some change was impending. By degrees I learned that when the Russian invasion of the Turcoman territory was impending, the Shah sent a messenger to Merv, inviting the Khans to visit him at Teheran, and to try to come to some agreement with him by which Persian supremacy at Merv would be acknowledged. Upon this

Baba Khan and Aman Niaz Khan, fearing that they might be detained as hostages, called a council, and retired temporarily; Kadjar was elected Ichthyar and sent with a following to Teheran, where he remained some months, and afterwards returned without coming to any arrangement. Thus it was that I found him holding the supreme rank.

After sunset he came to my hut to try and win me over to his side, but I declined, telling him that several chiefs had told me of the real position of affairs. This sent him into a passion. He told me that if the other Khans came into power my life would not be worth a moment's purchase, and he then went away. Soon after his brother, the moullah, came, evidently on the same tack. He pointed out that Kadjar Khan was my friend, but that I had omitted one indispensable ceremony, that of presenting a *zat* or present to the chief. I replied that I had only been waiting for a favourable opportunity, and, as I declined to send one by him for fear that it should not reach its destination, he took his leave.

Among other articles intended for presentation I had a silver casket, richly engraved and embossed, and set with turquoises and rubies, for which I had paid about twenty-five pounds sterling. I placed within it some ruby and turquoise rings, folded it in paper, and, after sealing it, despatched it by my servant to the Khan's residence. In the meantime Aman Niaz came in, accompanied by his uncle and several followers, evidently with a view of preparing me for coming events. He had scarcely taken his seat when Kadjar Khan again appeared. He was, clearly, highly displeased at the presence of Aman Niaz Khan, but it was also easily to be seen that he did not care to say too much in presence of the latter. He simply drew from his pocket the casket which I had sent to him, saying, 'What is this?' I replied, 'Khan, as you see, it is a jewelled silver casket.' 'What is it for?' he continued. 'To keep as a tribute of my respect,' I replied. 'What is it worth?' said the Khan. I mentioned its value in Persian money. 'Ouallah Billah!' he cried. 'Six hundred krans! why, I would not give you two for it!' Then, throwing it contemptuously on the carpet close to me, he said, 'Take back your box, and give me the money!' I must admit that I was considerably taken aback by the manner in which my present was treated. However, I had, at a bound, gained an enormous insight into the mental temperament of Turcoman chiefs. I replied, 'Certainly, Khan, if you wish; but I thought you might be offended if I merely offered you the money.' Then, with an affectation of great magnificence, I drew from my pocket the twenty-five pounds in gold, and handed it to him. 'By God!' exclaimed he, 'that is right; I am satisfied.'

Hereupon a new comedy arose. During this scene Aman Niaz Khan had been glaring at me from between his bleared eyelids, and when Kadjar, happy in the possession of his wealth, left the *ev*, the Otamish chief elevated both his hands behind his ears, in expression of amazement at the manner in which the present had been dealt with, and said: 'Sahib, you can see that Kadjar is no Khan. Had such a present been offered to me by a Dowlet Adam (a man of the state), I would not part with it for four times its value, not even if ten horses were offered to me in return.' Of course this was too broad a hint to be passed lightly over. I replied, 'Aman Niaz Khan, there are Khans, and Khans; I recognise you as a true Khan. Will you accept this casket as a slight token of my regard?' Whereupon he again raised both hands behind his ears, bowed low, as he sat in a kneeling posture, and, stretching out his palms, received the coveted gift. All his followers were loud in their exclamations of admiration at my generosity; and the Khan's uncle volunteered the statement that all that his nephew possessed, and all his clansmen, were at my service. 'Not,' he took care to remark, 'because of the present, but because I can at once perceive that you are really a Dowlet Adam.' These were some of the opening incidents of the bloodless revolution which was to take place in the near future.

Almost every moment from this time forward I could perceive signs of the approach of something unusual, and also that events were rapidly turning in my favour. After the visits of Kadjar and Aman Niaz Khans, one of Baba Khan's chief cavalry officers called upon me with a soda-water bottle full of arrack as a present from the Toktamish chief, and Beg Murad, the fat, humorous-looking ruffian to whom I have alluded when describing my arrival at Merv, and with whom I had ever since been on very indifferent terms, sent me a gift of a shaggy, big-tailed sheep. At the same time, the leading persons of Kadjar Khan's party were unremitting in their efforts to get from me an assurance that I would acknowledge as Ichthyar no one save their friend. Failing to obtain this assurance, they endeavoured to effect small loans of money from me, in order to make sure of something before their faction went out of power.

On this same evening I received a note, written in Russian, from Kidaieff, a young Russian gunner who had been imprisoned in Merv during the preceding seven years, coupled with a verbal message from him, asking for some pecuniary assistance, and bespeaking my good offices towards obtaining his liberation. The bearer, by name, I believe, Ana Geldi, was the individual in whose immediate power Kidaieff was. Having failed during so long a period to extract any ransom from the Russian authorities, he was trying to raise all the money he could, in one way or another, before Kidaieff should slip through his fingers, as, at the moment, seemed far from impossible. However, as a proof of his belief in my non-Muscovite character, and as an intimation of good-will, he remarked that I had only to say the word, and the throat of the captive would immediately be cut in my honour. I used all my efforts to point out that I should consider it the reverse of an honour to have anybody whatever, even though a Russian, killed in the way suggested. On this occasion I sent the money asked for by Kidaieff, but I very much doubt whether he ever received any of it. I also sent him word that as soon as possible I would come to see him, and hear his story from his own lips.

Kadjar Khan came in again somewhat after midnight, accompanied by Dowlet Nazar Beg. They sat up the livelong night with me, talking about the state of politics in the oasis, and the necessity of preventing what they called the pro-Russian party from coming into power. Shortly after their entry, I was puzzled by the sound of digging, in the immediate neighbourhood of my house. It was continued with the utmost persistency. I began to be alarmed, lest some trick was about to be played upon me, or that they were even digging my grave, but I received from Kadjar Khan the assurance that preparations were being made to do me honour, and that a ditch and breastwork were being drawn around my *ev*, in order to keep intruders and noisy people at a distance. When morning dawned, I could perceive that my dwelling was nearly encircled by a small trench, at a distance of a few feet from its walls.

CHAPTER XX.

A fresh council—Political questions—I become a Khan—An expedition—A visit to Baba Khan—Merv vegetables—Peculiarities of teeth—The ride to the ruins—An ancient city—Traces of the past—Crumbling palaces—Old tombs—Giaour Kala—Rampart and citadel—A Caravanserai—Brazen vessels—Manners of prayer—Religious customs—Traditions of Alexander—Treasure-seekers—Tomb of Sultan Sanjar—Melon-growing—Strange offerings—The voiceless wilderness.

On the day following, between one and two o'clock in the afternoon, as I lay drowsily upon my carpet, awaiting the turn of events, I was summoned to attend a meeting of the notables of Merv. I was conducted by the messenger to an *ev* of more than ordinary dimensions, situated about two hundred yards to the north of my own. I found there assembled some twenty-five persons, including the Khans of the Toktamish and Otamish divisions. The interior was decorated with rich carpets, hung round the walls, and the floor was covered with equally costly material. I was given to understand that a general council had been held earlier in the day, but that no definite result had been arrived at, save that the council of Khans and Kethkodas had received power to organise a new and vigorous executive, calculated to deal with the pressing circumstances of the moment. The leaders had come to the conclusion that the time had arrived for the resumption of power by the hereditary Khans, and the removal from office of old Kadjar, who had acted during the previous twelve months as their figure-head and mouthpiece. I was very tired and sleepy, after my night-long interview with Kadjar Khan and his companion, and felt in anything but the humour to undergo the cross-examination which evidently formed part of their programme. But as I surmised that my liberty of action for a considerable time to come might depend upon the manner in which I bore myself before this council, I tried to answer their queries as best I might. I was asked point blank, 'Are the Russians coming to Merv, or are they not?' Thanks to the news now forwarded to me weekly from Teheran, I was aware that the Russians had promised not to advance further eastward than Askabad, and I was able to answer that they were not. Then I was asked of the position of the English troops, and whether they were coming to Merv; what advice I would give the Mervli, and whether the Queen would be willing to accept them as servants; and, lastly, whether England would give them a subsidy to pay for two thousand horsemen. I told them I could only give my opinion, for I had no authority to speak; but they seemed satisfied with my words and the course I pointed out, and, finally, being utterly wearied, I was allowed to retire.

When I left the place of assembly, half a dozen Turcomans accompanied me; but instead of leading me in the direction of my former residence, they conducted me to an open space lying between the northern and southern lines of *evs*, and which had hitherto been entirely unoccupied. To my great surprise, I found that in its midst was being constructed a kind of redoubt, seventy or eighty yards square, on which nearly a hundred men were busily engaged. In the centre of this space was an *ev* in course of erection. The wooden, cage-like framework was already reared, and half a dozen women were occupied in adjusting the felt walls and roof. To this I was led by my escort. I had become too accustomed to the vicissitudes of fortune, and the unforeseen whims of the Turcomans, to be surprised at anything, so without question I paced along the narrow causeway which served as one of the entries to the redoubt, and entered the half-completed dwelling. My saddles, arms, bedding, and other effects were piled within it, and the two Turcoman servants whom I had hired since the departure of Gholam Riza were busily engaged in adjusting the carpet. Turning to my conductors, I said, 'Why have you changed my *ev* from the place in which it stood to this? And what is the meaning of this breastwork which you have thrown up around it?' 'This,' they answered, 'is your residence as a Khan; for the *medjlis* has decided that you are to be accepted here as the representative of the English Padishah.' This was almost too much for my gravity, but, retaining my self-possession, I simply bowed, as if all this were only a matter of course, and, sitting upon the carpet prepared for me, made note of the circumstances.

The revolution was now practically effected, though not consummated in a public form. Kadjar Khan had ceased to administer public affairs, and for the moment the eastern and western divisions of the Turcomans arranged their state concerns apart, under the guidance of their own immediate chiefs, Baba and Aman Niaz Khans. As both these gentlemen had been very civil to me since the meeting of the privy council, I thought there was a good opportunity of disregarding old Kadjar's recommendation to keep myself aloof from them, and accordingly, the same evening, I asked Aman Niaz Khan whether it would not be possible for me to visit the ruins of the old cities of the plain. He was very fond of expeditions of the kind, and willingly assented to my desire, telling me that on the following day he would accompany me, with the necessary escort. This he undertook to do without any permission from Baba Khan, for now that no Ichthyar or chief commander was in power, Aman Niaz considered himself quite on a footing of equality with his brother Khan of the eastern division, though the latter was by courtesy styled the senior of the two.

A little after dawn, according to appointment, Aman Niaz Khan, who had stayed specially in my neighbourhood during the preceding night, his own residence being a considerable distance away, came in to drink green tea with me before starting. He brought with him his maternal uncle, Nazarli Beg, a kind of scribe called Moullah Baba, and half-a-dozen of his own immediate clansmen, the Sitchmaz, that subdivision of the Otamish to which his family belonged. He wore the silk cloak, irregularly splashed with brilliant tints, which he habitually affected, and which he carried when I first saw him in my pavilion tent. As usual, he looked extremely sallow and worn, and the edges of his eyelids were bloodshot. He looked quite a wreck of a man, though, as I had subsequent reason to know, he could hold out as well as the best of his men in traversing long distances. He told me that he felt far from well; that he had smoked too much opium on the preceding evening, and that he had also drunk more arrack than was good for his health.

The sun was getting pretty well above the horizon as we mounted, each one fully armed, as if he were going on the war path instead of on a peaceful promenade. The Khan, besides two formidable horse-pistols in his holster, carried at his belt a Colt's revolver of an antiquated pattern. At his back was hung a remarkably handsome double-barrelled fowling-piece of English make, and at his side appeared the inevitable sabre. With the exception of the revolver and pistols, all his men were similarly armed.

We directed our steps towards the great entrance of the now nearly completed fortress, with the intention of crossing it, and making our exit by the opposite gateway. In doing so we had to pass through a group of *aladjaks*, in which, surrounded by the greater number of the captured Persian guns, was Baba Khan's residence. Early as the hour was, the latter chief was seated on a carpet before his door, attended by his immediate henchmen. As we drew near I could hear from some of the villagers muttered expressions of discontent, and queries as to whether I had obtained Baba Khan's permission to proceed to Makdum Kuli's village. I heard Aman Niaz say, *sotto voce*, that we had not got Baba's permission, and did not want it, that his own was quite sufficient. Still, I thought it would be only courteous, under the circumstances, to make known my intentions to the senior Khan, so, dismounting, I drew near the group. Baba and his entire company rose to their feet as I approached, and received me very politely. I stated the object of our expedition, and the senior Khan at once gave consent, saying that he was sorry that circumstances prevented him from accompanying me. He despatched a few horsemen with us as far as the next village, this being an evidence of politeness usual on such occasions.

A Turcoman, when not on the war path, but merely travelling, as we then were, takes every possible opportunity of stopping, now to light his pipe, and now to enter some *ev* in which to partake of the food that is invariably offered. At Baba Kalassi we drew up, especially as the people of the place, seeing the Khan and his horsemen, and his distinguished Ferenghi guest, coming up, insisted upon our dismounting and partaking of breakfast with them. This my companions were in no wise loth to do, so leaving our horses to the care of the attendants we entered the elder's house. The elder invariably entertains strangers, and in compensation receives a small subscription from each villager, either in money or kind.

A very substantial *pilaff* of boiled corn, well greased with sheep's-tail fat, and mingled with slices of *kashir*, or sweet yellow wild carrot, which abounds in Merv, and, indeed, all over the plain extending westward to the Caspian, was served. Boiled in the manner I have described, in combination with fat and corn, the *kashir* is exceedingly agreeable to the taste, and much sweeter even than the red carrot. In size it is rarely over a foot in length, and three-quarters of an inch in diameter at its thickest portion. I have no doubt that under cultivation it would attain much more respectable proportions, but vegetables, such as the carrot, turnip, &c., are never cultivated among the Turcomans.

Another singular vegetable was laid before us, viz., the bulbous root of the wild tulip, or Lala Gul. This plant often attains a height of from two and a half to three feet, the flower assuming the dimensions of a large tumbler. It is of a brilliant crimson colour. The bulb varies in size from that of a small onion to three inches in diameter. It is eaten raw, and tastes like a very tender sweet chestnut, but with rather more of the flavour of the hazel nut. It appears to be wholesome, for though I have eaten large quantities I have never suffered any inconvenience therefrom.

I had often been puzzled, when riding across the plains, to see holes of a foot in depth, evidently newly scraped up, and I now learned the cause of these. The jackals and foxes are very fond of the tulip root, and dig it up with their paws. The wild boars also consume it largely.

After the corn *pilaff*, a wooden dish, filled with bread and mutton broth, and on the surface of which were some half-picked bones, was served. These bones, ribs of a young lamb, the Turcomans scarcely deign to pick. They crunch them up bodily, together with whatever meat may be attached to them, for as a rule their teeth are wonderfully fine, and seem to continue undeteriorated by age. From the very first my attention had been attracted by the beauty of the teeth of the Tekkés, and I had also noticed a peculiarity which I at first set down as a natural abnormality. Almost without exception the two upper middle incisors of a full-grown Tekké exhibit, each in its midst, a deep angular notch, reaching to a depth of fully a quarter the length of the exposed portion of the tooth, and rendering it bicuspid. I had taken note of this fact, and, with a view to ascertain whether it was a general peculiarity of the race, I lost no opportunity of observing, and subsequently discovered its origin. The melon and water melon form a large portion of the diet of the Mervli. Their numerous seeds are laid by and dried in the sun, partly for sowing purposes, and partly to be eaten in leisure moments. In most of the towns on the border one sees, in the grocers' booths, large sacks of these dried melon-seeds. One side of the flat seed case is more or less rounded, but the other side presents a sharp, hard edge. In eating the seed the rounded edge is placed upon one of the lower incisors, and the sharp edge pressed with one or other of the upper ones. It requires considerable pressure to cause the two carpels of the seed-cover to separate so that the interior may be extracted.

As the Turcomans, even when on horseback, are continually eating these melon-seeds, in the end their sharp edges produce the serration of the teeth of which I have spoken, and that, too, only in the upper incisors, owing to the rounded margin of the seed being placed lowermost. That it has nothing whatever to do with the natural formation of the teeth is evident from the fact that in young children there is no sign of this peculiar marking. Besides, the Tekkés were at some trouble to explain to me its cause.

Breakfast over, we resumed our march, passing close to the base of an ancient mound, Marma Khan Tepé, where, to judge from the great amount of brick and tile scattered around, buildings of considerable size must have formerly stood. The Turcomans told me that a town of large dimensions once existed there. Not far from it is the village of Yussub, where a second bazaar is held. Thence we pushed on, almost in a due easterly direction, save when the unpleasant inundations with which we met at every few hundred yards forced us to make a *détour*. For though it was early in May, the heat was excessive, and irrigation was absolutely necessary to prevent the young corn from being utterly dried up.

Our ride was consequently slow and hindered by a marsh, full of gigantic cane-like reeds, as well as by the water. The canal here had cut very deeply into the soil, the steep banks being fifteen to twenty feet in height. Passing over three different rude bridges, composed of tree-trunks and osiers, we continued our march towards the head-quarters of the Vekil, young Yussuf Khan's village, where, for the moment, Makdum Kuli Khan, the great Akhal Tekké chief, dwelt, surrounded by the three or four thousand adherents who remained faithful to him after the overthrow of Yengi Sheher.

Owing to the delays we had had upon the road, and the slow pace at which we proceeded, it was near sunset when we approached Yussuf Khan's premises. We were very kindly received by the two Khans.

The next morning, after a copious breakfast of bread, mutton broth, and boiled mutton, preceded by green tea, we set out for the ruins of the ancient cities, the centre of which lay almost due east. Half-an-hour's ride, through very flooded grounds, brought us to the eastern limit of cultivation. Then the ground rose slightly, putting its surface above the reach of the present irrigation system. Here we came in view of an immense wilderness of ruined buildings, forming a semicircle in front of us to the north and south. Between us and the domes stretched, in an apparently unbroken line for four or five miles, a belt of ruined wall and shattered houses, apparently the remains of former suburban villas and gardens. This belt, running due north and south, was over half a mile in width. Even still nourished by the scanty rains and still scantier moisture of the earth itself, the withered gardens displayed remnants of former greenness, choked with masses of ruin. Snakes swarmed on every side, with black eagles, sparrow-hawks, and vultures. Clearing this belt of dilapidated wall and building, at a distance of a quarter of a mile before us stood the western front of Bairam Ali, the youngest of the three cities, each of which in its turn has borne the name of Merv. This front was a line of embattled wall, two hundred yards in length, flanked by circular towers, and having a large guarded gateway in its centre. The wall, fifteen feet in height, is further strengthened by an exterior ditch, spanned at the gateway by a brick archway, now piled and cumbered with broken material. These walls were partly of baked and partly of unbaked brick, and in a very fair state of preservation. Passing beneath the low, vaulted gateway, we stood within a square place, a complete wilderness of ruins. What had once been a street, crossing the square, was flanked by the remains of brick houses. On its southern side, and near its eastern extremity, were the vaulted remains of extensive baths. This first, or western square, was apparently a later addition, and intended for the accommodation of the caravans which frequented the place. The real town of Bairam Ali itself adjoins it. It is a quadrangular enclosure, two hundred yards from east to west, and about two hundred and fifty from north to south. Its western wall is common to both squares. Its walls are, however, higher than those of the other, owing to their being built upon a low embankment of six or eight feet in height. Entering this by a gateway similar to the first, but of larger and more massive proportions, we again stand in the midst of complete ruin. Near the centre are the tolerably well-preserved remains of a mosque, its cupola forming a salient feature of the group of remains. Its courtyard has well-built cloisters of brick, and adjoining the mosque itself is a large building, probably the residence of the moullahs. In the northeastern angle is the brick 'arg,' or citadel, some eighty yards square. Its sides are parallel to that of the town itself, and two of them, the northern and eastern, are identical with those of the city. Entering by the gateway in the southern wall, we came into a kind of courtyard, lined all round by what were once elaborately ornamented buildings, three storeys high, the palace of the former sovereigns. One could still trace the arabesques and other decorations, stamped upon the stucco-plastered walls, and the chimney-places are still black with the smoke of the last fires. Near the entrance of the palace I noticed the broken remains of a subterranean aqueduct. It was brick arched, eighteen inches in height by twelve in breadth, and carefully plastered on the inside with some kind of hard brown cement. Here and there were numerous wells, now completely choked up, and the resort of immense numbers of snakes and of small birds, especially hoopoes, who take refuge in them against the broiling heat. This latter bird is never molested by the Turcomans, who hold it in great esteem. A moullah who accompanied us informed me that it was one of the principal servants of Solomon, whose life it had on one occasion saved by conveying to him intelligence of some deadly peril which awaited him. Round the mouths of these wells were broken parapets, piled with masses of rubbish overgrown with a creeping species of *berberis*, a very disagreeable thorn when any piece of ground covered with it has to be traversed. It bears a large fruit, in size and shape closely resembling a green fig, the five carpels of which dehisce, separating and bending backwards, so that with their crimson interiors they might easily pass for the blossom of the plant itself.

This Bairam Ali was the last of the towns of Merv, if I except Porsa Kala, the Saruk settlement which I have already described. It is named after Bairam Ali Khan, its last defender, who was killed here in 1784, when the town was attacked by Begge Jan, *alias* Emir Masum, sovereign of Bokhara. In the midst of all this waste of crumbling palaces and baths and ramparts, excepting the snakes, a few birds, and an occasional jackal, no living creature is to be met with, save, indeed, an occasional Ersari robber or treasure-seeker; for here, as in almost every other part of the East, the popular imagination enriches these ruined vaults and foundations with secret treasures stowed away beneath them.

We left Bairam Ali by its eastern gate, for the double enclosure has two entrances. Immediately in front, and a thousand yards away to the eastward, rose a long line of earth bank, indicating the site of Giaour Kala, as one of the ruined cities is now called. We did not proceed there immediately, but directed our course in a north-easterly direction, to a group of buildings some two hundred and fifty yards off, occupying the brow of an undulation of the ground. There was what resembled a large triumphal arch, forty feet high and about the same in breadth, built of hard flat-baked bricks of a yellowish-brown colour, and ornamented with oblong tiles enamelled of a bright blue, the alternate ones being a shade darker than those next them. Nowhere else among the ruins of Merv is the slightest trace of similar enamelled bricks to be found. In contact with, and to the south of the arch are two covered buildings, the sides of which are quite open. A low, open-worked brick balustrade runs breast-high around them. These buildings and balustrades are sparsely ornamented with blue tiles, like the triumphal arch. Both buildings are exactly alike, and inside each stands an oblong tomb of bluish-grey marble, beautifully and elaborately sculptured with inscriptions and arabesques, and divided into panels. Each tomb is about seven feet in length, two in breadth at the top, and four in height. The sides and ends have a slight incline. Apart from the arabesques and inscriptions, which are cut in very slight relief, the outline of the tombs is perfectly plain. Adjoining the more easterly of the buildings were the remains of what had probably been large baths, if one might judge from the extensive underground vaults with brick groining, closely resembling those within the *enceinte* of Bairam Ali. The Turcomans who accompanied me could tell me little concerning the history of these tombs, or of the persons interred beneath them. They only spoke of them as very holy 'sheiks,' for here this word, which in Arabia and Syria simply means a military or political chief, indicates an individual celebrated for sanctity. The tombs were known as those of the *Sahaba bouridal*, literally 'the beheaded gentlemen,' and my informants told me that they had been murdered in the cause of religion; when, or why, they could not give me the slightest idea, though they prayed as devoutly before their resting-place as if they knew everything about their history. The entire area between these old tombs and the triumphal arch was completely covered with *débris* of bricks and tiles.

From this point we turned in an easterly direction, descending a pretty steep incline, towards a very deep irrigation canal which was in course of construction some hundreds of yards further on, in continuation of one which brought the water almost level with the north-western angle of Bairam Ali. When I saw it, the water had not yet been made to flow to this point. A shallow valley intervenes between the eastern face of this latter town and the western one of Giaour Kala. Crossing the valley, we proceeded towards the south-eastern angle of Giaour Kala. The great earth ramparts by which it is surrounded closely resemble, in size and construction, those of Kouchid Khan Kala, which would almost seem to have been copied from them. At a distance the ramparts of the old town exactly resemble a great railway embankment. The ground upon which it is situated rises considerably towards its northern side, while the level of the top of the walls on each side is exactly the same. Consequently, the southern line is much higher than that along the north. At the south-eastern angle the ramparts are at least sixty feet high. Urging our horses at full speed, we galloped with difficulty obliquely along the great slope, and succeeded in gaining the summit. At this point the *turbé* of some holy person of the wilderness had been erected, and a pole, bearing a piece of tattered linen floating bannerwise at its extremity, had been planted beside it. The walls, which at a guess I should say were eight hundred and fifty yards from east to west, and six hundred and fifty yards from north to south, enclosed a regular quadrangular space. Immediately below us, and occupying the whole of the south-western portion of the enclosure, was what apparently had been a small lake in which water was stored for the use of the inhabitants. Through a gap near the north-western angle of the ramparts formerly entered an irrigation stream, the bed of which is still distinctly traceable, and which, I am informed, flowed from the ancient dam at Bent-i-Sultan, on the Murgab, a day's journey beyond the present Saruk dam of Kazakli.

Almost in the centre of Giaour Kala stands a large mound, on the summit of which are the traces of walls and towers. This was probably an old palace, or a defensive work of some kind. The *arg*, or citadel proper, was here, as in every other ancient town in this part of the world which I have examined, in its north-eastern angle, and consisted of a square enclosure, of which the northern and eastern sides were identical with the main rampart itself. The *terre pleine*, or inner area, of this redoubt-like work, is considerably above that on which the central mound stands. I made the entire circuit of the ramparts, proceeding first along its southern, then its eastern, and lastly its northern side. Towards the middle of the northern side still exist some traces of rampart, of upper parapet, and of embattled wall; but I should say that these were of a far later date than the great embankment on which they were built. The whole of the area within the ramparts is littered with the *débris* of broken tiles and earthenware vessels, many of the fragments exhibiting the most beautiful tints, and, in some cases, prismatic colours. I did not come upon an entire utensil of any kind.

Standing on the ramparts of this old city, the view ranges far away to the eastward, over slightly undulating ground largely covered with tamarisk growths, while here and there are traces of ruined walls and buildings, scattered sparsely in the present wilderness. This Giaour Kala is the oldest of the three remains, and was doubtless the first walled city erected upon the spot. It was destroyed by the Arabs towards the end of the seventh century, when the lieutenants of Omar, having overrun Persia, pushed away northward towards the Oxus.

Descending from the northern ramparts, we wended our way in a north-westerly direction towards some large ruins, distant a few hundreds of yards. Some of them had been ancient palaces, to judge by the elaborateness of ornamentation of their interiors. Others had evidently been religious structures, and some may have been storehouses. Continuing still further in the same direction, and leaving the old town of Sultan Sanjar to our left, we reached the only building which in all the vast extent of crumbling remains is now used for any human purpose. It is the last caravanserai at which caravans from Meshed, proceeding through Merv to Bokhara, halt before entering upon the waterless expanse beyond. It is known as the caravanserai of Khodja (or moullah) Yussuf Hamadani. It consists of two enclosures, one about a hundred yards square, and another, some thirty yards to the northward, of half that size. The latter is simply a wall-girt space, within which camels and other beasts of burden are assembled at night, and in the corner of which is a deep well, furnished with a bucket and lift. The entrance to the caravanserai is in the northern side of the main enclosure. Right and left of the doorway are extensive vaulted apartments of brick, occupying the entire length of that side of the enclosure. More than half of the western side is taken up by a small mosque, the entire eastern front of which is open to the air. It is termed the mosque of Mehemet Hussein Herati, a nobleman of that locality who came hither on a pilgrimage and caused this mosque to be built in honour of Yussuf Hamadani, whose tomb occupies the centre of the main enclosure. In the vaulted chamber to the left, or east, of the doorway, are two enormous brazen pots, nearly five feet in diameter, set in a bed of brick arranged so as to allow of fires being lighted underneath them. In these huge utensils is prepared, simultaneously, the food of the members of the caravans. There are two attendants in the place—*sofis*, as my companions styled them—two exceedingly dirty-looking, cadaverous individuals, wearing large white turbans, and who are supposed to keep on hand various small stores to be disposed of to travellers. These men informed me that the pots were presented by Emin Khan of Urgenz (Khiva) when he came to this place upon a pilgrimage very many years ago—how many they did not know; it might be a century, or three centuries. The groined roof overhead was sadly blackened by the smoke of the fire, but here and there I could make out that the surface of the bricks had been silvered, or, I might rather say, leaded over, by being rubbed with a piece of metal. The attendants told me that this silvering had been done by order of Abdullah Khan, of Bokhara, who came upon a pilgrimage to the tomb of the saint. This may or may not be true; but while I could distinctly see the metallic covering on the surface of some of the bricks, it appeared quite confined to separate ones, those alongside being entirely without any trace of metallic tint. Had I not been told of the origin of the metallized appearance, I should have decidedly said that it was some lacquered surface, developed in the process of baking the brick itself, and that, too, unintentionally. However, I give the story told me by the guardians of the caravanserai.

These vaulted chambers formed a very welcome refuge from the glare of the sun, resembling so many ice-houses when we entered them after a quick gallop over the blazing marly plain separating us from the ramparts of Giaour Kala. A tomb, which stood in the very centre of the enclosure, was evidently the original building round which the others had been erected at a later period. It consisted of a rudely-built, flat-roofed house, two storeys high, some thirty feet wide by fifteen in depth. It was entered by a strongly barred door. Behind it, and adjoining it to the southward, was a balustraded, roofed enclosure similar to those at the tombs of the 'beheaded gentlemen,' and within which stood a somewhat similar tomb.

Before proceeding to eat or rest, my companions performed their orisons around the tomb of the blessed Yussuf Hamadani. They drew up in a line on its western side, with their faces towards the tomb. They prayed for a few minutes in muttered tones, and then all advanced to the balustrade. Each person, laying both his palms upon it, applied them to his face, drawing them downwards towards his chin. Then they began to circle slowly around the tomb, proceeding towards their right hands. At each two steps they placed their hands upon the balustrade, repeating the operation of stroking down their faces and beards. The balustrade was covered with dust and sand, and as, owing to the heat of the day, my companions were perspiring pretty freely, it may be imagined what appearance they presented, after twenty or thirty applications of the dust-covered hands had been made to their countenances. Arrived at the eastern side of the tomb, they again formed line, this time kneeling, still facing the tomb, and praying in the same manner as before. They then repeated the march round, with the same peculiar ceremony. Then we went to visit the mosque, which was little more than a large deep recess, furnished with a *mirhab*, or devotional station. Above the principal recess, or chamber, was a vaulted room, surmounted by a small cupola. My conductors prayed for awhile within this building, and I was surprised that they made no objection to my presence within the sacred precincts, even during the religious ceremonies. I remarked, too, another peculiarity. They did not uncover their feet, as is invariably the custom in Constantinople, or in any Persian mosque that I have seen. On subsequent inquiry I learned that when, as was the case with all the party, long brown leather riding boots reaching to the knees were worn, it was not usual to remove them, either when entering a mosque or paying a visit to the house of a friend. These long boots are never worn except by a horseman, and the fact of his having been mounted presupposes that he has not soiled his feet in walking across the muddy ground.

Having got through a due allowance of prayers, we next proceeded to prepare green tea at the fire which the two *sofis* lighted for us. After the usual meal of griddled bread and weak tea, we indulged in the siesta for which the extreme heat and our long ride had fully prepared us. For my part, I could get but little repose, for the *singak*, as the Turcomans call the common house-fly, swarming about the spot consequent upon the offal left by the passage of caravans, made existence almost intolerable. While we were endeavouring to rest, one of our companions took his station as sentinel upon the tomb of the little mosque, and kept a sharp look-out for the possible approach of Ersari robbers, who make the ruins of Merv a trysting-place when they organize an *aleman*, or raid, upon any of the Vekil villages.

After a brief rest, and having recompensed the *sofis* for their trouble with a few pieces of silver, we wended our way towards the remains of some earthworks lying about three hundred yards to the westward. Here was a rectangular space, its sides, like all the other enclosed areas of the place, looking towards the cardinal points, and each side being about five hundred yards in length. It had evidently been an encampment of some sort, but the traces of the fortifications were now very indistinct. The Turcomans call it Iskender Kala, and say that Alexander the Great's army was camped there when on its way to India. This is the local tradition, but in these countries Alexander, or, as he is styled, Iskender, comes into every story connected with ruins of remote antiquity. A moullah, a brother of Makdum Kuli Khan, who was explaining to me the local traditional history of the place, informed me that Alexander had foretold the destruction of Merv, and that he was a great *pihamber* (prophet). I ventured to express a doubt as to whether the Macedonian soldier had ever been endued with the gifts attributed to him by my informant, whereupon he flew into a violent rage, saying that it was easy to see that I was a giaour, and unacquainted with the truth of things in general.

After having examined the old entrenchments, we turned southwards, and approached the northern side of the ancient city of Sultan Sanjar. This is a great quadrangular enclosure, measuring about six hundred yards on each side, and surrounded by a well-preserved wall with numerous flanking towers, a *fausse braye*, or lower secondary exterior rampart, as at Meshed, being added. This town is said to have been destroyed by the son of Zenghis Khan, Tului, about the year 1221. It must, however, have been occupied at a later period—at least, the fortified walls—for in the flanking towers at the corners and gates are artillery embrasures. It is provided with four gates, each well defended by massive towers of baked brick, a material which also enters largely into the circuit of the walls, especially their lower portions. With the exception of the mausoleum of the Sultan himself, standing exactly in the centre, at the point where the two great causeways running respectively north and south and east and west cross each other, of all the buildings that once stood within the walls there is not now one brick remaining upon another. One is puzzled to imagine how such thorough and complete ruin could have been worked, and still more mystified by the occurrence, in close vicinity to each other, of pits of from four to five feet deep, dug all over the surface. I was told that these pits were made by treasure-seekers, a caravan scarcely ever passing by the place without many of its members trying their fortune by digging these holes, in hopes that they might perchance stumble upon a pot of gold or jewels. That quantities of ancient money and vessels of precious metal had been found here from time to time, Yussuf Khan assured me. The entire destruction of the foundation, and the upsetting and scattering of the material, is probably due to this continued digging. Moreover, the materials of the houses have evidently been transported from the spot, and made use of in the construction of the later city close by—Bairam Ali. The Easterns appear to have a superstitious dislike to rebuilding upon the site of a former town. In the older city, Giaour Kala, there are only fragments of brick and pottery scattered over the surface, the great mass of the building material having, I believe, been made use of to construct the city which succeeded it, Sultan Sanjar. In like manner, when the last-named city was destroyed, the material was utilized for the erection of the most modern city. In Bairam Ali the buildings still extant can be seen, as well as the materials of the others, scattered about in great quantities, for, no other town having been built in the locality at a later period, the *débris* of the former one was not removed.

The tomb of Sultan Sanjar is a place of pilgrimage, and no Turcoman ever passes this spot without paying homage to the sanctity of the departed potentate. The tomb itself is of commanding size. It cannot be less than sixty feet to the summit of its cupola. Its form is very similar to that of Ferdusi's tomb at Toos, but it bears traces of having been still more elaborately ornamented. Its greatest diameter is at least forty feet. Its ground plan was that of a square, with the corners flattened; within, the walls still preserve a large portion of the stucco and white plaster with which they were formerly coated, and on which still remain, in many places, blue and red arabesques upon a white ground. The doorway is on the western side, and the floor seems to have been excavated, probably for the purpose of removing the pavement, so that one enters by an inclined plane, leading downwards, and can plainly see that the present floor is at least six feet below the level of the original one. In the centre stands the tomb, about the size and dimensions of those of the *Sahaba bouridal*, not far off. It was doubtless originally of stone. Now it is of plastered loam, or the original, at least, is covered with that substance. My companions drew up in line in front of this, and went through the same ceremony as at the tomb of the holy man at the caravanserai. As before, I looked on, taking no part in the ceremonial. Then we mounted again, and rode away along the causeway leading to the southern gate. Here, on the right-hand side, and a hundred and fifty yards from the mausoleum and its cupola, are two large piles of broken brick and tile. These, I was informed, were the graves of the 'enemies' of Sultan Sanjar; who or what these enemies were, no one could give me the least idea. The group of horsemen halted about fifty yards short of the heaps, and then each dashed by at full speed, discharging his musket at one or other of them. Those who happened not to have their pieces loaded rode up, dismounted, seized a fragment of brick, and hurled it furiously against the pile, uttering curses and maledictions upon the Sultan's enemies.

Issuing from the southern gate, we entered into a very shallow valley, which separates the ruins we were leaving from those of Bairam Ali, which lie due south, and about five hundred yards distant. This shallow valley, after clearing Sultan Sanjar, turns sharply to the south, intervening between the latter town and Giaour Kala. Taking advantage of this depression, some of the Vekil Turcomans had led a slender thread of water in this direction from the easterly branch of the Novur canal. The water had been brought opposite the northwestern angle of Bairam Ali, and half-a-dozen men were trying to lead it still further by cutting a very deep trench. At this point some scanty melon-beds were being attended to, as the fruit can be sold at a great profit at this, the last station on the Merv line to Bokhara. On the southern bank of this irrigation trench are three Imam Zadés. The more easterly two are small covered structures of unbaked brick, with rough, loam-plastered tombs within them. Here my indefatigably pious comrades again dismounted, and before each of the tombs again offered their vows. These two sepulchral edifices bear the name of the Imamlar. One hundred yards westward was a small enclosure, having in one corner a roofed chamber. This was the tomb of a person of sanctity named Pehlvan Ahmet Tabanji. Both he and the other two individuals are described by the general name of 'the Sheiks,' this being, as I have said, understood to imply a religious and holy personage. The latter celebrity seems to have been very distinguished indeed for piety, for his tomb is literally covered with souvenirs of all kinds, brought from afar by pilgrims. There were morsels of marble and earth from Mecca, and, among others, was a very droll offering. It was a marble cannon-shot, over twelve inches in diameter, and by some accident had been broken in two. The energetic piety of a pilgrim had caused this offering to be conveyed all the way from Mecca to the heart of the Merv desert.

Around and between the ruined cities, and reaching far and wide to the north and east, were blank aridness and desolation; save the usual desert shrubs, the chiratan and tamarisk, nothing in the nature of verdure was to be seen. The sun was getting low, and as I was tired of dismounting whenever my comrades took it into their heads to go praying and walking round these tombs, I was glad when we turned our horses' heads westward, and made our way towards Makdum Kuli's home. As on our return journey we reached the belt of dilapidated gardens and tumble-down houses which intervenes at a short distance between the cities of the plain and the Vekil settlements, I could perceive the vast extent of the ground formerly built upon, for the suburbs of the walled towns cover a much greater space than the towns themselves. I climbed to the summit of a ruined building, half dwelling-house, half fortalice, whence a commanding view was obtained over the crumbling expanse of cities. A feeling of oppressive loneliness comes over the spirit as the eye ranges across that voiceless wilderness, so deserted, so desolate, yet teeming with eloquent testimonies of what it had been of old.

CHAPTER XXI.

Mad racing—Imitation raiders—Ready for combat—Heat of the desert—Hospitable customs—A Turcoman belle—Danger of whistling—An antique lamp—Troubles of the night—A cure for wounds—Value of stones—Snake-killing.

RETURNING from my visit to the ruined cities of the plain, I had a good opportunity of seeing how Turcomans amuse themselves when abroad. The ground over which we were riding, owing to deep trenches, slippery mud, and occasional deep flooding, required all the horseman's vigilance to keep himself and his beast from coming to grief; but it was only over such spaces, disagreeable as they were, that I had any peace or quietness. The moment anything like firm ground was reached, some one of the party suddenly uttered a wild whoop, and put his horse to the top of its speed. All the others were, it seems, bound in honour to follow suit, myself among the number, and then a scene of wild, headlong racing commenced, varied by different performances. Each person was expected to unsling his rifle, and, going at full speed, to take deliberate aim at some object and fire. Then re-slinging his piece, he would draw his sword, and, racing up to the person next him, exchange passes and flourishes. This was all very well on unbroken ground, but the sudden occurrence of a deep trench or mud-hole became a serious matter while one was engaged in displaying his martial accomplishments, his horse going at the rate of twenty miles an hour; and, as it was sore against my will that I engaged in such antics, it was with unfeigned satisfaction that I witnessed occasional catastrophes in the shape of some gallant Khan—horse, armament and all—coming down with a crash in attempting to clear an unusually wide mud patch, and getting up the reverse of pleased with himself. But these people take a pride in showing their stoicism, like North American Indians; and the man who had come to grief was the first to initiate a fresh stampede. A great source of amusement was to charge full speed at a party of villagers returning on foot from some market, with their asses laden with goods, and send men, women, and asses flying right and left, often dashing some of them to the earth. As the parties thus assaulted were invariably armed, I had fears of the consequences; but we went at such a speed that, before the victims could pick themselves up and unsling their guns, we were far beyond the chance of being hit. We entered each *aoull* in the same style, sending goats and sheep flying, women and children madly rushing to the first place of refuge, under the belief that we were a party of Ersari raiders executing a foray, for this is exactly the way in which an *aleman* is carried out. The raiders approach quietly; but when within 'a measurable distance' of the village they are bent on plundering, they put their horses to the top of their speed, and, sword in hand, dash like lightning into the place, cutting down everyone before he can run to his house for arms. Then, seizing on everything movable, including children, they are away again before resistance can be organised. Entering one village in this fashion, a group of old men were seen talking together in the middle thoroughfare. The brother of Makdum Kuli Khan charged them at racing speed. The old men, fully believing that we were Ersari horsemen, rushed right and left. There was one who could not get out of the way quickly enough. The rider, a moullah or priest to boot, directed his steed straight at him and dashed him senseless to the ground. I was obliged to keep with the rest of the party, for if I held back I ran imminent danger of being massacred by the enraged villagers when I came up. So long as no actual harm was done beyond scaring the people, and as I saw it was one of the customs of the country, I did not mind these simulated forays; but, after the incidents referred to, my face wore such a grave expression of disapproval that Makdum Kuli himself felt called upon to say something. Riding to my side, he asked me whether in Frangistan we did such things. I replied rather curtly that we did not, and relapsed into silence. After this the Khan forbade such exhibitions during the remainder of the ride.

It was sunset as we drew near Makdum Kuli Khan's present residence. Within three or four hundred yards of the place my companions all dismounted, and, leaving their horses to the care of one of their number, went through the rather lengthy prayers which all Mussulmans repeat at the close of day. Having washed their hands and faces in a neighbouring irrigation trench, they retired into a small grove of fruit trees hard by, and then went on with their orisons without removing either their sabres or their riding-boots. Were they at home, the invariable custom is to wash feet, as well as hands, before prayer, as well as to undo the sword-belt; but the exigencies of the desert require that, when abroad, no man disarm himself for a moment, or in any way make himself unfit for instant combat.

Yussuf Khan's house—or rather his establishment, for he had several houses—is to a considerable extent a departure from that of the ordinary Turcoman Khan.

There was a pretty extensive grove of trees—mostly fruit trees of one kind or another, the *jujube*, with whity-green foliage like that of the olive, figuring largely amidst the darker tints of the apricot and pomegranate. In the midst of this grove was a large open space, where were the immediate dwellings of the chief's family. There was a massive-looking square tower about twenty-five feet wide by thirty-five in height. It was built of unbaked brick, plastered over with fine ochre-tinted loam. A low doorway, closed by a rudely-carved wooden door, gave access to the ground floor, a large room lighted by four narrow loopholes, and paved with flat bricks from the neighbouring ruins of Bairam Ali. In somewhat less fiercely sunny weather than then obtained this quadrangular grotto would doubtless be cool enough. After a day's absorption of heat by the entire building, on coming into it from riding in the evening breeze one feels as if he had stepped into an oven. The place was for the moment uninhabitable. A rude flight of stairs on the outside of the building led to the upper storey, which was ventilated by four large windows besides the door. Here the breeze had free access, and the temperature was delightful. The terrace above, surrounded by a low embattled parapet, was only used for sleeping on at night. In the square space around the tower were ranged half-a-dozen of the usual beehive-shaped huts, and a couple of long raw-brick buildings—the latter serving as stables. The two Khans dwelt in huts, a Turcoman as a rule having a strong objection to live in any other kind of residence. The tower is only added as an adjunct of state, and as quarters for visitors who know no better than to dwell in such an un-nomadic dwelling. The Khans had ridden on before, and, as I dismounted at the entrance to the dwelling, came forward to receive me. They were dressed in the usual Turcoman robes of the upper class—a long tunic of coarse crimson silk reaching nearly to the ankle and with a narrow combined stripe of black and yellow. This was girt at the waist, rather high up, with a voluminous white sash of cotton, in the front knot of which was stuck a highly decorated sheathed knife, a foot long; wide pantaloons of white cotton, red leather slippers, and an enormous grenadier hat of black sheepskin, completed the attire. These chiefs came forward in the politest manner, surrounded by a crowd of retainers. On such occasions the proper thing is to walk with a slow, pensive step, the palm of one hand laid upon the back of the other, and with a dejected expression of countenance, such as a man might wear if he had woeful intelligence to impart. All this is meant to convey intense humility, and the idea of being the humble servant of the new comer. The host suddenly thrusts out both hands towards him, he following suit, each taking one hand of the other in his two. Then follows a series of minute inquiries after our relative healths, and as to whether there is any fresh news going, as if we had not seen one another for six months or more. We took our seats upon a raised earthen platform, such as is to be found alongside the door of every person of consideration, and where he sits during the evening hours with his friends. It is surprising what a difference this elevation of a couple of feet makes in the temperature of the breeze. The layer of air in immediate contact with the earth, still heated by the sun's rays, is as hot as if it passed through a furnace; while a little higher up it is cool and refreshing. As for the conversation of the select party with which I found myself, it was like that of most Turcomans, distressingly inane. I tried to turn its current towards the subject of the old ruins we had visited during the day; but I could elicit little more than a parcel of the most uningenious tales about gins and divs and *pihambers,* or prophets who had stuck their thumbs in the ground and made water spring from the desert, or who had driven the Giaours from their stronghold by a puff of their breath. I was becoming fairly distressed in mind, when a matronly woman came forward and announced that dinner was ready. The matron was the widow—one of them—of the late Noor Berdi Khan, of Yengi Sheher and Merv. Her name was Gul Djemal (the Beautiful Flower). She wore a long shirt of dark purple silk, reaching almost to the ankles, and closely fastened at the neck by a massive silver arrow. Around her neck was a ponderous collar resembling that of a Newfoundland dog, and from it, suspended by numerous chains, was an engraved plate chased with gold arabesques and set with cornelians, not unlike the urim and thummim of a Jewish high-priest. On her wrists were ponderous bracelets, set also with flat cornelians. The breast and stomach of the shirt were so set over with closely-hung large silver coins as to give her the appearance of wearing a cuirass of silver scales. On her head was a casque of open silverwork, showing the red cloth beneath, and surmounted by a spike like that of a German soldier's helmet. Her entire appearance in her silver panoply was Minerva-like in the extreme.

Makdum Kuli led the way up the precipitous stairs to the *bala-hané* or upper chamber of the tower, where our evening repast was laid out. A number of hungry attendants sat cross-legged around, eyeing the bowls with wolf-like eyes, and no doubt inwardly anathematising the extensive appetites that were rapidly lessening their contents, for the remnant of their superiors' repast was all they had to expect. However long I might live amid such surroundings, I could never get accustomed to them, or insensible to the wolf-like eyes of the attendants; and often on similar occasions I have given over eating before my hunger was half appeased, lest I might have too heavy a weight of maledictions to carry; for the greater part were sure to be levelled against the unbelieving Giaour who was thus consuming what should more properly find its way into the stomachs of true believers.

Supper cleared away, we sat in the gloaming looking out over the dimly-lit plain, listening to the lowing and bleating of the homeward-driven flocks and herds as they entered the various walled enclosures where they were placed for safety during the night. A curious Turcoman superstition here came under my notice. As, lost in reverie, I sat by the window, half-unconsciously I commenced whistling softly some snatches of tunes. I noticed a general movement of dissatisfaction among my companions. They shifted in their seats, looked uneasily at each other and at me. At length Makdum Kuli touched me on the shoulder and said, 'For God's sake, Sahib, don't whistle any more.' I feared that I had unwittingly committed some great breach of decorum, and accordingly, excusing myself, relapsed into silence. After a while I whispered to the moullah beside me, and asked why Makdum Kuli objected to my whistling. 'Is it possible you don't know,' returned the priest, 'that at this hour the ghouls and gins are abroad and are wandering to and fro? If they hear you whistle they will suppose you are calling them; and, Bismillah, we have no desire for their company.' I afterwards learned that to whistle in the daytime is a token of defiance, and not considered proper when others are by. A primitive lamp, excavated from among the ruins hard by, was brought in, and shed a flickering smoky light over the swarth countenances of the group within the chamber. The form of this lamp struck me; and, on examining it, I discovered that its material was white bronze. It was doubtless a relic of the earlier days of Merv. Our host, Yussuf Khan, informed me that it had been found while excavating some irrigation trenches in the vicinity of the old cities. Seeing that I was greatly interested in it, he generously presented it to me. It is about four inches in height, and of the form of the ordinary antique lamps sometimes found in Greek and Roman sepulchres, save that the neck between the cup and the stand is taller than usual. The side of the spout had been damaged, and the resulting holes soldered up with pure gold; the composition of the original material being at the time apparently unknown. A portion of the margin of the stand had been melted off, probably during some conflagration, and replaced with iron rudely riveted on. The handle had disappeared, but two small protuberances marking its position remained. The opening in the top was closed by a rude iron cover, the hinge of which worked in the original old bronze sockets. It had probably been added at a comparatively late period. Around the top of the lamp is a series of straight and curved scratches—whether attempts at decoration or inscription I am unable to say. Among the Vekil Turcomans, earthen lamps of the old Greek form are frequently met with in daily use. In all likelihood they are obtained from the neighbouring ruins. Among the Turcomans generally, one sees quite a different form of lamp (*chiragh*), an iron rod, a third of an inch in thickness, two to three feet in length, and sharply pointed at its lower extremity. It branches at its upper end into four, supporting a rude, shallow iron cup, of about four inches square, the corners of which project in the form of short spouts, and serve to hold one or more wicks of crude cotton. The flame is fed with oil or melted fat. The pointed extremity of the support is stuck in the earth of the floor.

With the lamp came myriads of those pests of this country, the *chirin* or sand-fly, which makes night for all but the natives of the place a time of groaning and swearing. How I envied my companions as, having divested themselves of their tremendous hats and lengthy tunics, they stretched their limbs on the felt matting and went soundly to sleep. After a weary vigil I had the questionable advantage of seeing the faint saffron morning come up palely, throwing the cupola of Sultan Sanjar into bold black relief, as the sable ibises, swans, and other aquatic birds fled with shrill cries across the flooded fields. Apart from the natural irritation caused by the loss of a night's rest after a pretty fatiguing day's ride, the recollection of an undertone conversation I had overheard among my companions of the previous evening as they disposed themselves to rest was not calculated to put me in good humour. Makdum Kuli had gone downstairs to his own wigwam, and I was left alone with my route companions. The speakers were the Khan of the Otamish division of the Tekkés, and a miserable *khodja*, or scribe, to whom I had lent one of my horses to enable him to come with us.

Said the Khan, 'Did you see the Ingles sahib to-day when we were praying at the tombs of the Sheiks? He was leaning on his sword and looking on as if he didn't care anything about us or our prayers.' 'After all, he is only a kafir' (unbeliever), said the scribe half apologetically. 'What are we to do to-morrow?' replied the

Khan; 'we can't stop here any longer, we have received our three days' hospitality.' 'But,' said the scribe, who was evidently hungering after the unwonted meals which Makdum Kuli's flesh-pots afforded, 'you know that a Mussulman has a right to *nine* days' hospitality.' 'Yes,' returned the Khan warmly, 'Mussulmans—yes, but a kafir like that!' and he intimated me with a movement of his head, 'a *Yaman kafir* (wicked unbeliever) like that, we couldn't share hospitality with him for more than three days.' All the foregoing was spoken *sotto voce*, and in the belief that I was asleep. Then the Khan added, with a good deal of bitterness, 'He gives presents to *haram-zadés* (scoundrels, good-for-noughts), but he gives nothing to Khans.' 'Yes,' returned the scribe, to whom I *had* made presents, 'it is only to such people he gives anything.'

We were early astir; but Makdum Kuli would not let us go without another meal, washed down by green tea. While we were on our horses at the gate taking our final pull at the water-pipe which was handed round as a valedictory ceremony, a number of men, old and young, gathered round us to hear what news was going, and to ask the usual absurd questions about things in general. A cousin of Makdum Kuli, who had lately been despatched to Askabad as a *jansus*, or spy, and who had been severely wounded in the right hand by a rifle bullet during the storming of Geok Tepé, wanted to know if I could give him any *moomia* to apply to the injury. This *moomia* I was for a long time at a loss to make out. I subsequently learned that it is bitumen. The Turcomans look upon it as a kind of panacea. They apply it to wounds, and take it internally, an infinitesimal portion being swallowed as a cure for nervousness, and a larger amount in cases of fever. It is to be found, I was informed, in the mountains of the Derguez, usually in inaccessible places, whence the nodules of it are dislodged by firing bullets at them. Matthi, the Jew trader at Kouchid Khan Kala, asked as much as two francs for a piece of *moomia* less than the eighth of an ounce in weight. When Makdum Kuli's cousin had done speaking, an old man came up to me to ask whether some minute objects he held in his hand were valuable. On examination they turned out to be small pieces of semi-transparent quartz, looking as if water-worn. Their owner informed me he had taken them from the gizzard of a *doornah* or stork. As there are absolutely no stones of any kind in the Merv oasis, even the smallest fragment of a material like quartz which is picked up, as in the present instance, is supposed to be something very much out of the common, and of exceeding worth. Just before turning our horses' heads from the door, some of our party drew from their pockets small pear-shaped gourds, from which they poured into the hollow of their hands a quantity of an olive-green, damp-looking powder, which they placed under their tongues, allowing it to remain there during the remainder of the journey, much in the same fashion as tobacco-chewers do. This powder is named *gougenasse*. It is of vegetable origin, probably the same as I found in the giant hemlock-like plants at Khivabad, but what its European or scientific name is I have been unable to ascertain. *Preusské*, or ordinary tobacco snuff, is sometimes put in the mouth in the same way.

Our course homeward lay due west, by a great mound here also known as Geok Tepé, from which we made for another known as Marma Khan Tepé. We found a waste space of brick fragments alive with snakes a couple of feet long, of a leaden-grey colour mottled with black, and extremely slender for one-third of their length immediately below the head. We spent half an hour hunting these up and killing them with our whips, in consonance with the invariable Turcoman custom. Within half-an-hour's ride of the north-easterly ramparts of Kouchid Khan Kala we stopped at the house of Kara Khan, the Karaoul-bashi, an officer charged with the direction of the patrols told off to look after the Ersari raiders on this side of the Murgab. Here we had some fermented whey of camels' milk, a very peculiar beverage, and very refreshing, in hot weather, and soon after reached the capital.

CHAPTER XXII.

The revolution—Coming of the Khans—A singular spectacle—Overthrow of Kadjar—The triumvirate—A theatrical spectacle—Dress—Differences of clan—Making presents—Festivities—My surprise—Playing the host.

DURING my absence at the old cities of Merv, the revolution, the commencement of which I have already described, had been growing daily more complete. Though Kadjar Khan was practically no longer the director of affairs at Merv, the fact had not been publicly announced, and it was resolved that a demonstration should take place, which, by manifesting the number of adherents of each party, would leave the matter no longer in question.

On May 14, 1881, my house was all day long, and far into the night, filled with various Turcomans of prominence, who talked over the political prospects, and the chances *pro* and *con.* of having to fight the Russians. I learned definitively that each of the two hereditary Khans had resumed his old jurisdiction over his respective division of the Tekkés, and on the morrow would come to take up his residence close by where my *ev* was pitched—the spot which had been settled upon as the administrative centre of the oasis. I was further told that I was to be associated with the two Khans in the direction of affairs, in the capacity of representative of the English nation, and intermediary between the Mervli and the English Padishah. I had over and over again protested that I had no pretensions to represent the British Government, and that my mission to Merv was undertaken purely with a view of ascertaining the true state of affairs, and keeping the British public informed as to the relative positions of Russians and Tekkés. All my efforts were in vain.

It was early on the morning of May 15, as I slept profoundly upon my felt mat after a night's weary wrestling with the mosquitoes—the interregnum between the departure of these pests and the arrival of their daylight successors, the *singak*, or house-fly, and the only portion of the twenty-four hours during which I was ever able to secure any rest whatever—I heard an unusual tumult around, and, not knowing what might be the matter, I sprang from my couch, and throwing my sheepskin *kusgun* around my shoulders, rushed to the door. Everyone was astir, and the main avenue of Merv was thronged with a vast concourse of people, mostly newcomers. Many were on horseback, and fully armed. At my door I found the attendants who had been told off for the service of my establishment, the chief of whom was named Mehemet Nefess Beg, a Kethkoda of some prominence. I asked him what was the matter. He informed me that the two hereditary Khans were making their entry into the capital, and that they were about to take up their abodes close to my redoubt.

Away towards the western end of the ramparts of Kouchid Khan Kala a large crowd of horsemen was seen approaching. In their midst, borne on a high pole, fluttered a red and white standard. In front, and on either side, armed horsemen dashed to and fro, their sabres gleaming in the early morning light, some of them, careering at full speed, rapidly discharging their muskets. As the body of men, numbering four or five hundred, drew near, those gathered together in Merv, both mounted and on foot, moved out to meet them. When within a hundred yards, I could make out that at the head of the approaching cavalcade rode Baba Khan himself, and that it was at his side that the red and white ensign was carried. Around him were his kinsmen and Kethkodas, all decked out for the occasion in their finest costumes. Many of his followers bore lances—an arm which has now almost disappeared from among the Turcomans, and which is only carried on state occasions, and then rather for show than anything else. Most of them were decorated with banderols of the same colours as the Khan's standard.

Mehemet Nefess now hinted to me that it would be only courteous on my part to go forward to meet Baba Khan, and, as I knew this to be the proper etiquette, I followed his advice. When within fifty yards of the front of the advancing cavalcade I dismounted, and awaited the approach of the Toktamish chief. As soon as I appeared outside the parapet of my redoubt, I was surrounded by a great mob of the inhabitants of Merv, all eager to catch a sight of one of the rulers of the place in his new capacity. Surrounded by the crowd of sight-seers as I was, Baba quickly espied me, and immediately, in pursuance of Oriental courtesy, dismounted, and advanced on foot to salute me. Holding each other's hands, we advanced slowly to a space, near the parapet of my redoubt, on which a large felt carpet had been spread, and where the *medjlis* of Merv had already assembled.

It was a singular spectacle. The morning light fell slantingly on the circle of grenadier-hatted, swarthy councillors who awaited the approach of the cavalcade, with its gaily-attired warriors, glinting bannerets, and flashing sabres, headed by Baba Khan and myself, our hands joined in friendship. At the same moment, from the opposite direction, clouds of dust announced the approach of another procession. Aman Niaz Khan was drawing near, surrounded by a retinue similar to that of Baba Khan. The latter chief and myself, accompanied by the principal elders, went forward to meet the ruler of the Otamish. The latter dismounted some distance from the assembly, and we all three marched solemnly towards the carpet of honour laid at one extremity of the great felt mats placed for the accommodation of the councillors. Aman Niaz also brought with him a standard, but of plain white, which, together with Baba Khan's, was reared close to the spot upon which we took our seats, and around which the entire council gathered, backed by an enormous crowd, hemming us in on all sides. The cannon boomed from the ramparts, where some had been placed expressly for the occasion. Neither Kadjar Khan nor his partisans attended the council, protesting by their absence against the revolution, the consummation of which was being celebrated. The discharge of artillery continued long into the afternoon, sometimes from the fortifications, and at other times from an open space some three hundred yards distant from us. The courtesies usual on such occasions were exchanged, and then the most gorgeous water-pipe which had come under my notice while at Merv was handed round. At Merv, that portion which in the Constantinople *nargheelah* is made of glass is invariably fashioned of wood, if it be not a bottle-shaped gourd. In the present instance it was of wood, slightly ornamented with silver. On the sides were lozenge-shaped panels, set with rough turquoises, and what I suppose were pieces of green glass, for they would have been of fabulous value if genuine emeralds. The upper portion, bearing the lighted tobacco, was of silver, and richly decorated with small turquoises and rubies.

We remained half-an-hour thus seated, receiving various newly-arrived elders and chiefs; and, when the entire number had arrived, the two Khans, each taking me by the hand, led me back through the entrance of the redoubt to my residence. Here I found, lashed to the door-post, a tall flagstaff, from the summit of which floated a bright crimson banner of silk, about three feet square, which, I was told, was the emblem of my office as one of the triumvirate, and, as I afterwards discovered, the president of it. It was also supposed to represent the English flag, and the hoisting of it at my door was intended to indicate the formal adhesion of the Merv nation to the British Government, whose envoy they did me the honour to insist that I was.

A large number of rich carpets had been spread upon the ground in front of the door of my *ev*. Upon these myself and the Khans, accompanied by the principal members of the *medjlis*, took our seats, those of lesser grade seating themselves in a circle upon the ground, outside the margin of the carpets.

It was a curious sight that I gazed upon from my door. The Murgab flowed sluggishly by; the huge mass of nearly completed ramparts rose against the morning sky, covered with thousands of spectators, who availed themselves of every coign of vantage to catch a sight of the doings within my redoubt. From moment to moment the guns thundered out, their echoes rolling away across these historic plains, the snow-white smoke-clouds from each gun sailing glidingly in procession through the still air until they were lost to view in the far distance.

The crimson flag flapped and fluttered above our heads; and the warriors and chiefs of Merv, in their best and brightest apparel, grouped around, some sitting, some standing, presented a spectacle the theatrical effect of which was only surpassed by its political interest. Then followed the political discussion, the chiefs calling upon me to explain the state of affairs existing between Russia and England, and asking my advice as to the best course to be pursued. To the best of my ability I gave these explanations, and then my opinions, which may be condensed into the following advice: that if Merv was to preserve its independency, its occupants must refrain from making raids against Persia or Bokhara.

Here I was indignantly asked how the Mervli were to live if there were to be no raids on one side or the other. I, however, kept to the text, and also insisted that no more prisoners should be held to ransom, even offering a thousand francs if the young artilleryman Kidaieff were set at liberty without delay; but this offer was declined. Baba Khan then inquired: 'Would the English Padishah be willing to receive the people of Merv as *naukers?' i.e.* servants, or subjects. 'That,' I said, 'is a matter about which I have no information; but you can easily be informed about it by forwarding a document, bearing all your seals, and testifying your desires, to the English representative at Meshed, to be forwarded by him to England.'

At last the council broke up, and the rest of the day was devoted to festivity. Rude games of different kinds were set on foot. There were horse-racing and wrestling —the latter being a sport upon which the Tekkés pride themselves very much. Indeed, the title *pehlvan* (wrestler) is one of honour among them. Prizes were offered by the two Khans and myself for the victors in these games. Baba Khan sent me an extraordinary silken mantle, of pale salmon tint, striped with dark emerald green and crimson, with intermediate groupings of embroidered flowers; and Aman Niaz presented me with a robe similar to the singular one which he himself usually wore, in which all the colours of the rainbow, and especially vermilion, yellow, and purple, were splashed in irregular dashes. With it was a *beurg*, or skull-cap, such as the Tekkés invariably wear under their great sheepskin shakos. It was of cloth, finely embroidered with silk, in yellow and pale purple, with a little admixture of green. Makdum Kuli Khan had on a previous occasion given me another similar cap, and I was able to compare the different patterns of each, which, like the Scottish plaids, distinguish the Merv and Akhal Tekkés from each other. The Merv skull-cap was covered with ornaments in the form of small Saint Andrew's crosses, grouped in rows, while that bearing the Akhal Tekké pattern was decorated with rows of upright ordinary crosses. This is the only difference I have ever been able to distinguish in the colours or patterns of the dresses worn by the two nations. There are, however, not only these distinctions, but others in the dresses of the various tribes or clans of the Mervli. On asking once how the difference was marked—for to my eye there was nothing in the dress, like the Highland tartan colours, to distinguish the wearers—a native pointed out that a peculiar way of knotting the sash and wearing the hat always indicated a member of the Sultan Aziz clan, a peculiar tie of the sword belt one of the Burkoz, and other minute points of dress the members of the other clans. My eye could never be sufficiently trained to tell a man's clan at first sight by the cock of his hat, or the tie of his sash; but my Turcoman friends never erred in the matter, which is a somewhat important one in their society.

Aman Niaz, too, sent me a thick cotton stuff quilt, covered with dark red-purple silk, heavily embroidered with gold and silver; and Murad Bey, the maternal uncle of Makdum Kuli, presented me with a rude four-legged bedstead, with rope netting as a support for the bed, and thick, double-folded felt mattress. The bedstead was styled a *takht*, and is one of the very few articles of furniture raised above the floor to be met with in Turcoman households.

I was at a loss to know what to give in return, for I was at the end of my selection of presents brought out from Meshed, and all my European goods had long since been given away. To Baba Khan I sent a large prismatic compass. To this I added a gift of money, and handed the same to Aman Niaz Khan and Murad Bey. All these gifts had to be supplemented by donations to the bearers of the presents to myself, and then we (*i.e.* the members of the triumvirate) had also to do with the public crier, and several poets who recited odes in our honour. The mode of proceeding was for a couple of poets to enter one's *ev*, and, after pronouncing a series of the most fulsome compliments, and drinking some tea, to recite an ode, extempore or composed, I could not make out which, couched in terms the most laudatory possible of their momentary host, one taking up the theme the moment the other had exhausted his stock of verbiage or imagination. I had by me a large bag of silver krans, and when the performance was at an end I gave a handful to each—twelve or fifteen shillings' worth, perhaps—whereupon the public crier, who had taken his stand outside the door, uttered in a voice that could be heard for fully half a mile, 'Dower! dower! dower!

Bahadur Sahib Khan gives so much money to the poets!'

Following the Tekké custom on such occasions, I had a sheep killed for the entertainment of my own immediate retinue, which by this time had swollen to most alarming proportions, and there was general rejoicing within the parapets of my redoubt. I was introduced to celebrated robbers—serdars (generals), as they were called by courtesy—people who had deserved the gallows a hundred times—hook-nosed ruffians, with buff-leather boots, like stage brigands, and who entertained me with stories of their successful raids, and the number of Persians they had made captive and sold in Bokhara and elsewhere. These men, almost without exception, freely drank arrack, as I found to my cost, for mounted messengers were kept constantly plying between my house and the establishment of Matthi the Jew, bringing up the necessary supplies in soda-water bottles. These bottles had made their way into Merv from Bokhara and Khiva, and bore stamped on the glass the names of Russian manufacturers. The arrack, however, was manufactured by the Jew himself in Merv.

An hour after sunset, Aman Niaz Khan, doubtless having learned that arrack was to be found, presented himself, accompanied by his maternal uncle, Nazar Ali Beg, and a small regiment of acolytes. The house, by this time, was as full as it could hold, and some of the persons of lesser rank were obliged to go outside to make room for the newcomers. In his following was a noted raider, the Khan's right-hand man, in fact, a serdar, named Meredh Ali, an exceedingly picturesque-looking vagabond. The Khan strongly recommended him to me, and told me that he was one of the men most deserving of a 'zat.' This was an unmistakable hint, and the result was that I handed the serdar two pieces of gold of the value of twenty francs each.

To judge from the expression of the Khan's face, he was evidently keeping some pleasant surprise in reserve, but it was only an hour afterwards, when under the influence of the arrack, and when the entire assembly was becoming boisterously hilarious, that I perceived what was in store for me. Aman Niaz suddenly pulled from under his silk robe a wretched, tawdry-looking, two-and-sixpenny concertina, which he had purchased from Matthi the Jew, who had procured it either from the bazaar at Meshed or from Bokhara. It was made of stamped gilt paper—one of the toys usually given to children. The Khan intended to astonish me with this unwonted marvel. He had not the slightest idea of how it should be played, and sawed away until I felt dazed and stupefied. He seemed to think no explanation or introduction whatever necessary. The thing was too novel, too magnificent, too overpowering, in the eyes of the mass of the auditory, for any prelude to be requisite. The worst of it was that his improvisations had the effect of attracting all the loafers within earshot, who came crowding round the house and crushing through the doorway, their mouths and eyes agape with astonishment at the unwonted and extraordinary scene. I really believe that unless some of the serdars had jumped to their feet and driven off the crowd, the house would have come down over us. The Khan felt himself to be the hero of the moment, and sawed away unceasingly with his concertina, grinning and giggling with exultation. When the Khan was tired, the vile instrument had to be passed round from one to another, and each one must needs try his skill upon it for fully five minutes.

I had now erected my *takht* at one side of the apartment, and covered it over with the gorgeously embroidered quilt with which Aman Niaz had presented me, and there I sat throughout the night, cross-legged, observing the proceedings from my commanding point, devoutly praying that they would soon come to an end. So long, however, as anything in the shape of eatables and drinkables was going, while arrack or green tea held out, or dishes of cold mutton fat and bread and broth were to the fore, there was no possibility of getting rid of my visitors, and it was not until the morning had well broken that the festivities terminated.

CHAPTER XXIII.

A dilemma—Branding horses—A Georgian prisoner—Other captives—Prisoners in chains—The black present—A camel's bite—Dread of poison—Turcoman pipers—A morning scene—My pets—An oil mill—Offers of hospitality—The Khan's vineyards—Tea-drinking—Tea etiquette—The Guinea worm—The Russian prisoner—Torture of Kidaieff—Offers of ransom—A cure for fever.

THE first use to which I tried to turn my newly-acquired dignity was to secure a little more leisure, but to my dismay I was told that a Khan's door is always open, and he must see and entertain anyone who calls. It was deemed advisable to hoist a genuine British flag as soon as possible, and I was requested to draw a design from which an *ustá adam* would manufacture the necessary ensign. Pieces of red, blue, and white cloth were procured, and I was desired to begin at once. I thus found myself placed in a very serious dilemma; for I feared that, in case of compliance on my part with the desires of the council, I might get myself into some scrape for thus taking part in an unauthorised hoisting of the British flag, an act for which I might perhaps be afterwards called to account should events so turn that some indignity were offered to the colours. At length I hit upon an excuse for postponing the manufacture of the Union Jack. I pressed my associates to wait and obtain the necessary sanction from the Minister at Teheran, saying that for the present the red flag flying over my house would meet all requirements.

Another matter, however, cropped up, which it was impossible to escape. With a view of practically demonstrating a Merv-English connection, and at the same time putting an obstacle in the way of their cattle being confiscated, should by any chance Russia press on to Merv, Baba Khan proposed that all the horses should be branded with a mark similar to that of the English military steeds. Before this proposition was made, the Khan asked me to draw for him the Government horse mark. I did not know what mark is used in the service, but on chance I sketched a V.R. surmounted by a crown. The Khan quietly possessed himself of the design, and the same evening he showed me an iron brand bearing the design I had drawn, and which he had had made without a moment's delay. He would not postpone for a moment the execution of his plan, and forthwith ordered his own charger to be brought out and marked. When the brand was duly heated, a man rode the horse into the steep-sided ditch of my redoubt, so that the operator might be secure against harm in case the animal should kick. The brand was successfully impressed ; but as the maker had exactly copied my design, the mark on the horse was naturally reversed, and what is more, the operator turned it upside down.

During my absence at Makdum Kuli's village, and my visit to the ruined cities, a small raid had been made somewhere between Geok Tepé and Askabad, which had resulted in the capture of a considerable quantity of stores—among them some cases of champagne and a quantity of hams, together with a Georgian sutler from Tiflis, whose property the captured stores were. I was very anxious to obtain one or more of the hams, for I had not tasted any for a very long period, but I learned to my disgust that as soon as the raiders discovered

T

what they had got they immediately buried them. The champagne, however, was regarded with a more lenient eye, principally coming into the hands of Aman Niaz Khan, whose clansman had captured the convoy. The Georgian sutler was a prisoner, held to ransom. Like most of his countrymen, he had been very gorgeously attired when captured; but his red silk tunic, silver-laced cloth coat decorated with enamelled cartridge-tubes, his silver belt, decorated *handjar*, and lamb's-wool hat had all been taken from him, and he was given instead a wretched tattered garment of quilted cotton, a pair of dilapidated Turcoman drawers, and a very sorry hat of shaggy sheepskin. His long boots of Russian leather had been replaced by rude sandals of untanned cow-skin; and his outfit generally was of the shabbiest description. He presented himself before me, and begged I would try to get him released, stating further that he was unable to pay the ransom asked by his captors. I gave him some European clothes which I had by me and a pair of boots, of which he stood badly in need; and I further succeeded in getting his ransom cut down to something like two hundred roubles paper money—20*l*. He tried to pass himself off as a Mussulman; but I was given to understand that he broke down in the ordeal of saying his prayers. However, I was glad to learn that a few days later, his ransom having arrived, he was conveyed to within a short distance of Askabad and set at liberty. When once a ransom is paid, the Turcomans never fail to liberate a prisoner, partly owing to their own rude ideas of honour, and partly to the fact that did they fail in doing so on any occasion they might afterwards be forced to send in the captive before any money was paid, and in that case faith might be broken with *them*.

The next captive who came under my notice was a wretched-looking elderly Persian peasant, carried off but a few weeks previously from some village a few miles to the south of Meshed. His case was an unusual one. A Tekké raid was made in that direction, and one of the marauders had been captured by the Persian patrols. He was then a prisoner at Meshed, as usual, held to ransom. His brother, being either unable or unwilling to pay the required sum, solved the problem by executing a raid on his own account, and carrying off a captive from the same village whom he held as a hostage for his brother's safety and offered to exchange for him. Of course, under the circumstances, I could not possibly do anything to effect the release of either captive. The Persian exhibited to me his naked feet, blistered by walking over the scorching marl, and begged me to give him a couple of krans to purchase some kind of shoes. I gave him some money; but, as his captor was by, the money was doubtless very soon transferred to the latter's pocket.

One of the most interesting cases I met with was one of an Afghan merchant who had been captured during an attack on a caravan proceeding from Herat to Meshed. He was evidently a well-to-do man, and, in view of his being a Sunnite Mussulman like the Mervli, was comparatively well treated and not deprived of his clothes. Soon after, he was set at liberty, Abass Khan having, I was informed, written about him to his agent at Merv.

The only other prisoners beside the Russian artilleryman to my knowledge remaining were an unfortunate white-haired old Persian colonel captured many years previously during the disastrous expedition against the Merv Turcomans, and whose beard had grown white during his captivity, and two Derguezli raiders who had been caught in the act of cattle-lifting within the Merv borders. I had an opportunity of seeing these men every day as they sat listlessly, cumbered with their irons. Each had fetters confining his ankles, so that he could only shuffle very slowly along, and heavy collars, locked round the necks of both, were connected by a massive chain, each link of which was nearly a foot in length, the iron composing it being an inch in diameter. They looked the picture of misery as they sat all day long in the burning sun, for no shelter was afforded them. Their only occupation, so far as I could see, was that of removing the vermin which covered their rags, or perhaps, at the command of some matron, turning the heavy stone hand-mill with which the flour was prepared. The ransom asked for each was but trifling—something like 10*l*.—but even this sum was far beyond the reach of either of the families of these raiders, who rarely, throughout their lives, succeed in amassing any considerable sum in specie.

It was late in the evening of the day succeeding the entry of the Khans and the formation of a government that several horsemen from Dushakh drew up before my door. They were sent by Adjem Serdar, the first Merv chieftain of any importance with whom I had come in contact when on my way to the oasis, and who had warned me about the horse thieves in his village. Two of his relations, by name Chariar and Sariar, brought with them three silver watches with rather gaudily gilt and painted dial plates, which they offered for my acceptance on the part of the serdar. It seemed that after the fall of Geok Tepé and the occupation of Askabad, some bodies of Russian cavalry pushed forward to the eastward, escorting the officer who penetrated as far as Kelat-i-Nadri, on the Persian frontier.

Various presents were given to the Awlilis and other Turcomans inhabiting the border, with the view of winning their friendship. Among these were a number of watches. Two of these had been given to the *chaoush* (head man) of Kaka, and the third by some means had been sent to Adjem Serdar. Neither the *chaoush* nor the serdar had the slightest idea of what these mysterious articles were, or what their value might be. Knowing, however, that I was at Merv, they sent them to me as 'presents,' that is to say, as something they wished to sell. I was glad to receive them, for I was in want of articles for some of the Merv notabilities, so that I told the messengers I would gladly accept the watches. The only difficulty about receiving them was, as I have said, that at the moment I had not to spare the necessary funds with which to make the return *peshkesh*. I said that if the senders would trust me with the articles in question for a little while longer, I would unfailingly forward the money to them from Merv, or at any rate as soon as I should reach Meshed. Hereupon a Merv Tekké Serdar, who was sitting opposite to me, observed brusquely, 'Why not take them as a *kara peshkesh?*' (or 'black present'); meaning that I should receive the watches, or rather appropriate them, giving nothing whatsoever in return, inasmuch as they were in my possession, and there was no necessity for my parting with them; a course, doubtless, that he would himself have adopted under the circumstances. This, however, I declined to do; but the messengers, thinking perhaps that it would be unsafe to receive them back, as they might be despoiled of them before quitting Merv, said, willingly or otherwise, that I might keep them, and transmit the money I wished to give in return, at my earliest convenience.

I do not believe that such a thing as a watch had ever been seen in Merv before, and many were the visitors who crowded in to look at the extraordinary articles —the *sahat namehs*, or hour indicators, as they named them after I had informed them of their use. Before long the news had spread all over Kouchid Khan Kala that I had received the watches; and one of Baba Khan's noted cavalry leaders called upon me and said that the Khan was extremely desirous of seeing a *sahat nameh*, he never having beheld such a thing. I had destined a watch for Baba, and unhesitatingly committed it to the charge of the serdar.

From my seat before the door of my house I could see Baba Khan and his friends curiously examining the wonderful machine, and in half-an-hour the serdar returned to me, but without the watch. He said that the Khan was delighted with it; so much so, indeed, that he intended to keep it, and that he thanked me very much for the present. Though I had intended it for him, I had not said so to his messenger, so that the act was one of barefaced swindling. The only revenge I could take was to tell the serdar that the Khan was welcome to the watch, but that I had intended to give him a gold one later on. Now, however, I had countermanded the instructions which I was about to send to Teheran for the purchase of the more costly present. I do not know what was the precise effect of this message upon the Khan, but he seemed to be impressed with the truth of the proverb about the bird in the hand, and I heard no more from him on the subject.

During the day I had a visit from one of the more respectable of the Mervli, by name Owez Bey. A few days before his visit, an angry camel had taken his hand into its mouth, and inflicted a severe bite, the

long fangs of the animal piercing through the palm.
The hand was very much inflamed, and, in the extreme heat of the weather which then obtained, I was fearful that serious results would accrue. I prescribed for him what I considered the proper course of treatment, and, after having lanced his hand to give exit to the pus which had accumulated under the fascia, I ordered a cooling lotion of vinegar and water. I directed him to procure the vinegar from Matthi, the Jew, but to this he was strongly opposed. 'How do I know,' said he, 'but that that Moussai would give me poison?' Such was the estimation in which this poor Jew, one of the most honest men in the whole community, was held.

While Owez Bey was visiting me, a portion of the inaugural ceremonies, which had not been completed on the previous day, was carried out. Owing to the extreme heat of the weather, I had caused the outer reed mat of my house to be removed, and the thick felt wall lining to be raised at a point opposite the doorway, so that a free current of air could circulate through the room. I was thus exposed to the view of the passers-by, and in a very short time, as was usual whenever I made my appearance, a considerable number of people had assembled, and seated themselves on the ground immediately adjoining my lattice, two musicians appearing among them. They were what were styled *tweeduk adamlar*, from the kind of instrument on which they performed. The *tweeduk* is a kind of large clarionet, made of bamboo, and about three feet in length. It is furnished with six holes for the fingers, at the back being a seventh, which is stopped by the thumb. There are the *dilli tweeduk* and the *karga tweeduk*; the former being the treble instrument, the latter the bass one. Both are cylindrical, and neither is furnished with a bell-mouth. The end is finished off with a kind of flat brass ring. The *dilli tweeduk* produces a sound like the note of a thrush, while the sound of the *karga tweeduk* is not unlike the drone of a bag-pipe. The musicians seated themselves upon a piece of felt which had been brought expressly for them, and commenced a low, dirge-like tune, which grew gradually quicker, the principal exhibition of skill consisting of running up the gamut to the highest possible pitch, and then down again, on the part of the *dilli*, accompanied by a monotonous droning by the player of the *karga*. As the rapidity of the fingering increased, the performers seemed to get excited, rising to their feet, and piping faster and faster each moment. They piped to the right, then to the left, and then, making right about face, piped to the rear, at each bar bowing their bodies until the mouths of the instruments touched their feet. This turning, bowing, and piping continued until the pipers were completely exhausted, when they resumed their seats; but it seemed to be a matter of pride to recommence as soon as possible after gaining sufficient breath to blow their *tweeduks*. There was nothing that, speaking strictly, could be called an air, but simply a succession of notes which conveyed an impression of wild sadness, followed by a monotonous running up to frequent climaxes of acuteness. The second player never on any occasion varied his drone. On the whole, the performance was not disagreeable; at least, it did not seem so to me, so interested was I in this first serious musical display which I had ever witnessed among the Turcomans.

Having repeatedly received letters from the Russian prisoner Kidaieff, some in Russian, written by himself, and others in Jagatai, written for him by some local scribe, but neither of which I could understand, I resolved to seek an interview with him.

As his place of residence was under the immediate jurisdiction of Aman Niaz Khan, I applied to that chieftain for permission to visit the prisoner. Aman Niaz readily consented, and appointed the following day for the proposed interview, saying that at the same time we could visit his own personal estate about fifteen miles from Kouchid Khan Kala.

I rose very early on the morning in question, as we purposed starting shortly after sunrise, and as I stood at the doorway of my house, looking out towards the coming day, great flights of wild ducks, ibises, and cranes passed at intervals overhead, winging their way to the distant marshes of the Tejend. Now and then a broad-winged heron went flapping heavily by, bound in the same direction. Some sleeping forms were still to be seen outside the huts, for at this season of the year the Turcomans sleep out of doors, on account of the excessive heat within the houses. Here and there a huge sheepskin hat, protruding from under the blanket, showed where the sleepers lay. Around were the recumbent camels, which had not yet commenced their daily groaning chorus. The women, early risers at Merv, were dusting the carpets. A flock of sheep was bleating on its way to pasture. The saffron light of morning threw the huge mass of ramparts into bold relief as it dawned behind them. Then the eastern horizon burst into a blaze of light, and the sun peeped above the fruit-tree thickets beyond the walls of Kouchid Khan Kala.

My principal servant was engaged in feeding a number of pet animals which I had gathered round me in my *ev*, for the people of Merv, knowing that I was interested in natural history, had almost overwhelmed me with zoological specimens—for a consideration, of course. I had a beautiful specimen of the antelope of the plain, a gerfalcon, three young jackals, a wolf cub, two black cats, and a hedgehog. The Turcomans display great fondness for dumb animals, and it was remarkable to see men of known ferocity exhibit the greatest tenderness to various pets. One of my servants, a raider of celebrity, amused me by sitting and laughing himself into convulsions at the antics of a kitten running after its tail, he being a man who, on the war-path, would cut down woman or child.

The sun had hardly risen when Aman Niaz Khan rose from the platform where he had been sleeping out of doors, performed his ablutions, and soon after we were ready, and were accompanied by several people of standing across the river and treacherous portions of the muddy road. The hurdle bridges were too rickety to trust, and trenches and quagmires made the ground unsafe. Parting from our companions, we rode on past cultivated fields and castor-oil plants, while vineyards and groves of apricots and peaches formed an almost unbroken line along our route. There were large fields, too, where a plant from which the *Kundji yagh*, the oil used alike for cooking and illuminating purposes, is produced. It grows to a height of four or five feet; its square stems, opposite leaves, and lipped corolla indicate it to be of the labiate family. I do not know its botanical name.

In each of the villages through which we passed were one or more mills for the production of oil from the grain of this plant. The construction of these mills is peculiar. A stump of a large trunk, about four feet in height and three in diameter, was hollowed into a kind of rude mortar, in which was a pestle of hard, heavy wood, in shape closely resembling a large Indian club, and weighing, perhaps, two hundredweight. This was made to revolve while pressing against the sides of the mortar by means of a beam six or seven feet in length, which was in turn attached to a straddle fastened to the back of a camel. The camel walked round and round the mortar in the very small circle which the length of the beam permitted him to make. A rude thatched roof, raised upon four tall poles, sheltered the animal from the heat of the sun.

At each village the elders came out to salute us, seizing our right hands in each of theirs, as is their method of salutation, and then stroking their beards. Many were the invitations we received to dismount and partake of *gattuk* and sheep's-tail fat at the Kethkodas' houses. It was near mid-day when we drew near Aman Niaz Khan's country residence. Some twenty acres of ground, copiously watered by branches of the Alasha canal, were enclosed by a tall mud wall. One-half of this was under clover, which here grows to a very great height; the remainder was devoted to *arpa* (barley) and melon; while around the house, and enclosing the vineyards, were pretty extensive groves of apricot and peach.

The Khan's house, situated in the centre of a small grove, was an oblong structure of unbaked brick, plastered over with fine yellow loam, and still exhibiting some attempts at decoration about the entry and windows. It was two storeys in height, flat-roofed, and about fifty feet by twenty long and wide, and fifteen in height. The Khan told me that he seldom inhabited this, as he preferred living in an *ev*; moreover, he used it as a storehouse for corn and fruit. Though it was early in June, the grapes were rapidly approaching maturity. They were of a dark red variety, and very small, a fact probably attributable to the density with which they were allowed to grow, for in most instances the clusters were so compact that the grapes were forced at their sides into a hexagonal form by mutual pressure. I pointed this out to the Khan, and he said it was true enough, but that nobody could take the trouble to arrange them in any other way. In the vineyards which were better looked after, as in the case of those of Matthi the Jew, the grapes attained very large dimensions, some of the white varieties, of an ovoid form, being fully two inches in length. Close to the Khan's house were numerous villages, also surrounded with fruit trees and vineyards. They were inhabited by the chief's own immediate clansmen, the Kethkoda of each being a close relation of his own. He took infinite pains to show me over his ground, of which he appeared to feel very proud. We then pressed a short distance northward, to a rather populous village, of which one of his uncles was chief. Towards its western side was a kind of low square tower, with terraced top, to which access was given by stairs on the outside of the building. The lower storey, or the interior of this house, was used for the storage of corn.

We were entertained by one of Aman Niaz Khan's kinsmen in a spacious, well-carpeted *ev*, from the summit of which a pair of inflated *tooniks* hung conspicuously. Suspended against the wall was the only matchlock I saw in Merv. It was of exceedingly rude construction, and even the Turcomans themselves looked upon it much as we should upon some of the antique specimens preserved in an ancient armoury, for all their guns of to-day have percussion locks. Even flint locks are completely out of date among them.

Aman Niaz told me that he had sent for Kidaieff, the Russian prisoner, who would make his appearance a little later. Meantime we took our siesta, after which a number of visitors came in, to assist at a general tea-drinking.

Every Turcoman carries with him in his pocket a small bag filled with green tea; and should he happen to call at a house where the inhabitants are too poor to afford the luxury, he calls for hot water, and produces a handful of tea for the refreshment of himself and his host. It is only among those who are well-to-do that sugar is ever seen, and even then it is considered a luxury. It is generally white lump sugar, of Russian make, but one also frequently sees crystallised sugar-candy. It is brought here from Bokhara. The teapot is a tall copper jug, about a foot in height, and furnished with a cover. This, filled with water, is placed upon a fire, and when the contents boil, a handful of green tea is put in. Every Turcoman, when on the road, brings with him his tea-bowl, which is of Chinese porcelain, about five inches in diameter, and four in depth. It is white inside, and of a greyish olive on the exterior. These are the only domestic utensils in use among the Turcomans which are not either of wood or metal. They are carried in a peculiar leather case, resembling a hemispherical saucepan with a long handle, which is slung at the saddle-bow of the rider. The guests sit in a ring. The host, having two or three bowls before him, fills and hands them to his neighbours in the order of their seniority or dignity. The sugar— if he have any—he generally keeps in his pocket; and when he wishes to distinguish any person especially, he takes out a lump and pitches it across the ring to the favoured individual. I recollect that, on my first arrival at Merv, I was in the habit of placing in the middle of the circle of my visitors a large bowl of broken sugar. Each guest, before filling his bowl with tea, more than half filled it with sugar; and then, taking a large handful, he put it into his pocket by way of guaranteeing a supply for the next bowl, for he knew full well that unless this precaution were observed the others would take care to seize all that remained. A Turcoman likes to drink his tea as hot as he can possibly bear it. When he has finished his draught, the manner in which he returns the bowl to be refilled for some one else is a matter of nice etiquette. By a sudden twitch of the wrist he throws the vessel with a spinning motion into the middle of the carpet, affecting an air of nonchalance as he does so. When a stranger arrives from a distance, or any person of distinction comes in, he is supplied with bowl after bowl of tea until he chooses to desist, which he signifies by placing his tea-bowl upon the carpet, mouth downwards. Black tea is practically unknown among the Turcomans, nor will they drink it when offered to them, unless it be very highly sweetened. Green tea is willingly drunk without any sweetening. When the jug of tea is exhausted, the host shakes out the leaves into one of the bowls, and then, sprinkling them with sugar, proceeds to eat them, unless he favours some of his guests by sharing them with him.

After tea, Aman Niaz Khan sent for one of his nephews, who had returned a short time previously from Bokhara, in order that he might show me an example of the peculiar kind of entozoon termed the *rishté*, by which so many people of that country are tormented. The nephew was a lad of about fourteen years of age. A bandage was unwound from his ankle, and a small poultice of boiled vine-leaves removed, disclosing an inflamed spot of about an inch in diameter. From its centre protruded a yellow, thread-like body, which was wound round a morsel of twig. This was the *rishté*, as it is termed in Merv and Bokhara, the worm of Pharaoh, as it is styled in Abyssinia, or the Guinea worm, by which latter name it is known to English-speaking people along the shores of the Persian Gulf and in Africa. A caravan scarcely ever arrives from Bokhara without a large number of its members being afflicted with this disagreeable entozoon. Aman Niaz informed me that anyone who drinks the stagnant water of the rain-pools, or that of the tanks of the caravanserais, is certain to take into his system the egg of the *rishté*, which will then infallibly develop itself. It generally makes its appearance where the bone has little more covering than the skin, as at the ankle, the knee, or the elbow-joint. A small pimple is seen, which after a time opens, and a small black head, furnished with two minute hooks, is seen protruding. This is laid hold of and drawn gently, the body, which is of a bright primrose colour, and about the thickness of the E string of a violin, following, to the extent of about half an inch. This operation is repeated twice in the day, care being taken to draw the worm very gently, lest it should break. As it is drawn out, it is wound upon a quill, a fine twig, or some such small object. As it dries it loses its fresh yellow colour, and exactly resembles a violin string. Should the *rishté* break during extraction, serious results are apt to follow. The entire limb swells, and suppuration sets in along the track of the worm. After seven days of intense agony, the entire body of the creature is discharged, and the wound heals up. Should the constitution of the sufferer not be of the strongest, however, he is in great danger of losing his limb, which in such countries is almost equivalent to losing his life. Aman Niaz informed me that there is another method by which the *rishté* may be extracted, without the tedious process of drawing it out day by day, half an inch at a time, and which occupies occasionally a month or six weeks. The worm sometimes amounts to a yard in length. By a judicious pressure of the fingers, with a kneading motion, round the orifice whence the body of the entozoon protrudes, it can be gradually worked forward, and its entire length extracted in the course of a few hours. There are men who devote themselves especially to this, and, as Aman Niaz told me, they generally make use of a couple of small silver coins, with which to press around the orifice. The Khan himself had extracted as many as forty of these dreadful worms from his body in the course of a year. In many instances, he had not patience even for the process by which it is extracted in a few hours, but, on its first appearance, plucked away the head, thus causing suppuration to follow. It is a curious fact that while this *rishté* prevails all over Southern Bokhara, it is never found in the Merv oasis.

It wanted but two hours of sunset, as I sat alone within the *ev*; Aman Niaz Khan and our host having gone to look at some vineyards at a short distance. I was engaged in taking some notes of the day's occurrences, when the door opened, and some Turcomans entered. They wore their swords, and were booted as for a journey. In their midst was a man who had neither sword nor boots, although he wore the regular Turcoman costume. This was the Russian prisoner Kidaieff. Had I not been so informed, I should never have known that he was not a Turcoman. Though only about twenty-five years old, he looked considerably over forty. He seemed worn to little more than skin and bone; and his pale, leaden-coloured face was wasted, and ghastly to look upon. He resembled a walking corpse rather than aught else; and his dull, glassy eyes had a fixed and mindless expression. I motioned to him to be seated. He addressed me in Russian, of which, unfortunately, I understand but little. I then spoke to him in Jagatai

Tartar, which he spoke with some fluency. He thanked me for the money which I had sent to him, and stated that he was very grateful for the improved treatment which he had experienced since my arrival at Merv, the irons upon his ankles having been removed at my request. I asked him about the treatment which he had met with at the hands of the Turcomans since his capture, but could get but little information on this score, for his gaolers were sitting beside him, and he did not dare to answer. I could see, however, from his emaciated frame and the expression of his countenance that his sufferings must have been great indeed. The traces of these sufferings upon his lineaments had been still further emphasized by the use of opium, for his captors, occasionally taking pity upon him, supplied him with this drug to enable him temporarily to forget his miseries. Little by little he had indulged in this pernicious habit, until he had become a confirmed opium eater and smoker.

He told me that that was his seventh year at Merv, and that though he had repeatedly sent letters to Russia, imploring his friends and the public to ransom him, nothing had been done, the sum asked by the Turcomans being too large, amounting, I believe, to something like 2,000*l*. This was to a great extent his own fault; for he had given himself out to be an officer of high rank, notwithstanding his youth, when captured, and the Turcomans believed him. He had further stated that his father was a general, and Governor of a province. Hence the exorbitant sum demanded for his ransom. He had been subjected to all kinds of torture. During the cold winter nights he had been forced to sleep outside the house, securely manacled, so that he could make no attempt at escape. I learned, too, that his gaoler, to stimulate him to greater efforts to obtain a ransom, used to torture him by placing pieces of lighted charcoal upon the surface of his stomach, and afterwards washing the wound with scalding water. As I have this story from some of the Turcomans themselves, I suppose I may attach credit to it.

I again tried very hard to procure his release, renewing my offer of one thousand krans (40*l.*), but they treated the offer with contempt, pointing to the value of the food he had consumed during his long imprisonment. But I told them flatly that Kidaieff was only a private soldier, and that if, as they proposed, they sacrificed him sooner than part with him for a low ransom, the Russians would make them pay dearly for what they had done. He was taken back to his quarters, but I believe my argument made some impression upon his gaolers.

Before starting the next morning some Turcomans applied to me for medical advice and assistance, as was generally the case whenever I appeared at any of the outlying villages. One brought with him his son, whose hand was badly inflamed. I prescribed a poultice of bread and milk, and gave detailed instructions as to how it was to be made. The man listened with attention, and, thanking me, took his leave. When he had gone half a mile, he came back again, to say that I had omitted to tell him what should be the colour of the cow whose milk was to be used. He had, he said, a brown cow and a black one. A woman, too, whose daughter was suffering from fever, brought me a handful of camel's hair, and asked me to manufacture from it a charm for the cure of her daughter's illness. As I had not the slightest notion of what the nature of the charm might be, I addressed myself to Aman Niaz Khan, who immediately undertook to instruct me. By means of a spindle the camel-hair was spun into a stout thread, the Khan all the time droning some verses from the Koran, or some necromantic chant. When the thread was finished it was of considerable length, and, folding it three times upon itself, he respun it. Then he proceeded to tie seven knots upon the string. Before drawing each knot hard he blew upon it. This, tied into the form of a bracelet, was to be worn on the wrist of the patient. Each day one of the knots was to be untied and blown upon, and when the seventh knot had been undone the whole of the thread was to be made into a ball and thrown into the river, carrying, as was supposed, the illness with it. I had some quinine with me, which I unluckily gave her, the result being that I was nearly torn in pieces by a crowd of excited matrons who desired to procure some of the drug for their children who were ill of fever.

CHAPTER XXIV.

Bazaar day—An accident—The market-place —Food supplies—Punishments—Turcoman steeds—The town crier—Sheep-tail fat—Abundance of game—Breakfast difficulties—Starving out enemies—My sumsa stealer—Beg Murad's present—Turcoman life—Customs—Cleverness of women—Carpets.

THE bazaar at Kouchid Khan Kala is held twice in the week—on Sunday and Thursday. On each of these days there is a very large gathering of the inhabitants of the oasis; eight to ten thousand persons being usually present. On each bazaar day the annoyance which I underwent from inquisitive visitors was quadrupled, and from the earliest dawn my *ev* was filled with unbidden guests, all seeking for the news about things in general of which they supposed me to be the unfailing recipient. The day following that on which I returned from Aman Niaz Khan's country house was bazaar day; and, with a view of being out of the way when my troublesome visitors began to arrive, I rose shortly before daybreak, and walked towards the southern gate of the fortress. Clambering up the very steep ascent, I took my place upon the ramparts to watch the sunrise over the plains, and see the various dealers and customers arrive at the bazaar. For nearly an hour I was left in undisturbed quiet. Owing to my wearing Turcoman attire nobody had taken notice of me when crossing the inhabited portion of the ground. Very soon, however, the relays of workers on the ramparts began to arrive. I was immediately espied, and, as usual, a dense throng formed round me, persecuting me with their senseless questions. The sun was well above the horizon before there was any great influx of visitors to the market, but towards seven o'clock the throng became very large indeed.

From my lofty look-out post, I saw an accident which threatened to turn out fatally, and which resulted in serious loss. The tall, rickety bridge across the Murgab, which I have already mentioned, was, owing to the passage of the Merv people with their beasts of burthen, sadly shaken and dismantled. It was hardly safe to cross it on horseback. A Turcoman, with a laden horse carrying various commodities for sale at the bazaar, seeing the dilapidated condition of the bridge, preferred fording the Murgab to risking himself and his animal upon the shaky framework. The river was at this time rather high, though there were many places at which it could be crossed with ease. This Turcoman, however, chose a dangerous spot, where there was a hole in the river-bed. When half across, the horse lost his footing, and, with his load and rider, disappeared beneath the surface. The current was unusually strong, and when they next appeared they were twenty or thirty yards lower down the stream. The man had held to the bridle, and struggled hard to keep his own and the animal's heads above water. On one occasion they disappeared so long that I felt confident both were lost. At least fifty on-lookers threw off their scanty garments and dashed into the water. They succeeded in disengaging the struggling rider, who seemed none the worse for his ducking; but the horse, borne down by his load, remained at the bottom. Divers immediately set to work, but could not discover the carcass. Then about twenty persons formed a chain across the river and swam against the stream. At every stroke the swimmers allowed themselves to sink, until their feet touched the bottom, feeling for the drowned horse, which they at length succeeded in discovering. Several of them, diving, laid hold of it by the bridle, and, keeping all together, towed it ashore.

When the bazaar was well thronged, I came down to look at the proceedings, for up to this time I had not had an opportunity of inspecting a genuine Turcoman market. There are two parallel lines of mud wall, each one hundred yards long, and about sixty apart. From these walls spring short partitions of the same material, forming recesses at right angles to the general line, and turned inwards towards the interior of the bazaar, in which the habitual traders display their goods. Overhead, each one has a kind of rude roof of reed matting or felt, to keep off the sun's rays. Within these booths the merchants squat upon the ground, surrounded by their wares. Those who have not regular stalls sit out in the middle of the open space exposed to the full glare of the sun, and others under cover of curious square cotton umbrellas, such as may be seen any day in a southern Spanish market.

The people who throng the bazaar, to the number of 6,000 or 8,000, are principally Mervli, though there are a few Khivans, Bokharans, and, very occasionally, a trader or two from Meshed. No charge is made upon the merchants who frequent the bazaar for the accommodation afforded them in the stalls, except in the case of Jews, who pay half a kran (fivepence). The only expense incurred by the traders is that of keeping in repair the pathways across the fields and rude bridges spanning the irrigation trenches. That such repairs are sometimes needed will be seen from the anecdote about the drowned horse, given above.

The local Turcoman traders supply the bazaar with

corn, some kinds of oil, fruits, fresh provisions, and articles of home manufacture; besides horses, asses, and camels. Almost throughout the year the bazaar is plentifully supplied with fruits, all of which are of exquisite flavour. In fact, Merv has from time immemorial been celebrated for its fruits. Its melons are occasionally exported to Persia, in which country persons of rank send them to each other as presents. They are beyond all comparison superior to those produced along the frontier, or in the interior of Persia. The peaches are also delicious. One variety, the rind of which is of a deep crimson colour, known as the *shanik*, is smaller than the ordinary peach, and is without exception the most exquisite species of this fruit which I have ever tasted. Then there are apricots, and the jujube fruit which abounds at Merv. In external appearance the latter is very like a small date. It has also a stone like that fruit. The inside, however, is of a dry, husky nature, slightly sweet, and produces intense thirst. It is perhaps the fruit least adapted for consumption in an Eastern climate. The only other fruits I have seen at Merv are walnuts, which are chiefly brought from Persia, and apples. These latter are very poor and woody, the climate being apparently too hot for their successful cultivation.

The bazaar is always plentifully supplied with food—cheese, both soft and hard as stone, coagulated milk, and large cakes of bread. The principal meat is goat's flesh and mutton, but beef and camel's flesh are seen at times, with that of the antelope and wild ass. The sheep and goats are killed on the spot as wanted, on account of the heat. Pheasants are plentiful, and fowls and eggs can be obtained.

The merchants from Bokhara chiefly bring cloth of different kinds, coarse silk, cotton, and woven camel-hair.

They also offer for sale *tumbaki* for the water-pipes, green tea, and sugar—either ordinary white lump or crystallized candied sugar, both being of Russian manufacture.

The traders from Meshed deal in finer cloths, Russian calico, Chinese tea-bowls, tea-pots, and glass tumblers; while the Merv people, besides food, sell wooden spoons and dishes, clothes, sheepskin hats and overcoats, knives, and occasionally arms. Russian leather and long and short rifles were also to be had. Sometimes, but rarely, dried fish is exposed for sale. It is brought from Bokhara and Khiva, and is caught in the Oxus, I believe. The money in use is a mixture of Persian, Bokharan, and Russian.

Upon alternate bazaar days a kind of court was held upon an earthen mound about forty feet long by fifteen in height. Here the Kethkodas, assisted by an old Cadi, administered judgment. The punishments were fines, and a kind of pillory, the offenders' arms being tied behind, their hats removed, and then they had to stand for so long in the broiling sun. Thieves were bound to a stake; and in cases where people were remiss in obeying the Khan, the stick was used until it fell to pieces.

With the exception of meat, fruit, and corn, everything was horribly dear. Coarse tea costs from six to eight shillings per pound; and sugar, both ordinary white lump and crystallized candied sugar, called here *kand*, were over one shilling and eightpence for the same quantity.

I was very much amused by an incident which occurred during my promenades. As I was making my way back, after having traversed the entire length of the bazaar, a Jew merchant placed himself before me, and, making a profound reverence, presented me with a small bag of silver coin, containing about fifteen krans. In some surprise, I asked him what was the meaning of this proceeding. He replied that it was a gift to me from the

Jewish merchants of the bazaar, by way of testifying their respect. This is a common Eastern custom; a gift offered to a person of high position being intended to conciliate his good-will, and secure his influence on any needful occasion. He would not take back the money, so I handed it to the men for their trouble in accompanying me.

The western extremity of the bazaar is devoted to the sale of horses, asses, and camels. Some fine horses are to be seen at times, at prices varying from 30*l.* to 60*l.*; but, as a rule, animals of this price are not brought to the bazaar. They are generally of the Persian breed, being a mixture of Arab and Turcoman blood, but thoroughbred Turcomans are also frequently exposed for sale. I saw two fine ones on the day of my arrival. They were very richly caparisoned. Besides embroidered saddle-cloths and housings, they had heavy silver collars studded with turquoises and cornelians, and corresponding ornaments on every available part of the body. The value of the trappings must have equalled that of the steeds themselves. During my stay at Merv, and a pretty long one among the Yamuds, I had ample means of observing the merits of Turcoman horses, and of hearing their praises sounded by no cold partizans of the breed, viz., the Turcomans themselves. Yet I never witnessed or even heard of such exploits as European travellers mention in speaking of them. I have over and over again made searching inquiries about the powers of these Central Asian steeds. A first-class Turcoman horse, after a month's special training, and with ample and special food, will go from sixty to seventy miles a day, and keep up that pace for an apparently unlimited period. This sustaining power is probably their only excellence which has not been overrated. For mere speed over a mile or two they cannot hold their own against the higher class of European horses. As a rule, the Turcoman horse is very 'leggy,' but extremely graceful of limb. His chest is narrow, but very long, as is his shoulder also. His head is usually handsome, but in the main rather large; and the neck, far from having the proud curve of the Arab horse, is not even straight. It is slightly concave from above, and gives to some otherwise elegantly formed animals a lamentable likeness to a strangely abnormal camel. At the point of junction with the head, the neck is usually very constricted, giving the animal a half-strangled appearance. There are not generally more than half a dozen for sale on any given day. Asses are, however, abundant; but I never saw at any time in Merv the large white ass used by persons of distinction in Persia.

It approached mid-day, and the sun's heat was becoming intolerable, as I turned away from the bazaar. The town crier, mounted on a broken piece of mud wall, was announcing the disappearance of a child, and alternating his descriptions of its dress and appearance with the statement that at a certain stall the flesh of a sheep could be purchased at a reduced rate. There were some men, also, walking up and down the bazaar, and crying out the names of the articles which they wished to buy. In a European mart one would expect the sellers to cry out their wares, but at Merv it is the contrary. A man goes along the row of booths shouting, 'I want six eggs,' or 'I want two fowls.' Should the stall-keeper be sufficiently emancipated from his habitual reverie, or from quarrelling with his neighbours, perhaps he will reply, but no dealer ever takes the trouble to put his goods *en évidence*.

The camels were groaning laboriously, and the horses were standing around in dissatisfied silence in the white heat of noon. The frequenters of the bazaar were beginning to make their way to their own houses or those of their acquaintances, to indulge in the habitual siesta, and I directed my steps towards my redoubt. In the outskirts of the bazaar I passed large piles of the gnarled stems of tamarisk (*odjar*), brought from a distance of some twenty or thirty miles westward to be sold for firewood. Charcoal, too, in rude sacks, was being disposed of, for Turcomans of the better class use it for lighting their water-pipes, instead of the balls of dried horse-dung which the humbler citizens of Merv employ for the purpose.

At Merv a sheep usually costs from seven to twelve shillings. The animals are of the big-tailed variety, and all the fat of their bodies seems to concentrate itself in this part, which cannot, on the average, weigh less than twelve pounds, and is the dearest portion of the carcass. When a sheep is killed, the tail is first made use of. It is skinned, and cut into pieces, which are placed in a large hemispherical iron cauldron of about two feet in diameter. In this the fat is melted down to the consistency of oil, and, when it is at a high temperature, pieces of lean, chopped small, are thrown into it, and the pot is removed from the fire. The contents are then poured into a wooden dish, somewhat larger than the pot, which is placed upon the carpet in the midst of the guests. Each person dips his bread into the melted grease, now and again fishing out a morsel of meat. Owing to the high temperature of the fat, these morsels are quite calcined, and taste precisely like greasy cinders. It is a peculiarity of the Turcomans that they like their meat exceedingly well done. When all the meat has been picked out from the dish, and the liquid within has attained a moderate temperature, the master of the feast takes the vessel in both hands, places it to his lips, and swallows a pint or so of the fat. He then hands it to the guest nearest to him, who does likewise, and so it makes the circuit of the party. When nearly all the grease has been thus consumed, and if there be present any person whom the host especially designs to honour, he offers him the wooden dish, and the recipient gathers up what remains by passing his curved finger round the interior and conveying it to his mouth.

Pilaff is a favourite dish with the poor, and, whether of rice or barley, is often flavoured with prunes. Sheets of dough boiled in oil also form a popular food, the dough, from the extreme heat of the oil, being very light and flaky. Strange to say, though game abounds, very few indeed ever go in search of it, the Turcomans preferring to sit at home and munch their dry bread to taking the trouble and making the exertion necessary to procure it. Neither do they much care for it. In the majority of instances the pheasants and partridges are not shot. When a party of horsemen are abroad, and by chance cross a piece of ground affording any cover, they are sure to put up some dozens of partridges or pheasants, and then, forming line at short intervals, they drive them towards the open, the birds, after the first two flights, rarely ever again taking to the wing. They are then run down until exhausted, when the riders spring from their horses and catch them alive.

There is one preparation of meat which the Turcomans carry with them when they go far afield for any purpose. It is called *sumsa*. A thin, circular cake of dough, a foot in diameter, is covered with meat finely minced, and highly flavoured with spices and garlic, a little sugar occasionally being added. The cake of dough is then doubled over, and the edges are united. The whole is placed in an oven and baked for half an hour. This kind of mince pie is one of the most palatable dishes to be found among the Turcomans, especially when they can be prevailed upon by any means to lessen the ordinary modicum of garlic. I subsisted largely upon *sumsa*, which I had specially made by Matthi, the Jew merchant. Subsequently, however, I was obliged to abandon this diet. When it was once known that I was in the habit of ordering a dozen meat pies of the kind, I had always a large number of guests at my house, patiently awaiting the moment at which I should produce my breakfast or dinner, in order that they might partake of the *sumsa*, which they looked upon as a great delicacy.

This dish was the occasion of an amusing incident, which, at the time, however, was to me the reverse of diverting. Beg Murad was extravagantly fond of this minced preparation. I had, in my unsophisticated days, largely supplied all comers with it, Beg Murad among the number. Finding that there was an apparently never-failing supply, the old ruffian, far from being shy of continually repeating his visits, seemed to have grown to consider breakfast and dinner at my expense a standing institution. Observing this, I directed Matthi not to bring me any more *sumsa* until I should send him further word. Great was the disappointment of the pot-hunters when, on arriving each morning and evening, they discovered that I was confining myself to a diet of bread and *gattuk*, with an occasional egg. Turcoman etiquette made it necessary that I should offer my visitors a portion of what I was eating; and often, out of what would otherwise have been a substantial meal, I have scarcely been able to secure a couple of mouthfuls for myself. It was hateful to eat with these people. Each raced with the others, as it were, in eating, so as to obtain the greatest possible supply of food for himself. It was quite sufficient to prevent one from enjoying his food to witness the rapacity and eagerness with which they devoured what was laid before them, lest they might be outstripped by any of their companions. Sometimes, with a view of disappointing them, I have abstained from food for a whole day, leaving them, from early dawn to long after sunset, with no other nourishment than that which they could extract from their water-pipes. My own servants, who were highly disgusted at this system of abstinence, inasmuch as it forced them, as well as myself, to fast on occasional days, again and again urged me to tell my visitors to go out; but I did not wish to commit such a breach of etiquette, and preferred the more passive form of showing the intruders that I thought they were carrying the joke a little too far. When by these means I had succeeded in getting rid of the more rapacious of my acquaintances, I ventured to order a fresh supply of *sumsa*, which I kept concealed in my saddle-bags, pending a possible opportunity of consuming it unobserved. However, someone betrayed the secret of the hidden sandwiches to Beg Murad, who now made a practice of visiting my house about dawn, when I was asleep, helping himself from the bags, and coolly sitting down upon my carpet to enjoy his breakfast, after which he had the audacity to wake me up and ask whether I was not going to get him any tea. At first I was highly amused at his *sang froid*, but this system of breakfasting surreptitiously at my expense began at last to assume the form of a serious annoyance. I have often awakened, to see the last portion of my day's allowance of *sumsa* vanishing down Beg Murad's throat, he not feeling the slightest concern as to how I should procure my breakfast.

At last matters came to a crisis. Baba Khan and Aman Niaz Khan were desirous of consulting me upon some serious matter connected with the government of Merv, and, with several of their principal followers, one morning paid me a visit. Taking their seats, they waited patiently until I should awake, for, as I have said, it is a matter of strict etiquette among the Turcomans, at Merv especially, never to disturb a sleeper. When I awoke, I noticed, as usual, Beg Murad, rapidly swallowing my *sumsa*, and I could perceive by the broad grins on the faces of the others, that they had been informed of the joke, and were intensely amused at it. This was too much for me, and, with a very sour expression of countenance, I commenced to think over the means whereby I should put a summary end to the objectionable proceedings of the Beg.

The conversation turned upon the doings on the previous evening of some thieves, who had infringed the new regulations as to raiding upon their neighbours. 'Oh,' said Beg Murad, with his mouth full of mincemeat, 'I believe that the Bahadur Khan (myself) thinks we are all thieves at Merv.' This gave me the desired opportunity, and I replied, rather fiercely, 'I do not believe that you are all *ogri* here, but a great many are, and it is my opinion that you are the chief of them.' This provoked inextinguishable laughter among the audience, which had the effect of irritating me still further, and, resolving to push the matter to an extremity there and then, I continued, 'Beg Murad, finish that *sumsa* which you are eating, and then immediately go out of my house; and if I ever catch you within the door again it will be the worse for you.' With this I imperiously pointed towards the door. Beg Murad, who was a man of very high standing at Merv, was completely taken aback at this sudden change in my long-suffering attitude, and as he perceived from the demeanour of his superiors who were present that I should be supported in my command, he rose, and left the *ev*, darting an angry look at me.

I then explained to Baba and Aman Niaz Khans how for a long time I had been victimised by the Beg, and that no other course than the one I had adopted was left open to me. They said that I was quite right, and that Murad's reputation was the same all over Merv; that he was a very greedy person, and endeavoured as much as possible to live at the expense of others, while never on any account would he offer hospitality to his friends.

In the course of half an hour the Khans left me, and, as I was engaged in writing, I noticed an unusual stir outside my door. Then the carpet which hung curtain-wise before it was thrust aside, and two Turcomans appeared, dragging by the horns a large fat-tailed sheep. 'Stop!' I cried, 'where are you bringing that animal to?' 'It is,' said one, 'a present from Beg Murad.' It was, in effect, a peace-offering on his part, for he had thought it more prudent to try and be on good terms with me, especially as he had a suspicion that ere long some substantial presents might be distributed among the leading inhabitants. He had therefore pocketed the affront which I had put upon him. However, I would not hear of any compromise, and peremptorily ordered the sheep to be taken away, saying that I would have no dealings of any kind with a man of Beg Murad's character. Observing, however, the ludicrously dolorous expression upon the faces of my servants and henchmen, who, by my refusal of the sheep, saw themselves deprived of a prospective meal of sheep's-tail fat and mutton broth, I so far rescinded my original decision as to consent to buy the animal. I asked my chief servant to appraise its worth, telling him not by any means to undervalue it, as I did not wish to be under any obligation whatever to the would-be donor. He said that thirteen krans (nearly eleven shillings) would be ample purchase money, so I handed that sum to the man who had brought the sheep. To make my action all the more patent, I had the animal slaughtered upon the spot, and despatched a leg of it to Beg Murad's *ev*, with the message that, if so disposed, he could make *sumsa* out of it for himself. To do the Beg justice, I must admit that he saw the humour of the proceeding. When I subsequently became reconciled to him, previous to leaving Merv, he laughed heartily over the whole affair.

Eating seems to be the main object of a Turcoman's life, and, provided he has an adequate supply of the better class of nutriment, such as I have described, he will remain inactive and indolent. He will not even go upon a *chappow* or *aleman*, those species of raids which for the younger members of the community have the double advantage of mingling pleasure and profit. At the bottom the Turcoman is not fond of fighting; he would much rather supply his wants by some other means, though he decidedly prefers raiding, with all its concomitant risks, to anything like steady labour in the fields, or other industrial pursuit.

The everyday life of a wealthy Turcoman is a very indolent one. He rises a little before dawn, which he can well afford to do, inasmuch as he spends the best part of the middle of the day in siesta, and retires to bed at an early hour in the evening. Having washed, and lighted his water-pipe, he sits smoking, awaiting the production of the hot fresh bread which the female members of the household are preparing, and then, having made his breakfast, and smoked again for half-an-hour, he talks with the people who drop in to arrange his ordinary matters of business, whether in connection with his flocks and herds, or his traffic with Meshed. The rest of the day is spent in the idlest possible fashion. Those who are compelled to work proceed, immediately after breakfast, to toil in the fields, or follow their avocations as sheepskin-dressers, shoemakers, or the like. At Merv, those who follow any occupation of this kind are few indeed. Once a man passes the age of forty, he delegates all his work to the younger members of his family, and never dreams of doing anything himself. In the event, however, of raids or defensive fighting, men of comparatively advanced age deem it to be their duty to take part with the youngest in the necessary martial toils.

It often happens that a Turcoman's sons are so numerous that he cannot find occupation for them all upon the grounds which he cultivates, or in looking after his cattle while grazing. In cases like this, some of them either hire themselves as camel-drivers to and from Bokhara and Meshed, or else work at wages of two krans a day on the farms of some of the richer Turcomans, particularly at harvest and irrigation times. Should anyone feel so disposed, he has always plenty of unoccupied ground from which to choose a site for the planting of crops on his own account; but as a younger son of this description can rarely raise the necessary funds for the seed, and at the same time support himself while engaged in the preliminary labours of cultivation and until his crops have ripened, such as these are few indeed. It is only when a Turcoman marries, which he seldom does until he has accumulated or received from his parents some small capital, that he ever sets up as an agriculturist on his own account. He then purchases a house, a second-hand one, costing from seventy-five to a hundred krans (3*l.* to 4*l.*), and settles somewhere in the neighbourhood of one of the secondary irrigation streams branching from the Novur or Alasha canal, accordingly as he belongs to the Toktamish or Otamish, and proceeds to dig a minor watercourse for the irrigation of the land the cultivation of which he undertakes, which must be within the particular district inhabited by the clan or subdivision of which he is a member. Some, especially those inhabiting the western border of the oasis, the Sitchmaz, for instance, occupy themselves in collecting the tamarisk trunks which are to be procured in abundance in the neighbourhood of Dash Robat. These are sold, sometimes in their natural state, and sometimes burned into charcoal, both on account of the convenience of carrying it in this form and of its inherent value.

The female members of the family are mainly occupied in household duties. They do all the cooking and fetching of water, and the daughters for whom there is no other occupation occupy themselves in the manufacture of embroidered skull-caps, carpets, shirts, saddle-bags, and socks of variegated tints for the better classes. The silk and cotton robes worn by the men and women are made by special persons. The women manufacture their own garments, the cloth being purchased from the merchants at the bazaar. When a Turcoman is blessed with a large number of daughters, he contrives to realize a considerable sum per annum by the felt and other carpets which they make. In this case an *ev* is set apart as a workshop, and three or four girls are usually occupied upon each carpet, sometimes for a couple of months.

Each girl generally manufactures two extra fine carpets, to form part of her dowry when she marries. When this has been done, she devotes herself to producing goods for the markets at Meshed and Bokhara, where the Turcoman carpets fetch a much higher price than those manufactured in Khorassan or beyond the Oxus. Sometimes these carpets are made partly of silk, brought from Bokhara. They are generally twice the size of the ordinary ones, which are made from sheep's wool and camel-hair mingled with a little cotton, and are almost entirely of silk. They fetch enormous prices. I have known as much as fifty pounds (50*l.*) given for one measuring eight feet square.

CHAPTER XXV.

Religious proposals—Generous offers—A request to Teheran—Russia leather—Raiding—The Old Man of the Sword—Mourning customs—Effects of a storm—Shampooing.

MATTERS were going fairly smooth for me, and the Turcomans had begun to look upon me as naturalised among them. I was able to talk to them about Koranic doctrines; let them see that I was acquainted with the fact that Adam, Noah, Moses, and David were prophets, and had even renounced my heretical doubts as to Alexander the Great being one of the inspired elect. I had made such progress in the favour even of the moullahs, that one day a Seyd (descendant of Mahomet), one of their number, called upon me, and said that as I was so well acquainted with Mussulman tenets, he saw no reason whatever why I should not openly embrace the true faith. Issa (Jesus) and Moussa (Moses) were, he said, quite as much respected by the adherents of Islam as they were by my own co-religionists; and I required only a short course of instruction in the form of prayer, and some minor matters connected with the practice of the Mussulman religion, to enjoy all the privileges accruing to the membership of his faith. Even Makdum Kuli Khan entered into the matter with ardour. He was sorry I expressed any desire to leave Merv. He said that probably I desired to return to my wife. He could not believe that it was possible I was unmarried. 'Once you openly acknowledge yourself a Mussulman, we will find you another wife here, or two if you wish.' I was in no slight degree alarmed at this proposition, for it looked like the preliminary to an announcement that leaving the oasis was a thing not to be thought of. Grasping at the Khan's hypothesis about my being married, I replied that I couldn't think of marrying any other wives, as the Christian religion forbade it. 'But,' said the Khan, 'when you are a Mussulman, you will have the privilege of having even four wives if you choose.' My position was very precarious—I feared to give the slightest ground for saying that I was trifling with their religious and matrimonial proposals; and at the same time I feared to bring on a crisis by a peremptory refusal to entertain for a moment the propositions made to me in evident good faith.

About this time, during a political discussion, I had taken an opportunity of reminding my colleagues in the triumvirate of the advice I had given at the last *medjlis*, when I recommended them to forward to Teheran a document, bearing their seals, in which their views about an English alliance should be fully set forth, and I inquired whether any measures had yet been taken towards drawing up such an instrument. I was informed that it had not yet been sent, but that no time would be lost in preparing and forwarding it.

On the very next day a *Khodja*, or scribe—a man of great repute at Merv for erudition—was summoned to headquarters to act as amanuensis in the matter of this important State document. He was of Arab descent, and carried about with him in a long cylindrical tin box a roll of documents signed by the Sherif of Mecca, the Khans of Khiva and Bokhara, and other Oriental potentates, testifying to his direct descent from Ali, and to his right to the title of Seyd. The document was ultimately drawn up, and the seals of the Khans and Kethkodas were attached. Half-a-dozen horsemen conveyed it to Meshed, to be forwarded thence to the British Minister at Teheran. I took this opportunity of writing myself to the latter, informing him how matters stood, and that any summons on the part of Abass Khan requiring me to go to Meshed would be utterly disregarded by the Turcomans. I asked the Minister himself to address a letter to the Merv chiefs, saying it was absolutely necessary that I should come to Meshed, and to attach to it seals and signatures which they could understand, and whose importance they could realise.

Up to this time I had not extended my excursions to the extreme north of the cultivated territory. On expressing a desire to do so, a very intimate friend of mine, Owez Agha, whose *ev* was near mine, asked me to spend a day with him at his fruit-tree grove, situated due north of Kouchid Khan Kala. The intermediate country was exceedingly well cultivated, and rather too copiously watered to make travelling at all agreeable. The village towards which we directed our steps is called Har, and is close by the outlying fortalice known as Kara Shaitan Kala (the fort of the Black Devil). This place was, besides, the principal station of the *Karaoul bashi* of the Toktamish, who from this point kept an eye upon the movements of the Ersari Turcomans, and whose patrols radiated to all parts of the border in this direction. Owez's brother, who superintended the cultivation of the ground at Har, was, for a Turcoman, very well-to-do from a worldly point of view. To his profession of agriculture he added the trade of a boot-maker.

We stayed but one night at Har, and then proceeded to the last dam upon the main stream of the Murgab, at a place called Egri Guzer, where there is a very considerable *aoull*, its chief being Yaghmour Khan, the head of the Toktamish police. I was informed that from this place there is a considerable exportation of cow-hides to Khiva, and thence to Russia, the tanned leather being given in exchange for the raw material. The Russian leather, which is used by the Tekkés for the manufacture of boots, slippers, sword-belts, and military accoutrements, is very stout, of the natural colour on one side, and on the other of a bright crimson marked with diagonal lines crossing each other at right angles. It has the peculiar perfume characteristic of Russia leather. While in Bokhara and on the Afghan border the red surface of the leather is turned outwards in the long riding boots used by the people, at Merv it is the coarse brown side which is exposed, the Tekkés considering a display of so brilliant a colour to be effeminate.

On my return from the Egri Guzer dam, I found that a deputation of Saruk chiefs had arrived at Kouchid Khan Kala. They were from the neighbourhood of Herat, and their object was to obtain help from Merv to proceed against Ayoub Khan, Colonel St. John, the political officer at Kandahar, having, they said, asked their help. I learned a good deal about the political situation in Afghanistan, and when the chiefs departed I sent by them a letter to Colonel St. John, begging him to try and get me away from Merv. I subsequently learned that my letter did not reach its destination.

Apropos of the Turcoman practice of making raids, a most amusing incident occurred about this time. Aman Niaz Khan had sent to Meshed for a large consignment of tea and sugar, and rolls of cloth. This became known in Merv, and a troop of the worst marauders went out to intercept the caravan, and swept off the booty. The

Khan's rage was ludicrous at this want of honour amongst thieves, and, gathering a party of *yassaouls*, or police, he started off to wreak vengeance on the evil-doers. He recovered nearly everything, and brought in six prisoners, who, however, pleaded ignorance of the proprietor, and so escaped.

Another raid of great magnitude was at this juncture brought to my notice, and, as one of the triumvirate in power, I made a most strenuous protest, as it was a flagrant breach of the agreement entered into between me and the *Medjlis*. Some hundreds of Tekkés had gone out to raid in the Derguez, under Abdal Serdar, and I sent word to Baba Khan that it must at once be stopped. A council was summoned, and upon the strength of my protests Baba Khan gave orders for the freebooters to be pursued. Aman Niaz took the opposite side, and when I threatened to leave Merv, he told me I was perfectly at liberty to do so. Finally, the two Khans decided to take possession of the spoil when it was brought in, and decide the matter after; and on the strength of this I decided to remove myself for awhile from the immediate vicinity of the principal officials. A few days previous to this event Aman Niaz Khan had invited me to pay a visit to Matthi, at the Jews' village, about a mile and a half away, and this visit was now paid. While waiting for Matthi to prepare the upper storey of his castle for our reception, we sat within one of his magazines, in which was stored a most heterogeneous collection of articles of merchandise. There were fur-bound caps from Bokhara, cotton and silk from Samarcand, china tea-bowls, copper utensils, and a very extensive assortment of drugs of different kinds, for Matthi was a professed physician, as well as a general dealer. While Aman Niaz Khan and myself were turning over the Jew's goods, and endeavouring to select something which might be of use to us, I had a visit from Killidge-ak-Saghal—the Old Man of the Sword. We seated ourselves upon a kind of raised mud platform near the door, and smoked our pipes. The ak-Saghal fixed his eyes upon my horse, which was tethered to a tree near to us, and commenced a series of praises of the animal. This, among Turcomans, as I have said, is a preliminary to asking the owner to make him a present of the desired object. As, however, I seemed not to take the hint, he remarked that I had made very extensive presents to several of the Merv chiefs. 'What,' said he, 'have you given to me?' I replied that, as far as I knew, I had not given him anything. 'But,' he rejoined, 'what are you going to give me?' Then interrupting himself, he said, 'I do not require money,' which I considered a fortunate circumstance, inasmuch as I had not any. 'But I will willingly receive your horse, which I admire very much.' I reminded the old Kethkoda that I required a horse for my own use, and that I could not very well proceed any long distance—to Meshed for instance—on foot; but that, if it were possible to find a sufficiently good animal for my own use, I would willingly make him a present of that which had taken his fancy.

Shortly afterwards, I mounted a break-neck staircase, a little wider than an ordinary chimney, and arrived in the upper chamber, which was some twenty feet square. One third of the floor was occupied by barley, piled half-way to the roof, the remainder by large carpets and voluminous cushions, among which Aman Niaz Khan had already installed himself, surrounded by his water and opium pipes, and half-a-dozen soda-water bottles full of arrack. After he had imbibed the contents of a couple of bottles, he began to inveigh against Baba Khan's over-sense of propriety in endeavouring to interrupt the raid, observing that he could not see why a thing which had gone on for so long, and which had always been looked upon as perfectly permissible, should now be found fault with. I reminded him of the near presence of the Russians, and of the extreme danger of the raiding parties coming in contact with the Russian patrols, which might give the invaders an excuse for advancing upon Merv. The Khan's ideas, however, were very much of the 'après moi le déluge' kind, and he evidently thought that the Merv machine would hold out during his time. We remained two days in Matthi's castle, and I was heartily glad to get away, for the diet of sour milk and bread, with the accompaniment of arrack and water-pipes, was far from agreeable in the blazing heat which then prevailed.

On returning, I found that the mother of Baba Khan had died suddenly during our absence, and the senior Khan was confining himself within doors for three days according to custom—the women mourning among themselves. Wishing to testify my respect to Baba Khan I ordered my crimson flag to be hauled down to half-mast, an act which was directly looked upon as my declaration of a breach of agreement. People crowded round my redoubt, and the greatest anxiety prevailed until I had explained.

Soon after, the booty of the raiders arrived in charge of the police—six hundred sheep and seventy oxen being impounded—four hundred of the sheep belonging to a chieftain named Aliar whom I had formerly met in the Derguez. Finally, after much discussion, the decision was left to me, and I insisted upon all the cattle being restored. This was carried out on consideration of a small fine being paid for each head to the *yassaouls* by way of remuneration for their trouble. This settled, robbers and robbed spent the greater portion of the evening together in my ev, and it was truly amusing to hear the anecdotes which each related in turn. Abdal Serdar told Aliar of the various *ruses* by which he carried off his sheep and cows, at the same time escaping the notice of the patrols. Aliar seemed highly amused, and, on his own part, related other stories, explanatory of his method of capturing Mervli cattle. Both parties laughed very heartily, and complimented each other on the skill displayed.

This was on June 27, and I had the company of my guests the night through, consequent upon a violent storm, a very rare thing in these regions. The thunder and lightning were incessant, and by degrees the rain began to make its way through the roof, forming a most disagreeable fluid with the material that had saturated the felt. The fire had gone out, the lamp would not burn, and to add to our discomfort all kinds of venomous things—scorpions, and insects which ordinarily inhabit holes in the dried marl—were driven in by the weather. More than one person was stung. The storm ceased at sunrise, and when on the point of setting out Aliar and the other prisoners of the raid made a most elaborate toilet, which, to tell the truth, the latter were much in need of, considering the time they had been clothed in filthy rags and chained together. The barber, a Merv Tekké, produced a razor which, from its extreme size and extraordinary appearance, was doubtless of home manufacture. He proceeded to sharpen this instrument, using the blade of my sword as a hone. The Turcoman invariably shaves his head entirely clean, with the exception of the small scalp-lock upon the top. Even this is not always retained. The Persian, on the contrary, when he shaves his head at all, does so only from the top of the forehead to the back of the neck, leaving the hair upon each side of the head hanging over the ears. After passing through the hands of the barber, each guest underwent a singular kind of shampooing, consisting of his being trodden upon as he lay upon the floor. Sometimes, too, he sat upright; and the shampooer, mounting upon his shoulders, stamped upon them with his bare feet until the requisite amount of suppleness had been produced.

CHAPTER XXVI.

Diseases—Thirst for remedies—An unsatisfied patient—Plans for the future—A fast for liberty—The Khan's proposal—A change of front—Squeezing a Jew—Unwelcome visitors—Traits of the people—The Moullah's watch—Ink v. blacking—Marriage—Settlement of divorce.

I HAVE already mentioned the great prevalence of diseases of the eye, particularly *keratitis*; but affections of this kind were so common at Merv that the inhabitants had almost ceased to regard them as maladies, and I was troubled very little with respect to such diseases. But, at the very lowest computation, fifty per cent. of the population, male and female, had badly diseased livers, and scrofulitic and scorbutic ailments. The deranged livers I believe to have been the direct product of the consumption, during the exceedingly hot weather, of large quantities of melted fat, which it was useless to tell the people to avoid. Fever, too, was to be met with, though to nothing like the extent to which it prevails in the neighbourhood of the lower waters of the Tejend and among the Yamuds. As long as my quinine held out it was in great demand; but as I had from twenty to thirty applicants daily for this medicine alone it may be conceived that my store was very soon exhausted. For the Turcomans will linger on for months, suffering severely from the effects of intermittent fever, when two or three francs' worth of quinine would completely cure them. Knowing that I had some store of the drug by me, the fever patients were incessant in their demands for it.

A man would ride twenty or thirty miles, and spend two or three days in persecuting me on this score, when he might have procured as much as I was able to give him for a few pence at the Jew's shop. Any traveller who would bring to Merv a couple of camels laden with quinine, Epsom salts, croton oil, antibilious pills, and their much-esteemed *moomia* (bitumen), and would freely give away these drugs to all applicants, would be, while they held out, the idol of the people; but after the demolition of his stock he would fall from favour, as I did.

During the latter part of my stay at Kouchid Khan Kala, so great had become the daily influx of patients that I found it quite impossible to secure a moment for myself, either by day or night. At last, however, I hit upon a plan by which I secured a little more privacy than I had hitherto enjoyed. Happening one day to pay a visit to a neighbouring *ev*, I noticed a rude mosquito curtain, manufactured from a coarse muslin made at Merv, and which formed a sort of small tent, some seven feet in length, three in breadth at the top, six at base, and some four feet in height. I immediately purchased this treasure, paying a pretty high price for it, and had it conveyed to my house, where I at once set it up at the side of the *ev* opposite to the door. I then ordered the reed and felt covering of the adjacent wall to be removed, so that the air from outside might fall upon the wall of my tent, while I was at the same time sheltered behind its folds from the inquisitiveness of the passers-by. I could see with sufficient distinctness through the thin gauze, and was perfectly screened from the observation of those who presented themselves at the door of my *ev*. In this way I was able to go on with my writing in a manner which would have been altogether out of the question if I had tried to work under ordinary circumstances. I gave instructions to my servant to say that I was asleep, and, as etiquette is well observed among respectable Turcomans, I managed to secure some hours per diem for my own immediate work. However, crowds of patients continually collected, generally at the shady side of the house, waiting until it should please me to awake. Very frequently one of the more impatient, entering the *ev*, would thrust his head under the edge of my mosquito tent, and, discovering how he was being imposed upon, immediately summon his comrades.

When the croton oil had become entirely exhausted, a man one day pushed his way into my *ev*, and requested me, with evident anxiety, to give him a dose of it to carry home to some member of his family who was ailing. I showed him the empty bottle, and turned it upside down, in order that he might see that not a single drop remained; but he would not credit the fact. He said that he was sure I had a further relay of it concealed, which I desired to retain for more favoured individuals than himself. Again and again he importuned me to give him some, and as often I was obliged to explain that it was impossible for me to do so. Still he would not go. He sat patiently all day amid the ever-changing crowd, until towards sunset, when he again appealed to me, only to receive a repetition of my former answer. At last, rising, with a lowering expression of countenance, he exclaimed, 'Well, am I to go away your enemy or your friend? If I have to leave without the medicine I shall be your enemy for life.'

This was an extremely serious predicament; but I was partly relieved from it by one of my younger acquaintances, a bit of a wag in his way, who, drawing me inside the mosquito curtain, whispered to me to get some dust, or material of any kind, and to wrap it in a parcel and give it to the unfortunate applicant, as the latter would have the same faith in this as in the real remedy.

One day, while strolling within the ramparts of Kouchid Khan Kala, I discovered a locality where dandelion grew abundantly. This was an immense relief to me, as it suggested a plan which, to a large extent, would rid me of the importunity of my patients. On each subsequent occasion I prescribed the '*gulizar*,' or '*sarigul*,' as they style dandelion, and gave minute instructions how to pound and squeeze it so as to extract the juice. From that time forward one could not cross the inhabited portion of Kouchid Khan Kala without hearing the pounding of this herb and the extraction of dandelion juice going on in almost every house.

In the midst of my anxieties, arrived from Teheran the definite intelligence that Kandahar was to be evacuated within two months. This decided me upon the course of action which I should follow. The Turcomans entertained the belief that British troops would speedily march *viâ* Herat to Merv, if they were not already on the way. I felt that the inevitable disappointment of the Tekkés in regard to this matter would superinduce a state of affairs, so far as I was concerned, from which I should endeavour to dissociate myself. The moment had come for a supreme effort, and I began to arrange measures for quitting Merv, if possible with the consent of the Turcomans, but, if not, without it. As a whole, the Mervli honestly believed that I had done them considerable service, and that I had been the means of keeping the Russians from their doors. To this belief was owing, to a great extent, their unwillingness to part with me. At the same time, I had my suspicions that the people in power wished to extract from me as much as possible in the shape of presents before they acquiesced in my departure. I had already bestowed considerable gifts in money, jewellery, &c., and I feared that even with a solemn engagement on the part of the leaders to allow me to proceed to Meshed, a renewal of these presents would be only to tempt my further detention, as they would then think that I was not yet at the end of my money resources. In pursuance of the idea of the moment, one day, it being necessary to renew the store of corn for my horses, and to order some food for my servants, I declared that I had no money. Calling my chief servant, I told him to take one of my horses to the bazaar and dispose of him. The person addressed, Mehemet Nefess Beg, drew a long face, and, without saying a word, withdrew from my presence. He immediately went to report the state of affairs to Baba Khan. In a short time he returned, saying that the Khan would not hear of such a thing as the sale of one of my horses. He said that the Tekkés would feel themselves disgraced for ever if one of their guests were obliged to sell his horse in order to be able to live among them. Several would-be purchasers called upon me, but, learning from my servant that Baba Khan was opposed to my selling the animal, they immediately retired. However, I was determined to persevere in my course, at least until I could see to what extent it was likely to be successful. I remained one whole day without eating anything, my horses being in the same predicament, in order that it might be demonstrated to my neighbours that I was without resources. Then I had a visit from Baba Khan and several of his councillors. They said they were sorry to hear that I was at the end of my funds, but reminded me that I was among friends, that all they possessed was mine, and that I had only to command their services, &c. &c. To this I simply replied by pointing to my empty platters, and to the horses tethered close by, who looked for their accustomed food.

Baba Khan was thoroughly equal to the occasion. He said, 'You are a Khan among us, and you must not want. You shall have everything we can give you. You shall have clover and *jowane* for your horses; and mutton and sheep's-tail fat, and unlimited tea and sugar, for yourself.' He said this with a magnificent air, and an appearance of asking, 'What more on earth could you wish for?' I bowed my acknowledgments. The Khan continued, 'There are twenty-four *yaps* or tribes at Merv. We will levy daily upon each one a handful of corn, and that will more than suffice for your own bread and for the food of your horses; and the merchants at the bazaar will have contribution levied upon them for tea and sugar.' This, doubtless, was a very generous offer, from the Khan's point of view; but I steadily declined to accept it. I knew that in the end I should have to pay handsomely for the supplies offered to me, which, by the way, I had no occasion whatever for. The Jew merchants were quite ready to supply me with all the tea and sugar and other commodities which I might require, in return for my money orders upon Meshed, and many of my Turcoman friends would have supplied me with meat on the same conditions; but, as I have said, I wished to make it appear that I was utterly destitute, and that in remaining at Merv I was casting myself as a burden upon the people. I said to Baba Khan, 'I came among you as a visitor. I did not come to live at your expense. I had ample money to support me when I came, but I distributed it among you in presents. I now find myself destitute. I do not ask anything from you except the favour of being allowed to go to Persia, where I shall probably be able to obtain, in person, loans of money

which no letters from Merv would procure for me. I
will not receive any gifts; so that if you do not allow me
to sell my horses both they and I must perish with
hunger.' This brought matters to a crisis. Baba Khan
replied, 'Were I to allow you to sell your horses, I should
be for ever disgraced in the sight of the Tekkés as an
inhospitable person who would not afford means of sub-
sistence to his guest. I will send you everything that
you desire.' Upon this he rose abruptly, and quitted my
redoubt. Seeing that he was bent upon this course, I
changed my tactics, and resolved to try the patience of
the Turcomans to the utmost extent, so that when they
were tired of giving me the offered largesse, and saw no
return for it, they would be glad to be rid of me.

The same afternoon I heard the crier going round
the entire neighbourhood, proclaiming the order of Baba
Khan to the Toktamish that each *yap* should furnish a
certain amount of fodder for my horses and of bread
and meat for myself and my servants. Very shortly
afterwards a small mountain of freshly-cut clover was
piled close beside my *ev*, and a small sack of corn was
brought to my door, much to the satisfaction of my poor
hungry horses, who could with difficulty be restrained
from breaking from their tethering ropes at the sight of
the food which they had lacked all day.

Then Matthi made his appearance with a very woe-
begone aspect. He said he had received an order to
furnish me with tea and sugar, and everything else I
required, free of cost. He wished to know whether this
was by my instructions. I explained the situation to
him, and, taking him into my confidence, told him that
he might freely send all I wanted, feeling sure that, as
usual, I would pay him by order upon Meshed. I knew
that I could thus far rely upon his discretion, for I had

already a long credit with him. I owed him at least five hundred krans. He was a man of the most extreme prudence, and one who never spoke unnecessarily, either to friend or foe. This was the first time he had come to see me for many weeks, though I had repeatedly been to visit him at his mud castle. I asked him why he had not visited me oftener, as had been his wont when I first arrived at Merv. He said that he would have been only too glad to do so, but that Beg Murad, who looked upon himself, to a certain extent, as the supervisor of all my movements, had forbidden him to do so unless on each occasion he paid to the Beg the sum of one tenga; and Aman Niaz Khan had made a demand for a 'present' of a quarter of a pound of green tea on each visit, by way of going shares in the large profits which they believed the Jew gained by reason of his dealings with me. These exactions, Matthi said, would deprive him of all profit upon the articles sold to me during his visits to my *ev*. I felt very indignant at this, which I now learned for the first time; but, out of regard for Matthi's own safety, I said nothing about it.

I had the solemn assurance of all the people in authority at Merv that, as soon as the reply to the official document despatched to the British Minister at Teheran arrived, I should be at perfect liberty to go to Meshed. As, under the circumstances, I felt that this arrangement was fair enough, I was satisfied, and disposed myself as best I could to pass the interval in the most agreeable manner. I intended to devote myself to writing up my notes and *souvenirs* of Merv; but I found myself very much in the situation of Robinson Crusoe. My small supply of ink was rapidly drawing to an end, and my pens had become thoroughly impracticable, and I had caught one of my servants in the act of extracting a thorn

from the sole of his foot with my last steel pen. My
paper, also, was exhausted; and I was compelled to have
recourse to the curious parchment-like material brought
from Bokhara. It was all very well to resolve to take
notes and write, but in practice this was not so easy.
The general impression was that my stay at Merv was
drawing to a close. All manner of people fancied themselves entitled to call upon me, and to sit all day long
in my *ev*. Again and again I told my servants to explain to everyone who called that unless he had some
particular business with me I would rather be left alone;
but all in vain. The crowd continued undiminished.
Sometimes, when, in defiance of Turcoman etiquette,
notwithstanding the concourse of people sitting round, I
continued my note-taking and writing, some one would
lay his hand upon my paper, and say, ' Khan, when you
and I are here, there are two present; but when you are
engaged with this' (pointing to the writing materials)
'there is but one.' On one or two occasions I said that
that was quite true; but asked them to recollect that I
did not desire them to call upon me, and informed them
that I had a great deal with which to occupy myself. This
produced a rather morose silence on the part of the whole
company.

As in the case of my food, the result of these visits
was that I was obliged to spend whole days without tea,
unless I shared it with the two dozen people who seated
themselves upon my carpet. Sometimes, in sheer de-
spair, I was forced to order numerous copper jugs of green
tea, in the hope that it would stop the incessant gabble
and senseless questioning to which I was subjected; and
it must be remembered that on the borders of Afghanistan it was a question of fifteen to twenty shillings
daily, and that, too, at a time when my available

financial resources were of a very limited nature. It was not alone in the matter of tea and sugar that I was victimised. In these latter days, as soon as one had made a purchase even of hay and clover, it was known, by some species of intuition, all over the place, and a flock of harpies were to the fore, borrowing armfuls of fodder and nose-bags of barley, without the least intention of repaying them.

I lay a certain emphasis upon these peculiarities of the Turcomans, for no one could be more generous to the penniless fakir or poor traveller crossing their territory. It is only when some one having the reputation of being wealthy comes among them that all their covetous instincts are displayed. I met with one notable case of theft in a quarter where I least expected it. This was in a young student of the *médresse*, or college. He was the son of the old moullah, and nephew of Kadjar Khan. On one occasion he made me a present of a pair of hand-woven saddle-bags, and in return I entrusted him with two pieces of gold, out of which he was to retain ten francs for himself, spend a franc in a purchase on my behalf, and return me the change. This he promised to do, but after sending me the franc's worth of candles and an excuse, he finally repudiated the transaction, denying that he owed me anything. I applied to Yaghmour Khan, the yassaoul-bashi, but it was all in vain. Yaghmour could scarcely refrain from tears as he returned to me. He said, ' I know that you have given him the money; I know that he is a liar and a thief, and '—concentrating all objectionable epithets into one—' he is an *Eshek Irmeni* ' (an Armenian ass). It is curious that, while red-handed murder and robbery were a recognised means of existence among the Tekkés, thievery, in the sense of stealing from the person, or filching an article from a stall of the bazaar, was despised. It so happened that I had promised this young student a watch, but before it arrived he had been guilty of this shabby theft. Knowing that I had written for the present, old Moullah Baba came and said, 'I never stole anything from you, why not give the present to me?' I accordingly did so. I spent an hour in explaining the mystery of the machine, and in expounding the division of time. When he left my *ev*, with the watch in his possession, he had the air of a Minister who has just received his portfolio. He had risen enormously in the estimation of the Mervli; and might be seen, at any given hour of the day, surrounded by a crowd of from thirty to fifty persons, to whom he was lecturing upon the wonderful article into possession of which he had come. Later on he often affected airs of *hauteur* as regarded myself. One day, however, a collapse took place. Opening his watch to display to his wondering auditory its interior mechanism, some grains of sand lodged in the machinery, and—the watch came to a stand-still. It would be difficult to conceive a more terrible shock to personal dignity than that which now took place. The Moullah hurried to my abode. His haughtiness was gone. He was the personification of abject humility. His watch had stopped. He felt that he was at my mercy. He unwound several cloths, and ultimately produced the watch from its morocco leather case. If a young mother had laid her dying infant at my feet, and implored me to restore to it its fleeting breath, her accents could not have been more pathetic than were those of Moullah Baba when he said, 'Can you make the watch go on again?' Though not a watchmaker, I guessed that some dust or sand had lodged in the works. I was sufficiently acquainted with the Turcoman character to know that whatever I did to remedy the misfortune must be made a matter of mystery; so, drawing my large sheepskin coat over my head, I muttered in audible tones some presumably mystic sentences, and, turning the watch on one side, struck it sharply a couple of times in order to shake out whatever might be impeding its action, which it immediately resumed. Removing the covering which concealed me, I majestically handed back the watch.

However momentary, the gratitude of Moullah Baba was deep, and he swore by Allah and the Koran that if anybody ever persuaded him to open that watch again he hoped it might stop! He wished himself no worse than that—to his mind an overwhelming calamity. Notwithstanding his gratitude, however, he could not keep his hands from pilfering. Next day, while sitting among my usual throng of visitors, when the conversation turned upon writing he remarked that Ferenghi ink could not compare with that manufactured by the Turcomans. I challenged this statement, whereupon he produced a scrap of silk paper upon which were written some characters in a decidedly blotched style. 'This,' said the Moullah, 'is the result of writing with English ink.' Then he produced another slip upon which was some fairly written matter. 'This,' observed he, 'is Turcoman ink.' I questioned him still further on the subject, and asked him where he had obtained his 'English ink;' whereupon he produced from his pocket in triumph a flat tin canister of blacking which he had purloined from my saddle-bags!

One day the town crier, accompanied by half-a-dozen other Turcomans, entered my hut, each to present to me a new-born child. I could not catch the exact words; all I could understand was that one of the infants was O'Donovan Beg, another O'Donovan Khan, a third

O'Donovan Bahadur; I forget what the others were. It turned out that among the Tekkés newly-born children are, as a rule, called after any distinguished strangers who may be in the oasis at the time of the births, or have resided there a short time previously, or after some event intimately connected with the tribe. I felt relieved by the explanation, even though I had to give a *peshkesh* of five krans for each of my youthful namesakes.

The subject of children naturally brings one to the question of marriage. In Merv it is the rare exception that a man has more than one wife. He cannot afford to have his, for him, short meals cut shorter by the addition of unnecessary mouths. The Mussulman law, which permits four wives, obtains, but enjoins that a separate residence be provided for each—a provision which is usually religiously adhered to by the Turcomans. A Turcoman's courtship is not so difficult as that of his more westerly co-religionist. He has ample opportunity of seeing his destined bride every day, for, as I have had occasion to remark, the Turcoman women make no pretence of veiling their faces. A man, having resolved upon marriage, waits upon the father of the desired spouse, and, if he be at all well-to-do, proffers the sum of 40*l.* sterling in return for the young lady. Possession of the sum of 40*l.* argues an amount of eligibility which gainsays a denial, and a new *ev*, or, as they term it, an *ak ev* (white *ev*) is prepared at the expense of the father. This means a house with felt coverings as yet unblackened by the smoke of the fire. The affianced pair, with a number of their male relations, assemble in this dwelling. The Moullah asks the father, before witnesses, whether he is willing to give his daughter to the bridegroom. Some paragraphs from the Koran are read, a 'present' of a few krans is made to the Moullah, and the newly-wedded pair are left alone to the enjoyment of connubial bliss.

As far as my experience goes, divorce is altogether unknown among these semi-nomads. In the event of unfaithfulness on the part of the wife, a knife-stroke settles the question, and *no one* has a right to interfere.

CHAPTER XXVII.

Breach of etiquette—Important document—My ultimatum—Sale of a horse—The last arrow!—Largess—Summoned—An imposing spectacle—A Turcoman joke—My advocate.

It was close to the end of June. I cannot be sure of dates at this time, for I had lost all count of the days, and the Turcomans themselves never knew, within a fortnight, what their own month was.

I was lazily reclining within my mosquito-curtain tent, wondering what turn fortune would next take for me, when my servants announced the arrival of Baba and Aman Niaz Khans. These two gentlemen were rarely to be seen together, so that I felt that something important must have occurred. My curtain was raised, and I welcomed the Khans to my house. Baba held in his hands a portentous-looking document. The first words that he uttered were, 'The Ingles Vizir Mukhtar is evidently in error. He has addressed his letter to the Khans of the Otamish and Toktamish. The Toktamish chief is the senior, and I cannot understand why this slight has been put upon me.' As these Turcomans are hyper-sensitive upon such matters, I explained that it was through no want of respect to the senior Khan that the ambassador had so misdirected his letter, but that the mistake was owing to the latter's non-acquaintance with local circumstances; and thus this important point was disposed of. The ambassador acknowledged the receipt of the letter addressed to him by the Merv chiefs, in which they stated that the tribes over which they presided had resolved to proffer their allegiance to the British Government, and that they had hoisted a flag in the English name, and branded some of their horses with an English mark, in token of their proposed submission to the Queen of England. He also said that their communication had been transmitted to Her Majesty's Government. He was glad to hear that the Merv tribes were animated by kindly sentiments towards the British Government, and told them that they might rest assured of the interest which was taken in their welfare. He continued: 'It is my duty, however, to state to you, with reference to the proffer of allegiance to the British Government, that the proposal that the people of Merv should become British subjects is one that, owing to various causes, physical as well as political, cannot be entertained.' The Minister further reminded them that I was, as I had myself said, not an emissary of the British Government, but an agent of the British public, whose duty it was to keep the latter informed of events passing in the oasis. The British public, he said, had always evinced a lively interest in the welfare of the Merv people, and were consequently desirous to obtain accurate information respecting their condition and prospects. 'Mr. O'Donovan, having now resided for some time at Merv, is in a position to supply trustworthy information on these subjects, and it is now both desirable and expedient that you should, in accordance with the request that I have instructed the Agent of the British Government in Meshed to convey to you on my part, send Mr. O'Donovan at once to this country, in order that he may personally communicate to me such information as may have been furnished to him during his stay at Merv.'

The terms of this document were definite, and exactly what I had requested the British Minister to place before the Merv chiefs. Having perused the missive, Baba Khan told me that I was at liberty to go when I pleased. 'But,' he added, 'there must be a general *medjlis* before you leave us.' 'Let it be called immediately,' I rejoined. I knew what 'immediately' meant—a fortnight at the soonest, and, as it proved, I was right, for the delays were vexatious in the extreme. During these weary days a hundred peculiarities of Turcoman society came under my notice, but I had no heart to mark them: I was disgusted. Even when my brother Khans came to see me I wore an attitude of fierce defiance. I was resolved to let them know that I saw through their policy, and that I was not to be trifled with any longer.

At last the crisis came. I had been asking daily when I was to start for Meshed. There was always some obstacle in the way. The *medjlis* could not be got together, or one or other of the Khans was absent. On one day, one Khan was to the fore; the other had gone on a tour of inspection. When the latter was to be found, the former was sick, or he, also, had gone on a tour of inspection. Or, when both Khans were present, the waters at the Murgab dam were so high that every man was occupied, and no one could come to the *medjlis*.

It was now some time since I had been living at free quarters among the Turcomans. Corn and clover for my horses were freely forthcoming, and mutton broth for myself, and, as far as they knew, the supplies of tea and sugar brought to me by Matthi the Jew were at their expense. One day I made up my mind to send in an ultimatum. I despatched my chief servant to summon Baba and Aman Niaz and a number of Kethkodas.

They duly met at my *ev*. I said, 'I am going to leave Merv for Meshed within three days.' Objections were raised. I continued, 'I will hear of no objection; you have told me that since the arrival of the British Minister's letter I am free to go where I please. If within three days I be not in the saddle for my destination, I shall haul down my flag as a declaration of war.'

The chiefs begged time to consider. I would give none. I said, 'I have had quite enough of living on your charity. I do not require it any longer. I will not have it.' I sent for the serdar who had taken my watch to Baba Khan, and, pointing to my horse, said, 'I want to sell him as a bargain. There is no use in consulting with Baba Khan; if you do not buy him I will sell him to somebody else.' After some discussion we agreed upon a price, 20*l*., if I recollect rightly. The process of selling and buying was curious. We had an immense amount of haggling before we decided upon the 20*l*., but that was nothing to what came afterwards—whether I would give the bridle; whether I would give the new swathing wrapper; whether I would give the belly-band. All these minutiæ entered into the discussion, and at last, as I intended all this simply as a demonstration of my resolution to stay no longer at Merv, I exclaimed, 'Take everything; anything that belongs to him!'

As is usual in a community like that of Merv, no sooner had I effected the sale than it was known to every individual within the length and breadth of the place. A crowd of people of all ranks thronged my house. They begged and implored me to remain, asseverating that all that Merv was worth was at my disposal. I pointed to the serdar, who was preparing to lead away his newly purchased horse. I said, 'I am penniless. I have had to sell my horse in order to live. I will not accept your charity. I have asked Baba Khan to summon the *medjlis*. He is unwilling to do so. I shall mount and ride away. Prevent me at your peril.'

There were, fortunately, some circumstances which came to my aid. The Russian authorities were surveying the new frontier, and Tekké scouts brought word that Cossack horsemen escorted persons with divers wonderful and dreadful engines in their neighbourhood—the engineers with their theodolites, who were surveying the road to Sarakhs. I grasped at this as a drowning man at a straw. I imagined a meeting of the ambassadors of Europe at Meshed, convened for the purpose of deciding upon the new frontier; I declared that the fate of Merv depended upon that meeting. I reminded the chiefs that they were already cut off from Bokhara and Samarcand by the Russian protectorate of these places. Meshed and Herat were the only points from which they could derive their supply of percussion caps, without which their muzzle-loading rifles would be utterly useless. If the Russians were allowed to extend their line from Askabad along the Tejend to Sarakhs, Meshed, as a base of supplies, would be lost, and the proximity of Sarakhs to Herat would practically isolate the Turcomans from that point.

Even under the pressure which I brought to bear, the natural inertia of the purely Turkish mind was not to be overborne in haste. They were by this time very nearly at an end of their excuses for further procrastination, but there was still one undischarged arrow in their quiver. An important Kethkoda, by name Sari Beg, and who was remarkable for his gallantry with regard to the female sex, called upon me, and, in a last attempt to move my resolution anent going to Meshed, said that the ladies of Merv were greatly opposed to my going away!

It was towards the middle of July that the final council, in which I took part, met at Kouchid Khan Kala. It was an unusually large one, for all felt that a great crisis had arrived. The Bahadur Khan, the palladium of the Merv nation, was about to take his departure. Foreseeing the difficulties which might be awaiting me, I had resolved to sacrifice all the pecuniary resources remaining to me in a last effort to destroy any barrier to my departure which the cupidity of the leading men might raise up. I had determined that the last hundred pounds, which I had kept in reserve for a desperate crisis, should now be utilised, and I had despatched confidential messengers to Meshed to bring me that amount in silver. It may seem strange that I should have trusted a quantity of coin like this in the hands of professional robbers; but I knew enough of Tekké nature to be aware that when I devoted the sum as presents to their chiefs, through whose hands it must inevitably filter into the pockets of their adherents, I was perfectly safe in confiding in them.

On the night before the *medjlis*, the money arrived. Aman Niaz Khan's uncle, Nazar Ali Beg, and Koorban Pehlivan, a near relation of Baba Khan, were the messengers chosen. The money arrived in four bags, each containing silver to the amount of twenty-five pounds sterling. Without a moment's delay I despatched one bag to Aman Niaz, another to Baba, a third to Murad Bey, and a fourth to Yaghmour. In an hour's time, when the sun had set, and my lamp was lighted, the four recipients, surrounded by their henchmen, presented themselves. They saluted me ceremoniously, and seated themselves in silence around me. We exchanged the usual compliments, and then Aman Niaz Khan led the way by drawing from the pocket of his silk robe a heavy

sack containing my gift to him. 'Bahadur Khan,' he
said, 'this is the present which you have sent to me. I
thank you for it;' and he poured the contents upon the
carpet, so that all might be witnesses to the fact that he
had received them. Baba Khan and the others followed
suit in like manner.

Shortly after this little ceremony, Baba Khan left my
ev, followed by Yaghmour. Aman Niaz and Murad Bey
remained. The moment their brother potentates were
well away from my dwelling, Aman Niaz drew from his
pocket a quart bottle of arrack, which he presented to
me with great ceremony. With great show of hospitality
I poured out full measures for my guests, for, to tell the
truth, I was anxious to get rid of as much of the dele-
terious spirit as possible before being obliged to drink.
When the bottle was emptied, greatly to my relief, all
my guests left me but one, Allah Kuli, who gracefully
reminded me that I had given others presents, but left
him out. I, however, satisfied him by promising that
I would not fail to remember him directly I reached
Meshed.

It was July 19—a memorable day for me—when the
general council of the Merv representatives met at Kouchid Khan Kala. The morning passed. Mid-day came,
and yet I was not summoned. It was two o'clock when
Murad Bey waited upon me, and, with due solemnity,
invited me to appear before the council of the nation.
My horse was standing saddled at the door, for, among
the Mervli, a person of importance cannot proceed any,
even the smallest, distance upon foot.

At least fifty men, in their best attire, and fully armed,
were standing around. As I mounted my horse, they
all did likewise, and in solemn guise we marched slowly
to the place of meeting. The murmur of conversation

which was heard as we approached was suddenly hushed as I made my appearance. A large carpet was laid just within the circle formed by the chieftains and Kethkodas as they sat in an oval ring close to the water's edge. I took my place upon it. Behind me, to the left, sat Baba Khan, and near him was the Old Man of the Sword. Dowlet Nazar Beg, the former Vizier of Baba's father, sat by the senior, and close by was many a chief whose name and deeds had carried terror far within the Persian frontier. At the opposite extremity of the assembly sat some of the Otamish leaders. Aman Niaz Khan was absent, so was Kadjar Khan, though all his immediate followers were there.

It was an imposing spectacle, this gathering of chiefs beside the Murgab. Close by rose the frowning front of the newly-completed fortress. About me, in their picturesque garbs, were the redoubtable robber chiefs of Central Asia. Some thousands of people, grouped in knots, surrounded us at a short distance, and more than a hundred horsemen were close upon the edge of the circle, listening eagerly to every word that passed. There had evidently been a hot discussion in the earlier hours of the day as to the expediency of allowing me to depart, and at the time of my being summoned much that was interesting had passed by. I was sorry for this, for I should have wished to hear in their entirety the arguments adduced one way and the other. At the time of my arrival Baba Khan had evidently had it all his own way—in my favour. He asked me if I would say a few words to the council previously to hearing the final decision.

I spoke at some length, though I had little more to say than on a former occasion, on which I had pointed out what I considered the best policy for the Merv nation to adopt, in view of the near presence and aggressive

policy of Russia. I was listened to with the greatest
attention; the only interruption I experienced being the
continual going and coming of the individuals told off
to supply the members of the council with smoking materials.
In the further end of the space around which
the councillors sat was a deep, narrow hole excavated in
the ground, where a fire was burning, and from this the
water-pipes were lighted. When I ceased speaking, a
silence fell upon the assembly. Only Baba Khan and his
councillors whispered together. At length the tremendous
bass voice of the 'Old Man of the Sword' broke the stillness.
He proceeded to call the roll of the Kethkodas.
Without exception they answered to their names. Aman
Niaz and Kadjar alone were absent. 'Where is Kadjar?'
said the Ak Saghal. 'He is absent,' said Sari Beg. 'Why
is he absent?' 'He does not admit the jurisdiction of
the council.' 'Where is Aman Niaz Khan?' said the
Ak Saghal. One of the Otamish Kethkodas replied that
Aman Niaz was not at the council by reason of his eyes
being sore, and he being unable to support the brilliant
sunlight. Here the only joke I ever heard from Turcoman
lips was perpetrated. 'You say,' said the Old Man
of the Sword, 'that Aman Niaz's eyes are sore; how many
eyes has he got?' 'Why, two, to be sure,' said Sari Beg.
'He has got two eyes,' said the Ak Saghal, 'and yet he
is not here. Why, here is Baba Khan, who has got but
one eye, and yet he has come.' Baba Khan, as I have
said, had one eye completely destroyed by keratitis. He
tried to smile, but it was only a ghastly attempt. His
solitary orb flamed. It was more with indignation than
with pleasure that he heard this allusion to his infirmity,
common though it was at Merv. But apparently the
Old Man of the Sword did not care a straw about his
indignation.

The proceedings were now brought to a close. Baba Khan raised his voice, and asked whether there were anyone present who could say why the Bahadur Khan should not start for Meshed. A murmured conversation immediately arose all around the ring of councillors. Then, one ugly-looking Kalmuck-featured man said that he did not think adequate 'presents' had been made to all concerned. Baba replied rather hotly that he thought there had been. The ugly man rejoined, 'Oh yes, I know that yesterday you received a bag of six hundred krans; you are all right, but what about us who have got nothing?' I was now very much surprised by seeing the Old Man of the Sword rise to his feet, saying in an imperious manner, 'The Bahadur Khan came here to serve us, and he is going to Meshed to do the same. We Mervli may rob our enemies, but we do not rob our friends.' I felt deeply grateful to the Ak Saghal for his timely intervention in my behalf.

CHAPTER XXVIII.

Fresh delays—Turcoman inertia—Final presents—Sun-burning—The Tandara Pass—Down with fever—Back to civilisation.

AFTER the decision of the *medjlis*, one would have expected that, even among Turcomans, all difficulties were at an end. Not at all. It would fill another volume to narrate the various excuses given why I should not start at once. Baba Khan had sprained his ankle; Aman Niaz's sore eyes were a fruitful source of disappointment; and last, not least, there was the hypothetic anxiety on the part of the Mervli lest I might fall into the hands of the Russian surveying parties.

At last I overbore all resistance, and on the evening of July 28, 1881, I was solemnly informed, after a conclave of the *élite* of Merv society, that on the following day I could start for Meshed. As it was my last day at Merv, I paid a number of formal visits to the leading persons residing at Kouchid Khan Kala. I was entertained at a sumptuous banquet, at which sheep's-tail fat flowed in unlimited quantities, and even boiled eggs were served out to the guests. Arrack was brought from Matthi's establishment. Then I called upon my old enemy Beg Murad—he of the *sumsa*—who was dreadfully ill from having eaten an excessive quantity of greasy food. He had much desired, he said, to ask my advice as a Frankish physician, but since our last stormy interview he had not dared to do so. He begged me to give him some medicine. Fortunately I had a large bottle of pepsin, which I lavished upon the fat Beg. I subsequently heard, in Meshed, that the cure effected was marvellous; and, as I left the entire contents of the bottle with the obese chief, I trust he has managed to digest his fat sheep-tails to his satisfaction. When I presented him with the medicine he said he had one other favour to request of me, viz., that I should give him, with my *takht*, the rude four-legged bedstead of tree-trunks which Murad Bey had presented to me. This I gave him. I also sent back to Aman Niaz his gorgeous purple quilt, and, in fact, did all that I could in the way of little social amenities to restore a friendly feeling between myself and my associates of the past six months with whom I might have had any difficulty.

The following entry in my diary was made at this time:—'July 29, 1881, six o'clock A.M. I have put on my boots with the resolution of not taking them off till I reach Meshed. I found everybody asleep. There seems to be some inexplicable and ineradicable objection in the Turkish mind to prompt action. It seems against their principles. . . . Makdum Kuli Khan, who came in last night, has been cooking eggs for the past hour, with a view of giving me a parting entertainment. Therefore, there can be no hurry.'

Another extract. Three hours later:—'There is, truly, among these people, some ineradicable objection to do anything at once. It is now three hours after sunrise, and I sit here, waiting. Last night I delivered strict orders about being in the saddle at sunrise. I gave out the horse-shoes, even the nails. Now it seems that the "artist," the *usta*, as they are pleased to call him, has lent his hammer to some one who lives sixteen miles off. I am in a violent rage; but what can I do?'

These quotations will speak for themselves. I had everything packed up, and my horses were standing saddled at the door. But, like their relations the Osmanlis, the Turcomans wanted to gain some more time, even if it were only an hour, to see what might turn up. They knew that I was very much interested in obtaining the liberation of Kidaieff, the Russian gunner, so they kept the matter back by way of delaying me to the very last moment. Then came the chief Kethkoda of the Karatchmet, a subdivision of the Sitchmaz. He said that his people had decided upon setting Kidaieff at liberty, but before doing so he wanted an order signed by me to that effect, and also a letter to the Russian commander at Askabad to say that the prisoner had been liberated at the request of the British representative at Merv. I wrote the letter, and it was with the most heartfelt satisfaction that I signed the order for the release of the poor captive.

The last obstacle with which I had to contend was the clannishness of the Turcomans. I had to choose for my escort a fair representation of the twenty-four *yaps*, so that no one should be slighted. This was at last done, and at mid-day the escort assembled, when there was another delay. Presents had to be given in return for the money I had distributed. Baba Khan came in, followed by some attendants, and unfolded before me two genuine Turcoman carpets, of the finest style of workmanship. Aman Niaz Khan, not to be behindhand, brought me three, and Moullah Baba two. Allah Kuli presented me with another. I was sufficiently embarrassed with baggage, but I could not possibly refuse these eight carpets, though I knew they would sorely try the strength of my horses. Then old Kadjar Khan gave me a large copper jug, used in Merv for the preparation of tea, and Matthi, the Jew, begged my acceptance of an iron-headed pipe. Another gave me a porcelain tea-bowl in leather case; and lastly, Murad Bey came up, bringing me a suit of chain armour, and a huge steel helmet like a dish cover, which he said had belonged to one of his ancestors. Then arose the question of my flag, which I replied must remain until my return. My pets had to be distributed, and at last we started.

My escort consisted of some fifty horsemen, but in addition the chiefs were there with about a couple of hundred followers fully armed, and it seemed as if the whole male population of Merv had assembled to see me off; and now, anxious though I was to leave the oasis, it was not without some feeling of regret that I passed the entrance of my redoubt and rode away towards the rickety bridge spanning the Murgab, which I had crossed under such different auspices nearly six months before.

I pass rapidly over my journey back. For some distance it was over the same ground as I had followed in travelling to Merv, branching off at a place called Dash Lalung, to cross the Tejend at Kongali Guzer. Here the heat was frightful, the marl being in such a state that it was impossible to walk barefooted. In fact, the power of the sun was startling, and more than once I narrowly escaped sunstroke. Upon one occasion during this journey the day had been dreadfully hot, and yet, very incautiously, I had clothed myself lightly. I wore only a tunic-like shirt, of white cotton, and over it a long crimson silk tunic. The result was that the upper portion of my body, breast, back, and shoulders— was red and blistered by the sun-rays. It is a great mistake, under these circumstances, to wear thin clothing. The Turcomans, at such times, carry a stout camel-hair mantle, and if they are forced to proceed during the mid-day hours, add to it a great sheepskin *kusgun*, or overcoat, to save them still further from the baking rays. In fact, the habit of Western countries is entirely reversed. Along the borders of the desert a man wears a thick garment to keep himself cool, or, rather, to prevent himself from being roasted alive.

I could perceive no fish in the waters of the Tejend when we crossed, but it was thickly populated with an odd-looking, amphibious creature, some two inches in length, closely resembling a small turtle. Its colour was of the peculiar blue purple of an ordinary mussel-shell, from under one end of which protruded a small head and a pair of minute flaps, while from underneath either side of the rear end were swimming flaps of at least half an inch in length.

In due time we reached Chacha, which guards the entrance of the pass leading towards Meshed, being thus the key to one of the communications with the capital of Khorassan across the mountains. We traversed the Tandara Pass by moonlight. It was dreadfully steep and rocky, about three-quarters of a mile in length, and scarcely twenty yards across at its widest part. At its upper extremity, and on the left-hand side, was a group of Chenar trees, under whose shade was a rock-girt pool, the *Chashma*, or spring in which the Chacha river originates. Close by, and terminating the ravine, was the Derbend, or 'Gate,' itself. It was like a vast doorway, with Cyclopean piers, of black porphyritic rock, towering vertically on either side. It was not more than fifteen feet wide. Once beyond this, turning to the left and then to the right, we commenced the ascent of the tremendous Tandara mountain. It was a terrible climb. There was absolutely no road, nor even a track. We clambered over or scrambled between gigantic boulders, up an incline which sometimes caused the horses to kneel, lest they should slide backwards. Even the strength and endurance of Turcoman horses failed under the terrible ordeal, and the best mounted of our company was forced to dismount and lead his steed. We, however, crossed the mountains in safety, and leaving a portion of my escort on the road, I finally rode into Meshed with eight Turcoman horsemen, the remainder arriving next day, and calling upon me at the house of Abass Khan, where I had obtained lodgings. Giving them my engagement that a sum of two hundred and eighty *tomans* (100*l.*) should be distributed among them as presents, I bade them seek one of the public caravanserais and wait.

While at Meshed I had an interview with the new Governor of Khorassan, who proved to be my old friend the Sipah Salar, and he kindly insisted upon replacing my Turcoman garb with a suit of his own, which I could not wear, but which cost me 4*l.* in presents to the bearers.

I will pass over my stay at Meshed. I was very ill, and in no fit state for my journey when I started for Teheran on September 3. By the time I reached Sabzavar my horses were so broken down and sore-backed by the journey that I was forced to hire post-horses in their stead. While on the way to Shahrood a violent attack of fever completely prostrated me, and, unable to continue my road on horseback, I had to hire a pair of *kedjavés*. These are square wooden frames, like a large stool inverted, and which are hung, one on either side of a camel or mule. In one I put my luggage, in the other myself. My servant followed on horseback. I was more dead than alive when I reached Teheran, after a most painful and interrupted journey of twenty-seven days. The kindly hospitality of the British Legation set me on my legs again, and in a fortnight I was able to start on my way homewards. The journey from Teheran to Resht, on the Caspian, was very much as I have already described. I had hoped to be able to proceed to Tiflis by the new railroad, but discovered, to my sorrow, that it was only half completed. At Derbend, further northward, I found that the snow had rendered *troïka* travelling impracticable. I went on with the Russian mail steamer to Astrakan, only to find the Volga frozen, and to undergo one of the most disagreeable experiences of my life in reaching the nearest railway station, that of Zarizin, after a three days' voyage, broken by intervals of discomfort only to be experienced by those who try to travel in South-Eastern Russia at that time of the year—November. How I got on to Odessa, and thence to Constantinople, scarcely enters into the scope of this narrative.

I reached the shores of the Bosphorus on November 26, 1881, nearly four months after I had quitted Kouchid Khan Kala and the Turcomans, and close upon three years since I left Trebizond on my Eastward way.

THE MERV OASIS:

Travels and Adventures East of the Caspian during the Years 1879-80-81, Including Five Months' Residence among the Tekkés of Merv.

BY EDMOND O'DONOVAN,

Special Correspondent of the *Daily News.*

EXTRACTS FROM NOTICES BY THE PRESS.

'We feel sure that the almost unanimous opinion of the general reader will be that he has seldom taken up a more graphic or original book of travels than this is, and that Central Asia, despite its deserts, cannot be so uninteresting a place as has hitherto been supposed. There is not the least doubt that the author has written one of the most interesting and attractive books of travels in Central Asia that have appeared since those of Conolly and Burnes first drew the attention of our countrymen to the Khanates and the nomadic camps of Turkestan. And this is probably the most sterling service that anyone could render to the cause of Central Asian literature. What we want to learn is something of the inner life and character of those tribes and races of whose numbers and military equipments we have been accurately apprised, but whose individuality was not less shifting than the sands of their own deserts; and this is exactly the sort of information with which Mr. O'Donovan has abundantly supplied us.'—TIMES.

'Mr. O'Donovan's splendid record of his experiences to the East of the Caspian is a work that can hardly be too highly praised, and places him in the very front rank of explorers who, to indomitable pluck, add the invaluable gift of brilliant literary powers.'—STANDARD.

'The literary merits, which are by no means inconsiderable, are soon forgotten in the admiration excited by the fertility of resource, the resolute contempt of danger, and the intelligent observation displayed by the author during three years of varied and eventful travel. We can safely say that for some time to come these volumes, or the second of them, will be the text-book for all eager disputants about Merv, Sarakhs, and the possibilities of feeding large armaments in the desert, as well as of making railways, whether for strategy or commerce. There is an immense deal in these two volumes on which we can barely touch. The anecdotes of Eastern craft, ignorance, and credulity are always amusing. The descriptions of life and manners are graphic; and Mr. O'Donovan has a good eye for the colours—ochre, yellow, and red—of the landscape, as well as for the costumes of the raider and the merchant. His descriptions of ruined forts, mosques, tombs, and buildings of which the origin and use have perished, agreeably diversify his remarks on men.'—SATURDAY REVIEW.

'To the knowledge and character of the nomad tribes in the borderlands of Persia, and of the military and political situation in that interesting corner of the world, in which the concerns of Afghanistan, India, Persia, and Russia are intimately connected, this work is a distinct and notable contribution. Mr. O'Donovan writes like an intelligent appreciative traveller, with an eye for what is important as well as that which is interesting, and nowhere does he seem to write for mere effect; and the personal adventures are related modestly. Altogether, as a story of travel, as a record of adventures, and as a trustworthy account of a land of which little has hitherto been known, "The Merv Oasis" is of great interest and lasting value.'—DAILY TELEGRAPH.

'Mr. O'Donovan's description of his visit to Merv, and of his previous explorations on the Persian frontier, is sure to be allowed, by general consent, high rank among works on Central Asia. Indeed, as an interesting book of travels it may be doubted whether it has ever been surpassed by that of any other traveller in the same quarter of the world. The interest of these volumes begins with the very first page, when Mr. O'Donovan turns his steps eastwards from Trebizonde, and does not cease until he bids the reader farewell with his return to the Turkish dominions. Of course, the more fresh and interesting portion of the book is that describing his residence among the Tekké Turcomans at Merv; but the first volume, recounting his experiences among the Persians and Kurds of the Khorasan frontier, is also full of adventure and bristles with anecdote. We can heartily recommend these volumes as the most entertaining reading we know on the subject of which they treat.'

GUARDIAN.

'Mr. O'Donovan's visit, single-handed, to the Tekké stronghold during a time of wild excitement is an instance of daring to which we are precluded from applying the harsh term "foolhardiness" by the excellence of the present book. Anecdotes and incidents of travel are plentifully strewn through its pages, and the detailed descriptions of the trans-Caspian regions and their inhabitants supply us with information about an important region —a sort of half-way house between Europe and Asia in times past, and an arena of political interest at the present day. The description of Oriental towns given by Mr. O'Donovan is vivid and artistic. To have at hand so much positive, unbiassed, and recent information as this book contains regarding an area of proximate political importance should prove no small gain to our diplomatists.'—ATHENÆUM.

London: SMITH, ELDER, & CO., 15 Waterloo Place.

SMITH, ELDER & CO.'S PUBLICATIONS.

LEAVES from the DIARY of HENRY GREVILLE.
Edited by Viscountess ENFIELD. 8vo. 14s.

UNDERGROUND RUSSIA. Revolutionary Profiles and Sketches from Life. By STEPNIAK, formerly Editor of 'Zemlia i Volia' (Land and Liberty). With a Preface by Peter Lavroff. Second Edition. Crown 8vo. 6s.

The LIFE of LORD LAWRENCE. By R. BOSWORTH SMITH, M.A., late Fellow of Trinity College, Oxford; Assistant Master at Harrow School; Author of 'Mohammed and Mohammedanism,' 'Carthage and the Carthaginians,' &c. Fourth Edition. 2 vols. 8vo. with 2 Portraits, Maps, &c. 36s.

VICE VERSÂ: or, a Lesson to Fathers. By F. ANSTEY. Twenty-fifth Edition. Crown 8vo. 6s.

ANNALS of the EARLY CALIPHATE. By Sir WILLIAM MUIR, K.C.S.I., Author of 'The Life of Mahomet' &c. 8vo. with Map, 16s.
'Sir W. Muir has written a life of Mahomet, which for picturesqueness in its general effect, and for care and minuteness in details, has not, so far as we know, been equalled.'
SCOTSMAN.

CITIES of EGYPT. By REGINALD STUART POOLE. Crown 8vo. 5s.
'A better handy book for the ordinary reader who wants to form a correct idea of ancient Egypt by reading a couple of hundred pages it would not be possible to find.'
ATHENÆUM.

REPORT of the SMOKE-ABATEMENT COMMITTEE, 1882. With Reports of the Jurors of the Exhibition at South Kensington, and Reports of the Testing Engineer. To which are added the Official Reports of the Manchester Exhibition, 76 Plates of Illustrations, and 34 Tables of Results of Tests of Heating and Cooking Grates, Stoves, &c. Crown 4to. 15s.

NOTES from SICK ROOMS. By Mrs. LESLIE STEPHEN. Crown 8vo. limp cloth, 2s.
'The contents of this book should be learnt by heart by every sick-nurse.'
GRAPHIC.

ITALIAN BYWAYS. By JOHN ADDINGTON SYMONDS, Author of 'Renaissance in Italy,' 'Sketches and Studies in Italy,' &c. Crown 8vo. 10s. 6d.

LIFE of SIR HENRY LAWRENCE. By Major-General Sir HERBERT BENJAMIN EDWARDES, K.C.B., K.C.S.I., and HERMAN MERIVALE, C.B. With Two Portraits. 8vo. 12s.

EXTRACTS from the WRITINGS of W. M. THACKERAY. Chiefly Philosophical and Reflective. With a Portrait. Second Edition. Crown 8vo. 7s. 6d.

A DESCRIPTION of the HUMAN BODY: its Structure and Functions. Illustrated by reduced copies of the Author's 'Physiological Diagrams,' to which Series this is a Companion Work. Designed for the Use of Teachers in Schools, and of Young Men destined for the Medical Profession, and for Popular Instruction generally. By JOHN MARSHALL, F.R.S., F.R.C.S, Professor of Surgery in University College, London; Surgeon to the University College Hospital; Professor of Anatomy in the Royal Academy of Arts; and late Lecturer on Anatomy in the Science and Art Department, South Kensington. Fourth Edition, thoroughly Revised. Price, with small folio Atlas, 21s.

London: SMITH, ELDER, & CO., 15 Waterloo Place.

SMITH, ELDER, & CO.'S PUBLICATIONS.

WORKS BY ELIZABETH BARRETT BROWNING.

POEMS BY ELIZABETH BARRETT BROWNING.
Five vols. Thirteenth Edition, with Portrait. Crown 8vo. 30s.

AURORA LEIGH.
With Portrait. Seventeenth Edition. Crown 8vo. 7s. 6d. Gilt edges, 8s. 6d.

**A SELECTION FROM
THE POETRY OF ELIZABETH BARRETT BROWNING.**
With Portrait and Vignette. First Series. Twelfth Edition. Crown 8vo. 7s. 6d.
Gilt edges, 8s. 6d.
Second Series. Third Edition. Crown 8vo. 7s. 6d. Gilt edges, 8s. 6d.

WORKS BY ROBERT BROWNING.

POETICAL WORKS OF ROBERT BROWNING.
New and Uniform Edition. 6 vols. Fcp. 8vo. 5s. each.

**A SELECTION FROM THE POETICAL WORKS OF
ROBERT BROWNING.**
First Series. Seventh Edition, enlarged. Crown 8vo. 7s. 6d. Gilt edges, 8s. 6d.
Second Series. Third Edition. Crown 8vo. 7s. 6d. Gilt edges, 8s. 6d.

JOCOSERIA.
Second Edition. Fcp. 8vo. 5s.

DRAMATIC IDYLS.
First Series. Second Edition. Fcp. 8vo. 5s.   Second Series. Fcp. 8vo. 5s.

LA SAISIAZ: The Two Poets of Croisic.
Fcp. 8vo. 7s.

THE AGAMEMNON OF ÆSCHYLUS.
Fcp. 8vo. 5s.

PACCHIAROTTO, AND HOW HE WORKED IN DISTEMPER.
WITH OTHER POEMS. Fcp. 8vo. 7s. 6d.

THE INN ALBUM.
Fcp. 8vo. 7s.

BALAUSTION'S ADVENTURE;
INCLUDING A TRANSCRIPT FROM EURIPIDES. Third Edition. Fcp. 8vo. 5s

ARISTOPHANES' APOLOGY;
INCLUDING A TRANSCRIPT FROM EURIPIDES, BEING THE LAST
ADVENTURE OF BALAUSTION. Fcp. 8vo. 10s. 6d.

FIFINE AT THE FAIR.
Fcp. 8vo. 5s.

**PRINCE HOHENSTIEL-SCHWANGAU, SAVIOUR OF
SOCIETY.**
Fcp. 8vo. 5s.

RED COTTON NIGHT-CAP COUNTRY;
OR, TURF AND TOWERS. Fcp. 8vo. 9s.

THE RING AND THE BOOK.
4 vols. Fcp. 8vo. 5s. each.

London: SMITH, ELDER, & CO., 15 Waterloo Place.

WORKS BY AUGUSTUS J. C. HARE.

CITIES OF SOUTHERN ITALY AND SICILY.
With Illustrations. Crown 8vo. 12s. 6d.

WALKS IN ROME. Eleventh Edition. 2 vols. crown 8vo. 18s.

'The best handbook of the city and environs of Rome ever published...... Cannot be too much commended.'—PALL MALL GAZETTE.

'This book is sure to be very useful. It is thoroughly practical, and is the best guide that yet has been offered.'—DAILY NEWS.

'Mr. Hare's book fills a real void, and gives to the tourist all the latest discoveries and the fullest information bearing on that most inexhaustible of subjects, the city of Rome......It is much fuller than "Murray," and anyone who chooses may now know how Rome really looks in sun or shade.'—SPECTATOR.

WALKS IN LONDON. Fifth Edition. With numerous Illustrations. 2 vols. crown 8vo. 21s.

WANDERINGS IN SPAIN. With Illustrations. Fourth Edition. Crown 8vo. 7s. 6d.

'We recollect no book that so vividly recalls the country to those who have visited it, and we should recommend intending tourists to carry it with them as a companion of travel.'—TIMES.

'Mr. Hare's book is admirable. We are sure no one will regret making it the companion of a Spanish journey. It will bear reading repeatedly when one is moving among the scenes it describes—no small advantage when the travelling library is scanty.'—SATURDAY REVIEW.

'Here is the ideal book of travel in Spain; the book which exactly anticipates the requirements of everybody who is fortunate enough to be going to that enchanted land; the book which ably consoles those who are not so happy, by supplying the imagination from the daintiest and most delicious of its stories.'
SPECTATOR.

'Since the publication of "Castilian Days," by the American diplomat, Mr. John Hay, no pleasanter or more readable sketches have fallen under our notice.'
ATHENÆUM.

MEMORIALS OF A QUIET LIFE. 3 vols. crown 8vo. Vols. I. and II., 21s.; Vol. III., with numerous Photographs, 10s. 6d.

DAYS NEAR ROME. With more than 100 Illustrations by the Author. Second Edition. 2 vols. crown 8vo. 24s.

'Henceforward it must take its place as a standard work indispensable to every intellectual student.'—TIMES.

'Mr. Hare probably knows Italy better than almost any Englishman living. ......The information which it affords will enable anyone who cares, to see more of the genuine native life of Italy in a month than most pilgrims to the Peninsula see in a lifetime.'—WORLD.

'A delightful sequel to Mr. Hare's "Walks in Rome."'—SPECTATOR.

CITIES OF NORTHERN AND CENTRAL ITALY.
With Illustrations. 3 vols crown 8vo. 15s. each.

THE LIFE AND LETTERS OF FRANCES BARONESS BUNSEN. With Portraits. 2 vols. crown 8vo. 21s.

London: SMITH, ELDER, & CO., 15 Waterloo Place.

www.ingramcontent.com/pod-product-compliance
Lightning Source LLC
Chambersburg PA
CBHW020233240426
43672CB00006B/505